WRITER'S DIGEST

HANDBOOK OF MAGAZINE ARTICLE WRITING

ALL NEW SECOND EDITION

EDITED BY MICHELLE RUBERG
INTRODUCTION BY BEN YAGODA

WRITER'S DIGEST BOOKS

Cincinnati, Ohio   www.writersdigest.com

Writer's Digest Handbook of Magazine Article Writing. © 2005 by Writer's Digest Books. Manufactured in the United States of America. All rights reserved. No part of this book may be reproduced in any form or by any electronic or mechanical means including information storage and retrieval systems without permission in writing from the publisher, except by a reviewer, who may quote brief passages in a review. Published by Writer's Digest Books, an imprint of F+W Publications, Inc., 4700 East Galbraith Road, Cincinnati, OH 45236. (800) 289-0963. Second edition.

Visit our Web site at www.writersdigest.com for information on more resources for writers.

To receive a free weekly e-mail newsletter delivering tips and updates about writing and about Writer's Digest products, register directly at our Web site at http://newsletters.fwpublications.com.

09   08   07   06   05   5   4   3   2   1

Library of Congress Cataloging-in-Publication Data

Writer's Digest handbook of magazine article writing / edited by Michelle Ruberg; introduction by Ben Yagoda.—All new 2nd ed.
   p.   cm.
Includes index.
ISBN 1-58297-333-4 (alk. paper)—ISBN 1-58297-334-2 (pbk. : alk. paper)
   1. Journalism—Authorship. 2. Feature writing. I. Title: Handbook of magazine article writing. II. Ruberg, Michelle. III. Writer's Digest Books (Firm).

PN147.W67   2005
808'.02—dc22   2004043079
                                                               CIP

Edited by Michelle Ruberg
Designed by Terri Eubanks
Cover designed by Nick Gliebe at Design Matters
Production coordinated by Robin Richie

FOREWORD

By Kristin Godsey

As far as I know, you can't major in freelance writing at any college. But that certainly doesn't mean there's not enough to know on the topic to fill four years' worth of course study. First, there's all the journalistic background you need on constructing compelling stories, finding sources, getting good quotes, compiling your research, etc. Technique and copyediting skills are a must. You have to know where to find markets for your work, be able to construct query letters and pitches that editors will notice, and tailor ideas to a specific magazine's needs. Then there are those working-well-with-others skills: understanding how editors work, knowing what to expect in the revision process, and determining what you should—and shouldn't—take in terms of payment and rewriting.

That sounds like a lot of work, I know, but freelance writing can be a sweet gig. This is a great business to be in if you've got the drive, the writing talent, and the industry savvy. And all three of these components are equally crucial; don't let anybody tell you otherwise. In fact, I'll go as far as to say you need them in that exact order. Drive is critical. It takes the soul of a hustler to break into this business, and—especially if you don't have an address book full of contacts—the stamina to crank out a relentless onslaught of queries and ideas, all delivered cheerfully and professionally. Writing talent, under which umbrella I include learned skills and journalistic instincts, is what will *keep* you in this business for the long haul. As for industry savvy, it's all about getting past the gatekeepers so you have the chance to show off that writing talent. Proper query protocol, knowing the right people in the right positions, and honing your professionalism will prove to an editor that you're not going to be more trouble than you're worth.

This book is packed with practical information you can put to use today, whether you're just starting your freelance career or trying to keep pace with changing expectations and opportunities. As someone who's worked on both sides of the table, as a magazine freelancer and an editor, I can tell you that the advice between these covers can save you years worth of rejection slips and frustration. Most of us learned this stuff the hard way, through trial and error (after error, after error . . .). Who wouldn't prefer a little shortcut to success?

Don't get it into your head, though, that there's just one prescription for a rewarding freelance career. Consider the advice compiled on these pages as a starting point, but don't neglect your gut instincts, either. Read this book, find your voice, then get out there and start pitching.

—Kristin D. Godsey is editor of *Writer's Digest* magazine.

INTRODUCTION

By Ben Yagoda

The year was 1978. I had just left my first job, as assistant editor for a small magazine, and opened up shop as a freelance writer. I had no great prospects, but neither did I have children, health insurance, car payments, a mortgage, or even a lease (I was subletting a Manhattan studio), so the move was not quite as rash as it might seem. Each day I rolled out of bed, walked across the room to my typewriter, and worked on humorous essays. The market for these was hardly booming in 1978; in fact, I knew of only one magazine that published them, *The New Yorker*. But I didn't have children, etc., and really wanted to be published in *The New Yorker*. It seemed worth a try, for a few months at least.

For my first piece, I decided to produce a parody of John Leonard, who wrote a very idiosyncratic column for *The New York Times* called "Private Lives." For three consecutive days, I went to the New York Public Library Annex, which was on West Forty-third Street between Tenth and Eleventh Avenues. Each day I loaded microfilm into a creaky machine and studied Leonard's writing. I made charts of the frequency of his metaphors and long lists of his characteristic expressions. This kind of dutiful obsessiveness now strikes me as not the best way to go about being humorous, but at that point it was the only thing I had going for me. Anyway, I finished the piece, titled it "Personal Existence," sent it to *The New Yorker*, and promptly got it back, along with one of the magazine's small supercilious rejection slips, familiar to nine-tenths of the writers in this universe.

What to do next? A college professor of mine once mentioned a friend who was an editor at the *Village Voice*, the weekly newspaper. I sent "Personal Existence" to that man, and lo and behold, a phone call came back saying it had met with approval and would be published. The *Voice* would even pay me a sum of money for it, in the (very) low three figures as I recall. But the editor didn't know when the piece was going to appear and would probably forget to alert me, he admitted. So he advised me to check the paper each week. I was not a regular purchaser of the *Voice*, so the following Wednesday, when it came out, I went to a newsstand and looked for my name in the table of contents. It wasn't there. Three, four, five weeks went by. No ''Personal Existence.''

One Tuesday, I was sitting in my local library branch, flipping through the *Voice*. In a sort of no-man's-land after the feature articles ended and before the arts coverage began, wedged in between ads for escort services and futons, was my piece. I checked the table of contents. Nope, I hadn't missed it; mine was the only article not listed. I rushed out to the news-stand and bought the one remaining copy of the *Voice*, which had re-mained because its front cover was in tatters. It appeared to be the last available copy in New York City. My fantasy of phoning all my friends and telling them to pick up the *Voice* with my first published humor piece in it? It would have to remain a fantasy.

I tell this tale because, even twenty-seven years later, it seems to repre-sent all the important points about freelance writing. Getting a strong idea and identifying a market for it is key. You should give every article your best shot—maybe not to the level of reading microfilm for three days, but close. Most of the time, your first choice for the article won't work out, so you need to have or develop a plan B. Connections are essential; seek them out and cultivate them. Even if you have an idea or piece accepted, there is likely to be some unexpected and probably unexpectable disappointment.

Most important of all, freelancing is a good thing to do. I've been an independent literary contractor since ''Personal Existence,'' and today I get some satisfaction when I look at it and virtually every other article I've written. This includes the ones that never got published (because one or more editors were too thickheaded to appreciate them, naturally).

Once I branched out from humorous essays, I found that reporting was enjoyable, too. Freelancing has let me investigate a dizzying array of interesting subjects and hang out with a dazzling array of interesting folk. Among them: authors Peter DeVries, George Plimpton, M. Scott Peck, Elmore Leonard, and Bobbie Ann Mason; movie folk Barry Levinson, Uma Thurman, Jimmy Smits, and Susan Sarandon; NBA referee Danny Crawford; Julie Nixon Eisenhower; the secretary of the Navy; the director of the U.S. Census; the head of NFL Films; the executive editor of *The New York Times*; the coinventor of the first computer; jazz trumpeter Lester Bowie; athletes Mike Schmidt, Tim Henman, and Dirk Nowitzki; and entertainers Jay Leno, Robert Klein, and the Smothers Brothers.

I am an avid tennis player, and not long ago I had what I consider the ultimate freelance experience. *Tennis* magazine paid me to attend Roy Emerson's tennis camp in Gstaad, Switzerland, for a week, stay at a five-star resort, and write about the experience. Of course, it took me a quarter-century of freelancing to get an assignment that plum. But I wasn't complaining.

Here are the qualities a freelance magazine writer should have, starting with the most common, ending with the most rare: an ego that gets pleasure from recognition, a decent and adaptable native intelligence (what is called being "a quick study"), a fair amount of self-discipline and persistence, the kind of personality that can deal with rejection and solitude, a good general body of knowledge and/or expertise in a particular subject (obtained either through formal education or on your own), a natural curiosity, and a facility with and appreciation for the English language.

The necessary blend of these qualities is not exact, but before too long you'll know if you have the right stuff. If you do, I guarantee that you will get published. Go to a well-stocked newsstand or a super bookstore with a magazine rack, or look at *Writer's Market* or Yahoo!'s directory of magazines (http://dir.yahoo.com/News_and_Media/Magazines/). You will see that thousands of magazines are out there, and all but a handful get the majority of their contents from freelancers. (The exceptions are well-known, mostly news-oriented publications like *Time, Newsweek,* and *Sports Illustrated.*) Collectively, that's a pretty sizeable appetite for copy. I have been on both sides of the editorial desk, and I know that editors are always—that's A-L-W-A-Y-S—looking for good writers. Of course, some of them have pretty strange ideas of what "good" is, but there are plenty of other fish in the sea.

I'll close with a caveat. I have been a regular freelancer since "Personal Existence." But out of those twenty-seven years, I freelanced full time for only seven; the rest of the time I held down a day job. If you have the inclination and the ability and a reasonable amount of free time, freelancing as a sideline is a no-brainer. Full-time freelancing is for the strong of stomach and stronger of will—for those hardy souls able to put up with frequent disappointment, regular rejection, and occasional kill fees.

If you're unsure whether full-time freelancing is for you, here's a quiz, much like the ones you will devise if you ever write for women's magazines.

Give yourself ten points for each "yes."

- Do you have a mortgage?
- Do you have children?
- Would you take it personally if an editor didn't respond to your phone calls, e-mails, and letters?
- Are you over twenty-five?
- Are you over thirty-five?
- Are you over forty-five?
- Are you . . . well, you get the idea.

And now, give yourself ten points for each "no."

- Are PR work, corporate speeches, and annual reports beneath you?
- Will magazine editors actively seek you out instead of making you come to them? That is, have you won the Pulitzer Prize or National Magazine Award, do you appear regularly on television, or have you written a book that made *The New York Times* best-seller list?
- Do you have a trust fund, a winning lottery ticket, or a spouse with benefits?

If you "passed" the test and scored seventy or above, you might want to think twice about full-time freelancing. But if you "failed," and are in the mood for a rigorous but bracing challenge, why not give it a shot? I'm glad that I did, once upon a time.

—Ben Yagoda is author of *About Town: The New Yorker and the World It Made* and director of journalism at the University of Delaware.

CHAPTER ONE:
FINDING IDEAS

More than paper, more than ink, more than even those annoying subscription cards that tumble out at every opportunity, magazines are made of ideas. Behind every magazine is an idea. Behind every article within the magazine is an idea. Behind every sentence within an article is—or darn well ought to be—an idea. And where do all those ideas come from? Many come from writers.

Thinking up salable article ideas is a skill that some lucky writers may be born with but that most develop over time. When you are first starting out as a writer, you may worry that you'll run out of ideas any day now. But by the time you've been at it a few years, you'll be producing more ideas than you'll ever be able to use.

Ideas are writers' raw material. And like any other raw material, they're far more valuable once they've been refined. The most common problem that beginning writers seem to have is grasping the difference between a story idea and what's simply an interesting subject. One useful test is to write a headline for your proposed article. If it sounds like a book or a fourteen-part PBS series, you need to bring your idea into sharper focus. But if it sounds like a headline you might see in a magazine—particularly the magazine you want to propose it to—you're probably on the right track.

Great Ways to Generate Ideas

So how do you get article ideas? Where do they come from? There are numerous ways to find usable, salable ideas. Explore these and find some of your own as well.

1.   **Take a lot of showers.** Ask twenty successful freelance writers where they get their best ideas, and it's safe to bet nineteen of them will say,

"in the shower." There's even some science to back them up—possibly something about negative ions. But who cares, as long as it works?

2. Put your subconscious to work. Remember that one writer in twenty who doesn't get ideas in the shower? Odds are he would tell you that the best ideas seem to bubble up out of nowhere. That, some say, is the subconscious mind at work. But you don't have to sit back and wait for your subconscious to start bubbling. You can give it an assignment. Once, Napoleon Hill, one of the founders of *Success* magazine, was trying to come up with a title for a new book. He had a talk with his subconscious before he went to bed. "I've got to have a million-dollar title, and I've got to have it tonight," he said (and he said it out loud). "Do you understand that?"

Apparently his subconscious got the message, because at 2 A.M., Hill woke up, bounded to his typewriter, and banged out the title. Hill's book, *Think and Grow Rich*, went on to sell more than twenty million copies.

If you try Hill's technique, the results may be mixed. Some mornings you may wake up with an idea you've asked for. Other days you'll wake up with a good idea but on an entirely different subject. The rest of the time you'll just wake up.

3. Read everything you can get your hands or eyes on. The best writers not only try to keep up with the fields they cover but read just about anything in sight. Few of the things you read will pay off in an immediate story, but they all help feed that mysterious idea machine in your head.

Books. Poke around the library. Let yourself get lost in unfamiliar aisles. Check out the new releases at the bookstore. This can help you identify trends and see what people are interested in. Also check the sections that correspond to the magazine audience you are targeting.

Magazines. Read the ones you want to write for, of course, but look at others, too. You'll learn some new things, discover new ways to tell a story, and maybe even stumble onto a promising market or two.

Old magazines are another good source of idea fodder. Check out some of the great magazines when you're in the library and have nothing else to do: *Holiday, Look, Saturday Review*, to name a few.

Newspapers. Your local paper can be a terrific source of article ideas, especially if it's not a paper that magazine editors regularly follow. You may see a story in your local paper that's ripe for telling practically as is in a national magazine. More often, though, you'll find hints of a possible national story. It may be a local trend that's yet to be widely written about or a local person whose tale could be one of several in an article reported from a national perspective. So keep your scissors handy. When you travel, scoop up the local papers there, too.

Online. The Internet may be both the biggest time-saver and the biggest time-waster ever invented. It's an incredibly useful research tool but you may seldom discover any worthwhile article ideas, no matter how many hours you spend browsing. One possible exception: Web sites sponsored by local newspapers. They're rarely as rich in detail as the papers themselves, but they offer a window on the goings-on in different parts of the country. And, unlike the papers themselves, they're often free.

Junk mail. Everyone is inundated with junk mail on a daily basis, and you've probably considered all that mail to be worthless clutter. But with a change of perspective you'll find that it can be a great source for query ideas. Analyze those announcements for new products and stores, annual events, and human-interest subjects. Look at them all and save the most thought-provoking ones.

4. Listen up. Some of the best story ideas come from listening to your friends, neighbors, and co-workers talk about their concerns of the moment. Magazines pay a lot of money to convene focus groups of everyday people who sit around for an hour talking about their likes, dislikes, and whatever else they're asked to discuss. You can accomplish much the same thing for free by paying attention when someone starts griping about X, singing the praises of Y, or asking why no magazine has ever told the truth about Z.

5. Tap into your own experience. Forget for a moment that you're a writer. What's on your mind, just as a human being? If you've wondered about something, chances are other people have, too. The difference is you are a writer and can go out, investigate the matter, and maybe even get paid for coming back with the answer. Have a baby, and you'll find yourself jotting down child-related story ideas. Switch jobs, move to a new home, get a divorce, get a disease, win a trip for two to exotic Bora Bora—all of life's amazing twists and turns can supply you with fresh ideas. For instance, writer Steve Fishman turned a brain hemorrhage into an award-winning magazine article, then into a widely acclaimed book called *A Bomb in the Brain*. But you don't have to lust after any misfortune. Just remember that the events of your life—the good ones and the bad ones—are all part of your material as a writer.

6. Get to know some PR people. Public relations professionals often have great story ideas before anybody else. Many of them are former magazine or newspaper writers themselves. The trouble, of course, is that it's their job to put a spin on the idea that benefits their clients. The other trouble is that they're out to get their clients as much positive publicity as possible, so if you received a story tip from them, a few dozen other writers probably did, too. That said, you'll find PR people are worth paying attention to. If nothing else, they can sometimes get you access to key experts and provide background information that you'd otherwise spend a lot of time digging up on your own. Just remember that their agendas and yours aren't identical.

7. Keep a notebook handy. As you go through your day, you cannot even begin to anticipate everything and everyone that will cross your path. Nor can you anticipate every thought that will enter your brain. That's why you should always have a notebook with you—so you are ready to jot down any idea that might present itself. Don't trust your brain to store these ideas until you have time to write them down. Put them on paper immediately.

These are not the only ways to find good article ideas, but they are a good start if you're stumped. Remember there is no right or wrong way to find an idea. Always be open to receiving ideas. They are all around you.

Idea Matrix

Even with all the tips for generating ideas, there will still be times when you get stuck in neutral looking for that fresh idea. That's when you must remember the first rule of writing: Write what you know—or what you want to know.

When you hear those words of wisdom, you ask yourself: *Is it possible to make any money writing about my interests or what I know best?* Yes, you can make a profit by following that advice.

Interests can include hobbies, community and civic involvement, family, coaching, volunteer work (Boy Scouts, churches, hospitals), and your day job. Even everyday life experiences can provide endless opportunities to write profitable articles. One great method for developing new ideas is to make a matrix. This three-step process helps you:

- develop initial concepts or ideas and categorize ideas based on their strength
- expand and develop the final story ideas for additional future articles

Step 1: Format the basic matrix. The first step is to list your areas of involvement as the major headings in your matrix. As illustrated in the

THE MATRIX

Major Heading	Main Subject	Sub-Idea	Code
Hobby	Antique Bottle Collecting	Basic Facts of Bottle Collecting	1
		Digging for Bottles	1
		Trademark Identification	1
Community Projects	Pancake Breakfast	Pancakes for Profit	2
	City Beautification	Park Clean-Up	2
		Beach Clean-Up	2
Civic Involvement	Football	Fundraisers	1
		Playoff	3
	Boy Scouts	Food Drives	2

sample matrix, main subjects are listed next to the major headings, followed by a listing of subideas. Next to the heading of Hobbies, for example, writer Michael Polak listed the subject "Antique Bottle Collecting," since he has been collecting antique bottles for thirty years. Next, he listed these subideas: "Basic Facts of Bottle Collecting," "Digging for Bottles," and "Trademark Identification." The result? His first published article was "Basic Facts for the Beginning Bottle Collector."

Another example of a major heading is Community Projects, with the main subject, "Pancake Breakfast." Being the chairman of a July 4th Pancake Breakfast for twenty years provided Polak with the experience to write his published article "Pancakes for Profit."

After you focus on an article topic, determine if a viable market for your article exists. Use *Writer's Market* or WritersMarket.com as a resource, but don't forget the many other sources available, such as writer's conferences, Web sites, local newspapers, and magazines that may focus on your subject.

Step 2: Categorize and prioritize the ideas. Now you should categorize and prioritize each subidea: 1 = Strong, 2 = Medium, and 3 = Weak. There are a number of factors to consider in determining the rating.

- **Interest.** Is there a niche market for the subject and how strong is the market interest?
- **Resale market.** Is there potential to resell the article to other markets and how strong are those markets?
- **Indirect writing assignments.** What is the possibility of obtaining additional writing assignments based upon the quality and subject of your writing?

Polak's bottle collecting article resulted in a contract with Avon Books (an imprint of HarperCollins) for the first edition of *Bottles: Identification and Price Guide*, which resulted in numerous follow-up articles and another book, *Official Price Guide to American Patriotic Memorabilia* (not even related to bottle collecting).

Step 3: Expand and develop your ideas. As you develop your final story idea, format another matrix and list each of the final ideas across the top of the page with a sublisting of additional ideas below each of the major topics.

Go back to the initial example of "Antique Bottle Collecting," where Polak listed three subideas for articles, including "Digging for Bottles." He rated this as strong and chose it as a final idea for his second matrix. Under it he developed and listed these three other article possibilities: "Techniques of Digging Outhouses or Privies," "Western Privies vs. Eastern Privies," and "Tools for the Dig."

After completing this process with your own interests, you'll have two matrices that provide an excellent approach for not only increasing your number of articles and topics but also for increasing your profits. Never forget that what interests you can interest others. So develop that idea, find your market, write the article, and make the sale.

The Art of Anniversaries

The cardinal rule of marriage—remember the anniversary—is also one of the most useful freelancing tools and best ways to find ideas. "I think anniversaries are a good hook, and in our magazine's case, the more obscure the subject's anniversary the better," said Abigail Seymour, when she was managing editor of US Airways' in-flight publication, *Attaché*. "The only downside is that if many publications use the same angle, we can be at risk of coming out with stories simultaneously. That's why *Attaché* tends to stick to oddball anniversaries whenever possible."

To snag an anniversary assignment, you'll need three things: an interesting occasion, a unique angle, and pitch-perfect timing. Finding the anniversary is the easy part—it's as simple as opening up an almanac and focusing on relevant years. (A thirty-seventh anniversary isn't going to get an editor's blood pumping.) There are also Web sites, like a link on *The New York Times*' site (www.nytimes.com/learning) that offers an "On This Day in History" archive. But quirkier collections of facts and dates offer more fascinating fodder. Books like *The Optimist's Guide to*

History (which will tell you that the first banana split was created in 1904) and the *Pro Football Chronicle* (which informs you that the NFL's last successful drop kick occurred in 1941). Scour the fine print and the forgotten factoids, because sometimes it can be easier to sell a previously unheralded anniversary.

The key is to give even a well-known historical event a clever spin. "Those that go beyond the obvious anniversary angles are more likely to receive serious consideration," said Brian Cook, a magazine editor with custom publisher Pace Communications. "The ones that scratch a layer or two beneath the surface are especially appealing." An example: December 2003 marked the centennial of the Wright brothers' flying feats, which received widespread attention. But more obscure is the fact that a Cornell University graduate named Charles Manly attempted to pilot a Smithsonian-funded aircraft a few weeks earlier. Had the airplane's design matched the functionality of Manly's terrific engine, he would be the historical icon, and the Wrights would be mere footnotes. It's this kind of I-didn't-know-that angle that intrigued editors at *Cornell Alumni Magazine* enough to assign the story.

Date-specific stories take several forms. There is the anniversary as an annual event (John Steinbeck's hometown celebrates his birthday every year), as reminiscence (the Army-McCarthy hearings fifty years later), as comparison (the class of 2005 vs. the class of 1905), and as overview (celebrating a century of basketball). More so than most queries, your anniversary-based attempts should be well timed. Alex Gordon, managing editor of *Hockey Digest*, prefers a lead time of about a year. Cook and Seymour both prefer at least six to eight months. "Not so far ahead that we're not thinking about it yet," Seymour said, "but enough time to avoid a mad scramble."

So when you're at a loss for an idea, remember anniversaries and think of how you can make them relevant. Gordon emphasized, "Anyone can write a history, but it takes a skilled writer to analyze a historical event and place it in context." Develop this skill and you'll be on your way to querying great article ideas.

Evergreen Topics

In addition to anniversaries, there are other ideas out there just waiting for you to put your own spin on them. But writers sometimes can't see the forest for the trees. You constantly look for the breaking news that could lead to the perfect article for your favorite magazine, but you just can't break in. Yet that great opportunity has been there all the time. It's called the evergreen article, and it could be your ticket to publication.

Evergreens are the backbone of nearly every magazine. In the case of women's magazines, evergreens are the articles on health, relationships, parenting, and careers that appear each year. And every year, editors must present them to readers in new and innovative ways. Each magazine not only competes against the way it treated the subject last year, it competes against the other women's magazines covering the same story. "There is always a race to be the first and the best," said Nancy Clark, *Family Circle* deputy editor.

Each magazine has a lead time (usually between three and six months, though some want seasonal material a year in advance), and most have an editorial calendar of special stories and sections for the coming year. For example, almost all of the women's magazines run stories on weight loss and getting healthy in January. February is Heart Month, and October is Breast Cancer Awareness Month.

Get a jump on pitching seasonal evergreens by transferring to your own calendar the dates by which editors want to see queries, based on their guidelines and editorial calendars.

Even though women's magazines cover a lot of the same topics, each has a spin that it puts on that subject based on that magazine's tone and target readership. Go to the library and look at the way four different magazines handle any given evergreen story (such as weight loss or mammograms). One may give the readers ten tips; one may give quotes from experts in the field and more data on the latest research.

Sally Kilbridge, managing editor of Condé Nast *Bride's*, shared the way her magazine has handled wedding budgeting: "We've done it to death, but it's an incredibly popular topic for the reader, so we'd look for something clever and specific, like ten smart ways to slash $1,000 off your wedding budget, something from an industry expert, such as florists reveal their top secrets for saving money, or something trendy like a fashionista's tips for a wedding that's chic and cheap."

Keep a file of how your target magazine and its competitors handle an evergreen so you can find a different angle or one that hasn't been used for a while. It isn't unusual to see two or three magazines cover the same story in the same month, usually with a different take.

You've done your homework, picked a couple of subjects and angles that interest you, and matched your story ideas to the right publication. The next step is to come up with a tight, concise query that gives the old subject a new spin.

Remember, you're trying to sell an editor on a story that has already been covered, not only by her magazine but by her competitors as well. Your query letter needs specific details showing how you plan to make that subject fresh. If you're going to take hard data and boil it down into ten useful tips that the reader can put into action, make sure you spell that out.

If you have any personal experiences or special expertise, tell the editor. "We know the wedding industry inside out, but we'd love to find people who are true experts about subjects that may be too specific or involved for us to have mastered—i.e., someone who really knows the topic of diamonds, or a writer who can write knowledgeably and engagingly about planning a do-it-yourself wedding," Kilbridge said.

Evergreens are invaluable mainstays for magazine editors. It can be tough to come up with new angles for perennial stories, but once you get the knack of it, you'll realize there will always be a supply of article ideas out there to tap into.

Look for Ideas in New Ways

What if your ideas and articles are all starting to sound the same? What if you find yourself faced with the problem of being stuck for an ending? What if, when you hit upon the conclusion, you discover that you have used that same phrase to end your last five articles? Then you are stuck in a rut.

Your sense of wordplay might not be the only thing stuck—your article ideas are probably getting frayed from overuse as well. You may be querying the same business and career ideas over and over: how to succeed at a trade show, how to find a job online, how to market on a budget. Your ideas for health and women's magazines are most likely getting pretty stale, too: Ten Ways to Do X, Fifteen Reasons to Do Y. You realize that you've written on those topics so many times you could do them without cracking a book or even revving up your modem. Heck, you could pound out one of those articles using only 10 percent of your brain capacity, while the other 90 percent is busy watching *Iron Chef.*

Not that reusing ideas is inherently bad. It's wise, economically, to make the most bucks from the fewest ideas. And if you develop a few specialties in the writing world—business, career, women's interest, and health—it's a good thing to be able to whip out articles on trade shows or fad diets or time-saving cleaning tips with minimum brainpower.

But what's good for the pocketbook isn't necessarily good for the soul. When you're churning out your fourth article on how to ace a job interview, freelancing starts to feel less like an adventure and more like a tedious nine-to-five job. The freedom of having a five-second commute to your office at 11 A.M. is overshadowed by the drudgery of interviewing the same people, asking the same questions, and writing the same words. And your writing suffers when you fall into the groove of starting every article with an anecdote, ending every article with a cliché, and lacing every article with alliterative subheads.

To leap out of your writer's rut, you must play games with words. Find at least two other writers looking to rev up the idea-generating process. Have one person throw out a word, then each of you should try to think up ideas related to that word. For example, starting with the word "green" may lead to ideas, such as "an inside look at how money is made," "tips from golf course owners on how to care for your lawn," or "how to deal with friends who are green with envy over your successes."

The word "tea" could inspire ideas such as ten things to do with tea (antique linens, add shine to dark hair), how to brew the perfect pot, and a look at teapots and the people who collect them.

- **Read outside the box.** Another way to break out of writing ruts is to check out magazines that you don't usually read. Browsing through *Aeronautics Monthly* or *Modern Ferret* not only helps you find fresh ideas that you can reslant for other markets, it introduces you to a whole new world of writers and writing styles. And you can do this anytime you want, gratis, by going to your local bookstore/cafe, gathering armloads of magazines from sections you rarely peruse, and reading them over a cup of coffee.

- **Take on a new pursuit.** A humdrum life leads to humdrum writing. So one day, surprise yourself—and give your writing a shot of adrenaline—by doing something totally different like signing up for karate classes. You could spend four evenings a week kicking, punching, and yelling, which is pretty much the opposite of researching, interviewing, and stringing nouns and verbs. Boston-based writer Linda Formichelli did this and met kindergarten teachers, sound system engineers, and people who work with gibbons at the zoo—all with fascinating stories to tell. And, as Formichelli discovered, one of the most blessed benefits is having a few hours per week when you're too absorbed in something to worry about deadlines.

On top of all that, your new diversion will get the idea wheels churning, and you could end up selling an article on the benefits of martial arts to a women's fitness magazine.

Karate may be the answer, or it may be bowling, in-line skating, the local softball league—anything that gets the heart pumping and the mind off writing. Any class, from flower arranging to American history, can shake up your writing life.

- **Take time off.** Sometimes you have to empty your mind of all the junk that's bouncing around to make room for new, fresh ideas—and what better way than to take a break? Have you ever been hit with a writer's block the size of Montana? Everything you write is stale, boring, and lame? If so, clear a couple of days on your schedule, pack your bags, and head to a new location for some R&R at a B&B. Soaking in a hot tub and drinking port in front of a roaring fire will certainly help you forget about writing for a little while—and when you get back to the office, your writing might once again have that spark of originality.

Taking a break doesn't always require a lot of free time and cash. Even one day of reading on the couch instead of staring frustrated at a computer screen can bring an infusion of creativity. If you work through the weekends in a fit of Type-A pique, realize you can face Mondays with much more creative energy if you give yourself the weekend to read, explore the town, or hang out with friends.

• **Enjoy it all.** If you let writing turn into a burdensome, repetitive task, you pay for it in stilted prose and cliché ideas. That's why the tactics you use to climb out of a rut—playing games, doing karate, reading, taking time off—are all about having fun. A relaxed mind is an open mind, and an open mind is prepared to accept new and creative ideas. So above all other writing tips, remind yourself to enjoy the craft—no matter what.

Editors and Ideas

Many beginning writers often ask if magazines will steal their ideas. The best answer: Maybe, but it's not worth worrying about. The American Society of Journalists and Authors defines a story idea as a "subject combined with an approach." It says a writer shall have a proprietary right to an idea suggested to an editor and have first shot at developing it. Any editor with integrity will respect this ethical standard.

Even so, you may hear a few horror stories along the way, but idea theft is not a crime to lose a whole lot of sleep over. For one thing, a good writer is always generating ideas—far more than he can begin to use. For another, if a magazine wants to steal your idea, there is not much you can do about it. Writers try, though. Some are deliberately vague in their queries, hoping to tease the editor into giving them the assignment simply on faith. Others practically make editors sign formal nondisclosure agreements. The only thing a writer really accomplishes by such amateurish legal tactics is to insult the editor's integrity—a dumb marketing move if there ever was one.

Occasionally you'll see an idea you pitched to a magazine (and the magazine threw back) appear in that very magazine a month, a year, or a decade later. Did somebody swipe your idea? Possibly, but more likely the idea came from another writer with a somewhat different approach. Few ideas are so unusual that only one writer will think of them. So chalk it up to coincidence or to just being ahead of your time (and maybe avoid that magazine in the future). Then move on. You'll probably have better ideas tomorrow anyway.

You can boost your ideas' odds of success if you learn to step back and look at ideas the way an editor does. Not all editors think alike, of course, but if you could cut an editor's head open (and wouldn't writers all like to sometimes?), you'd probably see a thought process that works something like this:

1. **"Does this idea belong in this magazine?"** Sometimes the answer is pretty obvious: A magazine about dogs probably won't be interested in a story about cats. Other times, it's far more subtle: A dog magazine that last year ran a story called "Rottweilers: Those Gentle Giants" is an unlikely market for your proposed piece on "Rottweilers: Four-Legged Psychopaths From Hell."

What can you do? Look up what the magazine has run in the past year or two in the *Reader's Guide to Periodical Literature* or on a computerized magazine database at your library. Not all magazines are indexed in this way, but some surprisingly obscure ones are. Or check to see if the magazine has a Web site that has archived articles that you can read without a subscription. If you can't find out whether your idea conflicts with one the magazine has already done, just give it a shot. There's no shame in approaching a magazine with an idea that's just slightly off the mark.

2. **"Have we done this story before?"** And if so, how recently? Some magazines will return to the same topic month after month, as long as they can put at least the illusion of a fresh spin on it. Some women's magazines, for

example, run a diet story in every issue, for the simple reason that such stories, however unbelievable, sell copies. Other magazines won't touch a topic that they've covered in the past five or ten years.

3. "Have our competitors already done the story?" Even if the magazine itself hasn't touched the topic, an editor may consider the idea old if one or more of the magazine's competitors has. Magazines differ in what they consider their competition. Some will look only to their specific category (boating magazines, decorating magazines, teen magazines, and so forth), while others will consider newspapers, television, and every other type of media. Generally speaking, you stand the best chance with ideas that have received no coverage or only very local coverage.

4. "Is this the best way to approach this story?" Sometimes a fresh approach can inject life into a tired topic. For example, "Six Ways to Childproof Your Home" would be a familiar approach to most editors of parenting magazines. But something like "How Professional Childproofers Rip You Off" or "Childproof Accessories That Could Injure Your Child" might get their attention.

5. "Is this the best writer for the job?" As mentioned earlier, magazines will seldom steal your ideas. But in some cases they may turn a perfectly fine idea down if you don't seem like the right writer. In rare instances, they may offer to buy the idea from you and assign it to another writer.

What may make you inappropriate? Distance is one thing. If you come across a great story in Australia, but you happen to live in Albuquerque, the magazine may not have the budget to send you there. Or, if you are obviously a beginning writer, the magazine may hesitate to assign you what's sure to be a complex, ambitious story.

A magazine is most likely to take a chance on you if an editor there has worked with you elsewhere or knows your work from other publications. A powerful query and strong clips can also make a difference.

6. "Even if this idea isn't right, is the writer worth encouraging?" Some editors are too busy or too self-important to send personal notes to writers whose ideas may have just missed the mark. So don't automatically assume the worst if you receive a terse form letter in reply. Other editors will suggest a way an idea might be reshaped or urge you to try again with another one. If your query is impressive enough, an editor may come back at you with a story idea of her own.

Try and think like your potential editor to come up with the best and most salable ideas. The possibilities are endless; you just have to find the right idea at the right time for the right magazine. Keep working at it and you'll find the idea that brings you success.

Chapter Two:
Querying

Before you write an article, you need to sell it. Most editors want queries before assigning articles. The query letter is the traditional and most effective method for getting your article idea accepted at a publication. It is important that you craft the best query letter possible in order to have the best chance of selling your article. There is much to consider, but don't make querying harder than it needs to be. There are four primary purposes of a query letter—to sell your idea, explain how you will develop your article, show you are familiar with the publication, and indicate your qualifications. If you can do all of this you are on your way to making a sale.

Even before querying, though, there is groundwork you must do. Don't jump right in without considering things like writer's guidelines and actual published articles. Understanding these basics will set you apart from other writers and increase your chances of getting an assignment.

For the price of a self-addressed stamped envelope (SASE), most publications will mail writer's guidelines—rules and focal points to help would-be contributors understand just what the magazine is hoping to communicate and how. The first step is to request guidelines from each publication that appeals to you. (You can often find them at magazines' Web sites or in *The American Directory of Writer's Guidelines* (Quill Driver Books). And according to former *U.S. Kids* editor and seventeen-year freelance veteran Jeff Ayers, following those guidelines is the first step toward success. "Using writer's guidelines is essential to narrowing the focus of what a freelancer should write about," Ayers said. "You'd think that would be a pretty obvious first step. But I'd estimate 80 percent of the submissions I received weren't related to the mission and normal content of *U.S. Kids.*"

It's like flossing, said *Guideposts for Kids* editor Mary Lou Carney. "Nobody wants to do it, but it's terribly necessary. Nothing puts you on the inside track of a magazine like its guidelines. Magazines exist because they have distinctive editorial voices and biases. Don't think you can skim over the marketing process and hope to score sales."

Know the Magazine

After studying the writer's guidelines, sit down with several recent issues of the magazine you want to query (most editors suggest at least six) and read them cover-to-cover. As a beginning writer, you may resist reviewing the content of magazines to which you want to query or submit. You may diligently study the guidelines for a magazine, but if you avoid analyzing the actual body of the publication, you will sell little of your work. Only when you finally give in and start looking critically at the publications themselves will you place your work on a regular basis.

That advice is all well and good, but how exactly do you go about doing such a thing? Without fail, writer's guidelines say, "Analyze our magazine," but they don't give the first clue what to look for. Here is a list to get you on the right track.

When you're analyzing a publication, you want to look at:

- average article length
- tone of articles
- advertisers
- topics covered in the last six to twelve months
- distribution of short vs. long articles
- illustrations and photos
- who writes for them

The **length** is probably the key factor in placing a piece, especially for a new writer trying to break in.

If you want to pitch a dating story to the popular women's magazines— *Glamour*, *Cosmopolitan*, etc.—flip through them in the grocery store. You will see that almost every story is under a thousand words. You'll also notice that many have a preponderance of "number" pieces, i.e., "Five Ways to Get Ahead at Work" or "Top Ten First-Date Outfits." Janine Palley wrote a piece to submit to a women's magazine titled "How to Date a Glacier Without Getting Cold" as a funny personal essay. After looking through the women's magazines, she immediately went home and rewrote it as "Four Ways to Date a Glacier Without Getting Cold."

The **tone** of advice or service-oriented pieces, the mainstay of commercial magazines, has to be upbeat, and these articles are usually written in the second person. For example, in Palley's dating piece, she says, "Take a few minutes to consider the alternatives when the guy you're seeing is moving too slowly for you." Because she examined the magazine, she knew she had to write as if she were speaking directly to the reader.

Advertisers hold the key to who reads a magazine. Advertising demographics are the most accurate. Who advertises not only tells you who reads the magazine but how much they earn, what their personal tastes and dreams are, and where they spend their money. Is the publication advertising Royal Caribbean (lifestyles of the rich and famous) or Campbell's soup (families with small children)? The key to focusing your story lies both in the classifieds at the back of the magazine (vacation rentals, rare book dealers, summer camps) and the glitzy display ads up front (Lexus luxury cars, Stoli vodka, DeBeers diamonds).

Look at the **topics**, going back at least six months; twelve or more months is ideal. A year can give you an idea of how a magazine's editors handle seasonal material, which needs to be submitted well in advance. If you're not a regular reader or subscriber, go to the library. Almost any good public library will have a year's worth of recent issues on the shelf, with decades more on microfiche. Even if a topic was covered, you can still write about it. Use such an article as a springboard for a different slant, or even write an article that refutes the previous one.

The **distribution of long vs. short articles** will tell you a lot about your chances of getting in cold. Writing short features, the back page, and fillers are the easiest way for a newcomer to break in. Another advantage to starting this way is that you can submit a whole manuscript for a short piece instead of waiting for a query and assignment to turn around. Editors are reluctant to assign to unknowns, but they love work that's ready to plug in and will fill a last-minute hole.

Don't forget about **illustrations and photos**, which provide yet another route into a new publication. Some magazines—especially travel, cooking, and home design publications—rarely buy a piece without photographs or illustrations. Look at the type and quality of the photos: Are they black and white or color, small or large, realistic or abstract? Does the magazine use cartoons, line drawings, or fully rendered models? A picture is worth a thousand words. Good photos or drawings can make an otherwise average story stand out.

REMEMBER THE ART

One often-overlooked detail that can mean the difference between "sold" and "sorry" is photo availability. It's a key factor (apart from strong, accurate writing) in securing follow-up assignments—and that's the freelancer's primary objective. (Regular bylines pay the bills.) Any service you can provide that might make you part of an editor's regular team is worth the time invested.

"A good editor never forgets the impact of a great photo,'" said Mary Lou Carney at *Guideposts for Kids.* "So, after good copy, good photo research is the best thing a writer can deliver."

It's not essential to take photos yourself. In fact, many editors prefer to use professional photographers. "What's really valuable," Carney said, "are the names and numbers of people who may have suitable photos (newspapers that have featured this person, organizations that sponsor/photograph him). Busy editors remember which writers are thorough when it comes to photo details and give them assignments again and again."

But don't send original artwork until you're asked. "I love it when a freelancer lets me know that photos are available," said Jeff Ayers. "It's particularly handy if they send photocopies so I'm aware of what the visuals are. But I hate it when people send photographs I haven't requested because then I'm charged with returning them safely. It almost never works out and it's a red flag for lack of professionalism."

Lastly, see **who writes for the magazine**. If your competition is John McPhee, Hunter S. Thompson, or P.J. O'Rourke, it will be mighty tough to break in unless you have something absolutely stellar, like Julia Roberts and Tom Hanks are your best friends. This is not to say that you'll never get in, but it might be easier to set your sights a little lower when you're starting out. Every published clip, no matter how obscure the magazine, increases your chances of eventually selling a piece to a big publication.

Never underestimate how important the analysis of a publication is when targeting your pitch. The writer's guidelines are helpful, but an abstraction. The actual magazine is tangible evidence of which writing was selected. You will sell more work submitting to fewer, more accurately targeted markets than by blindly submitting to anyone who you think might possibly buy it. "Machine-gun" submissions waste a lot of postage, get dreary form rejections, and leave writers very disappointed. Analyzing whole publications might seem tedious and time-consuming at first, but stick with it. In the end, your upfront investment will pay a lifetime of publication dividends.

Writing Effective Query Letters

A winning query letter is well written, brisk, and energetic. At the same time, it must be highly professional. An organized letter sends a clear message that you know how to get a job done on time and accurately.

It's crucial to accomplish all these goals briefly; a query letter should be no more than one page. The type size should also be at least 11 point and preferably 12 point. Editors shouldn't have to work to read your letter. If they do, the chances that they'll set it aside are much, much greater.

Most consumer magazines prefer that you query them with a specific article idea. In an article query, you're selling two things: your idea and your expertise, in that order.

The first section, consisting of two to three paragraphs, should explain your idea and why it's important to the magazine's readers. A feature story about a woman's triumphant recovery from breast cancer and the subsequent founding of an unusual women's health support group might be of interest to *Good Housekeeping* or *Self*; chances are *Men's Health* or *National Geographic Traveler* won't care. As already mentioned, make sure you check the publication's guidelines to target the right query to the right publication.

The first section should also explain how you envision developing the article: the word length, interview subjects, and possible sidebars. Share why this article is right for this magazine.

The second section of the query letter explains why you're the right person to write the article. This is the place to list your credentials; it's especially helpful if the credentials are relevant.

For example, if you're querying *Bon Appétit* and have profiled chefs for your local newspaper, include that. If you haven't been published, explain why you're passionate about the topic or share any special access or interest you have. If you've been researching your family history for ten years and are querying a genealogy magazine, include that. If your next-door neighbor is a spokesman for an association that's key to your article, include that.

Think about what work each paragraph of your query letter is doing as you are writing. Below is a more specific breakdown of what your query letter should include.

- The first paragraph should establish a relationship and let the editor know your value. The first sentence or two must both sparkle and demonstrate a connection. If someone suggested you make contact, use her name.
- The second paragraph should give your credentials. Boldface or italicize the publications you've written for. Also talk about the time you've spent in your business and any awards or other honors you may have received.
- The third paragraph should showcase your skills and demonstrate some solutions. This is where bullets can come in handy. Once again, think of the publication you're targeting. Explain what you can do to meet the magazine's editorial needs.

- The fourth paragraph should close the letter and set a follow-up. Some people like to set a date, others a week. The key is to let the person know you will be following up, then make sure you do so.

Many writers conclude with an estimate of how quickly the article could be written upon assignment. It's also a good place to note that you've enclosed a SASE or e-mail address and, if appropriate, that this query is being sent to more than one magazine. Only send a query to

CRAFT QUERIES WITH PUNCH

"Even after seventeen years, the secret of the query was something I didn't fully understand until I wound up on this side of the desk," said Jeff Ayers former editor for *U.S. Kids.* "As an editor, I came to appreciate the beauty of a very brief pitch letter." According to Ayers, if the query is concise and to the point, the writer is more likely to handle an assignment the same way. "There seems to be a connection between the level of professionalism and the strength of that short pitch," he said. "The best queries come in at just under a page."

With less than a page to win a professional ally, it's important to start strong. "I get at least ten queries a day," said Jessica Solomon, former editor of two Chicago-based children's magazines no longer in publication. "If a writer doesn't grab me in the first paragraph or two, they're not going to make it. If they can't grab me with their query's lead, how are they going to grab the reader with the lead of their story?"

Make that first paragraph count. Start with the one thing an editor wants most—a well-written, publication-specific story idea. Once your concept is on the page, briefly explain why you're qualified to write the piece. Confidence is fine, but avoid idle boasting. "I shy away from writers who insist they'll be the best thing that ever happened to me," said former *Chicago Tribune* KidNews editor Devin Rose.

Finally, proofread your query before you submit. As Solomon said, "A writer loses credibility real fast if they spell my name or the name of the publication wrong. If you're unsure, call the office. If someone can't take a couple of minutes to double-check the spelling of the editor's or the publication's name, how can I trust they're going to double-check the facts in their story?"

more than one magazine if the topic is so timely that you can't wait for a response from one publication before sending it out to another.

Other Query Considerations

Although there are no hard-and-fast rules for query letters, there are techniques that seem to increase their impact on editors.

1. **Do your research.** Make sure the person you contact actually handles articles like yours. Consult the most recent print or Internet sources you can find. Most editors prefer not to be contacted by phone and generally do not return cold calls. Look at it this way: Most writers are not trained to pitch ideas convincingly on the phone. Put your efforts into writing a terrific query letter instead.

2. **Use your intuition.** It's all too easy to fall into the trap of making a query letter something of a form letter. That's a bad mistake. Yes, you can have a couple of stock paragraphs or phrases. But it's also important to think like a reader of the publications you're approaching. Figure out the issues the editors are facing and the problems they want to solve, and mention both in your letter. Identify with their needs and, even more important,

FORMATTING YOUR QUERY LETTER

- Use a standard font (avoid bold, script, or italics, except for publication titles).
- Include your name, address, phone number, fax, and e-mail.
- Use a 1" margin on all sides.
- Address the query to a specific editor (call to get the appropriate name, spelling, and gender).
- Keep it to one page if possible.
- Include an SASE or postcard for reply, and state in the letter that you have done so, either in the body or in a list of enclosures.
- Use block format (no indentations).
- Single-space the body of the letter and double-space between paragraphs.

(From *Formatting & Submitting Your Manuscript*, Writer's Digest Books) the needs of their customers. One potent tactic: If you're dealing with a specific industry segment, use at least one or two phrases of jargon to show you're an insider. People who think you understand their needs will be far more likely to hire you.

3. Respect their time. Editors are busy folks. Every day, thousands of writers mail out query letters. And every day, hundreds of agents and editors send back perfunctory rejections. Surprisingly, most of them want to say yes to writers. You can help! Your mission is to write a one-page—yes, one-page!—query letter that respects their time and sells your idea and yourself as a writer.

You have less than a minute to capture an editor's attention and interest. If she has to work to try to figure out what your idea is, forget it. Be straightforward and keep in mind what editors care about: a viable idea that fits their market.

4. Be clear and precise. Clarity is essential. That translates into simple declarative sentences, clear paragraphs, and a minimum of qualifiers. No "maybe this" and relatively few "I believes." Sharpness also involves word processing power: Bullets are very good, but don't go overboard.

5. Write as if you've got the gig. Query letters should radiate confidence and self-assurance. Act as if you're a precious resource. Convey the knowledge that you're the perfect one for the job, but don't sound like you are too wrapped up in yourself.

6. Demonstrate your ability to write. That doesn't mean you should tell the editor how good of a writer you are, but rather write your query letter in a way that shows your abilities. Don't be flashy or overdo it, but make sure your writing is captivating enough that the editor knows you can write in a way that will command readers' attention. Use your query letter to not only present your idea but also to present your writing skills.

The previous publications for which you've worked are indicators of your talent and legitimacy. Try not to mention a company more than once, but do drop as many different corporate, business, personal, and celebrity names as you legitimately can.

7. Enclose clips of your work. Do not include every clip from every newspaper or magazine you have written for. Instead, carefully choose the clips that would be of most interest to the publication you are querying and that show your best work. Include anywhere from three to five clips, and you can also direct the editor to a Web site where he can view more of your work if necessary.

8. Do not discuss fees or rights in your query letter. These are issues for contract negotiation. You can discuss these issues once your idea is accepted and not before.

Central to this entire exercise is to sell yourself honestly. Your ability to communicate directly, succinctly, and honestly in either a query letter or a conversation speaks volumes to your professionalism. That, ultimately, is what editors are hiring.

E-Querying

The digital age has supercharged the query and submission process and how editors communicate with their clients. What used to take a week or more now takes just a few hours, assuming the two parties are willing to go digital. But electronic submissions and queries take skill and tact to ensure you don't get branded as a difficult or bothersome writer. Using the Internet to stay in touch must be handled appropriately to maintain a human touch.

Simply put: The digital age requires electronic etiquette. E-mail queries and contact should suit an editor's personal preferences. If such submission guidelines are not listed in the publication itself, call the editorial office and request them. Follow these eleven pointers for writing—and sending—e-queries that sell:

1. Confirm e-mail acceptance. First, find out if the magazine accepts e-mail queries. This may seem too basic to mention, but there's no point sending out e-mail queries to publications that won't consider them. Check *Writer's Market* (the print edition or online at www.WritersMarket.com) or

December 10, 2004

Denise Foley
Prevention
33 E. Minor Street
Emmaus, PA 18098

Dear Ms. Foley,

Sales of vitamins and other dietary supplements have been doubling every four years, as consumer awareness of their health benefits grows. But the crush of publicity surrounding supplements obscures the growing confusion about proper dosages and formulations.

I have noted *Prevention*'s growing coverage of supplements and functional foods with interest. I believe many of your readers are now looking for a solidly researched guide to help them develop their vitamin and supplement regimens. The 2,000-word article I propose would be a primer on today's ten most popular supplements, including:

• how to know the right dosage

• how to evaluate quality, including understanding bio-availability and marker compounds

• how to find the best values

I would include a 200-word sidebar on how to find similar information on any supplement.

I have been a health writer for ten years, writing for such publications as *Your Health, Vim and Vigor,* and *Family Circle.* I can turn around a manuscript within three weeks of notification. Enclosed are some of my clippings and a postpaid reply post card.

Thanks for your time. I look forward to working with you.

Respectfully,

Beverly Goodnostrum
5 Freelancer Lane
Anywhere, USA 12345
(212) 456-7890
BevG@email.com

send a quick e-mail to the magazine and ask. Or use that quaint old tool, the telephone. Many magazines also spell out whether they take e-mail queries and where to send them in the writer's guidelines posted on their Web sites. The *Harper's Magazine* Web site (www.harpers.org), for example, asks that queries be sent by regular mail; *Travel + Leisure*'s Web site (www.travelandleisure.com) says the magazine accepts e-queries and gives a special address to send them to.

Also be sure to find out whether to send a document as a file attachment or copied and pasted into the body of the e-mail. Some editors prefer your file attachments be saved in a very specific format—such as PC, Mac, or .txt files. However, many refuse to accept any attachments for fear of viruses or worms. And, unfortunately, many attachments are also digital renditions of the sender's fancy, four-color letterhead. Frankly, most editors don't need or want colorful graphics; they hog memory and clog bandwidth during downloading. If you want an editor to see your beautiful letterhead, mail it.

2. Query with a strong idea. Remember that most basic of basics: The job of a query letter is to persuade a publication to give you an assignment. So whether it's printed on paper or glowing on a cathode-ray tube, any query you send should be built around a solid idea—one that's right for the publication and for which you are, of course, the ideal writer.

3. Take on a formal voice. Be a little formal. E-mail is often more casual than conventional letters. But if you wouldn't call an editor by her first name in a letter, don't do it in an e-mail. An editor accustomed to being addressed by strangers as Mr. So-and-So may not appreciate an e-mail that begins "Hi, Robert" or "Yo, Bobbo."

4. Spell check your query. Watch your spelling. Even in the world of e-mail, editors still expect you to know how to spell. Your e-mail program may have a feature to check spelling just as your word processing software does. If it doesn't, one option is to write queries on your word processor, spell check them there, and then paste them into an e-mail.

5. Use the subject line. Make the subject line work for you. The last thing you want to do is carefully write and polish a query and then have some harried editor delete it, unread, because it looks like spam. One simple way to prevent that is to put the word "query" prominently in the subject line of your e-mail, such as "Query about a new way to garden" or "Query for your upfront section."

6. Supply contact information. Provide enough contact information. Put your phone number and snail mail address on your e-mail. If you have a fax number, you might as well toss that in, too. Anything that makes it easier for a magazine editor to reply to your query increases the odds that one may actually do so.

7. Note your writing samples. Offer to supply samples of your work on request. But don't load up your e-mail with attachments since some editors won't accept them. If samples of your work are available at your own Web site or elsewhere online, by all means mention that, but don't count on the editor spending a leisurely afternoon reading them. In most cases you're still better off sending your samples in as plain old photocopies. That gives editors something they can scan quickly, pass around to their colleagues, and spill coffee on.

8. Keep the résumé at home. Save your résumé for job applications. Just because you can easily attach your résumé to an e-mail doesn't mean you should. As with any writing samples you attach, many editors won't give your résumé so much as a click. Far more effective is a paragraph somewhere near the end of your letter in which you sum up any experience and publishing credits you have that would be relevant to the story you're proposing. While it may take a little longer, try to adapt that paragraph for each query you send rather than treating it as interchangeable boilerplate.

9. BCC: Simultaneous submissions. Go easy on simultaneous submissions. Pitching the same idea to different magazines at the same time couldn't be easier than with e-mail. But unless your idea is so newsy that it can't wait, think twice. Even editors who are willing to look at simultaneous submissions (and many aren't) may be put off by a To: line with the e-mail addresses of all their competitors. When editors get those, they often just delete them, figuring that any writer who wrote to that many publications will never notice whether they replied or not. If you want to try that kind of scattershot approach, be sure to mention that it's a simultaneous submission, but send out separate e-mails with just one addressee each or use the BCC: option.

10. Allow response time. Don't expect an instant answer. E-mail can make it easier to churn out queries, but editors still need time to think about your ideas and respond, just as they would with a paper query. An idea is an idea, whether it arrives via modem or mailbag. If you haven't heard anything after the stated response time, there's no harm in e-mailing back with a gentle inquiry. But whatever you do, don't get testy about it. Editors felt overwhelmed long before e-mail, and it has only added to their burdens. Remember that the easiest thing any editor can do with your query is hit the delete key.

11. Save sent queries. Be sure to save your old queries on your computer. Even if a query didn't sell the first time around, hang onto it. A new market may open up or an editor who turned your idea down because it was too close to something the magazine recently ran may have a change of heart a year from now. You'll save yourself a lot of wasted time if you can retrieve your old queries, update them as needed, and shoot them off again.

Final E-Query Suggestions

Don't forget in all this querying to also track your contacts. All the data you collect about your editorial contacts should be gathered in a database. A contact management program like Outlook helps you keep track of names, data, dates, notes, and follow-up information. A spreadsheet like Microsoft Excel would be good for building that database as well.

Don't forget that just because you have digital capabilities doesn't mean you have to rely on them exclusively. Even in the digital age, don't forget the phone, fax, and yes, postal service. While they may seem antiquated and slow, some assigning editors prefer these communication media—at least as a tool of introduction.

When was the last time you called a client editor just to chat? E-mail is a good way to acknowledge a recent accomplishment or good issue of the publication. But hearing a voice can work wonders to solidify a relationship. Speaking of faithful and traditional correspondence tools, mail service also is preferred by some as the best way to say thanks. If you want to get remembered, mail a card, don't fire off a quick e-mail.

Even with fast, efficient, and functional tools of the digital age, try to retain some humanity along the way.

Take Cover

Cover letters are an often-misunderstood part of being published in a magazine. A near relative of the query letter, the cover letter is the first introduction an editor has to the piece you are submitting. Though not all situations require sending a cover letter to a publication with your manuscript, you should always include one. It's a simple, professional way to quickly summarize your piece and let an editor or publisher know why you were just the right person to write it.

Always think of your cover letter as a business document. It's a formal prelude to the piece you are submitting as well as a record that you sub-mitted it. It documents, for both you and the editor, what piece you sent and when.

Use a business letter format: your name, address, phone number, e-mail address, and company (if applicable) at the top center or left side, followed by the date. On the right side, just above your greeting: the name, company name, and address of the editor and publication where you are submitting.

It is important to know the name of the editor to whom you are sending your manuscript—"to whom it may concern" or "dear sir or madam" indicates inexperience and little knowledge of the publication. Your cover letter should be no longer than a page and should be written in the clear, concise, to-the-point style of a business memo.

Your letter should be tailored to the circumstances under which you are sending your article. Did you previously submit a query about this topic and receive a letter back from the editor expressing interest? It's crucial to mention that; editors are busy people and they may not remember encouraging you to send in your piece.

Any previous correspondence with the editor should be mentioned. Has the editor already seen the manuscript and sent it back to you for revisions? Let her know in your cover letter that this was the piece she looked at in November, and per her helpful suggestions, several revisions were made. Perhaps you queried her previously for an article in a genre she didn't feel fit the magazine (though that would never happen, because you're always familiar with the genre and needs of the magazine you are querying, right?), or on a subject she felt she already had too much on. Remind her of your previous query and tell her you've tailored the new article to her specific needs and interests.

Keep your cover letter brief and concentrated totally on the matter at hand—the manuscript is the important part of your submission; the cover letter simply functions as an introduction to your piece and a record of your submission. Make sure to always include the title of your article and its word count in the opening paragraph.

It is imperative to let the editor know of any special reasons why you are an authority on your topic or if there is something especially timely about the article. If you are a retired sea captain writing a how-to article on navigating a sailboat through a storm, mention your years of experience. It lends instant credibility to your writing.

Likewise, make sure to bring up any special events, publications, or occurrences that could coincide with your piece appearing in the magazine and make it appear timely and relevant. If you wrote a short history of science fiction literature and the biggest science fiction convention is being held at the end of the year, include that information in your cover letter. If a book you've authored on the same subject is being published in six months, let the editor know. This has a double advantage: It shows that at least one other editor thinks your work is good enough for publication, and it proves your authority on the subject. (If a book you've written has already been excepted for publication somewhere, it is best not to excerpt that work as an article. The rights and copyright issues could get complicated and potentially litigious. Avoid the possible problems altogether and use your knowledge of the subject to create an original piece.)

Avoid these common mistakes, and submit a professional cover letter with your professional manuscript.

1. It is best never to begin your cover letter with "Dear sir or madam." Never, never, never open it with "Dear sirs." The first sounds naïve and generic, and the second is archaic and will immediately prejudice any female editor against your work. Find the name of the editor of the publication, which should be listed in the masthead of their magazine.

2. Adjectives and flattery should be avoided at all costs. Do not describe your work as "riveting," "heart-wrenching," or "incredible"—if those things are true, your work will speak for itself. Keep your letter brief and businesslike. And do not flatter an editor by saying his magazine is "undoubtedly the best in the field" or "the only magazine today that really understands the needs of its readers." Editors will only see through this blatant attempt to get published on something other than the quality of your work.

3. Do not threaten an editor. Do not say, "If you reject this piece, I will have no choice but to send it to your competitors" or "I will be watching your magazine, and I'll know if you stole my idea." These are unprofessional and off-putting for a number of reasons, but I think the biggest deterrent for an editor is your tone—does a person who issues threats in her cover letter sound like someone an editor would want to work with? Probably not. Be polite, respectful, and keep the focus of the letter where it belongs—on your work.

4. Don't mention if the piece was previously rejected. Every writer starts his career with more rejection slips then acceptance letters, and

Sample Cover Letter

Jane Smith
1010 Writer's Blvd.
Anywhere, U.S.A. 10749
(123) 456-7890
Janes@email.com

Jan. 21, 2005

Susan Doe
Health, Fitness and Lifestyle Magazine
600 Publisher's Circle
New York, New York 10011

Dear Susan Doe,

Enclosed please find my 3,000 word manuscript entitled "Yoga and the Business World" to be considered for publication in your magazine. This submission is in response to your request of Dec. 15, 2004 to see the piece, after my query in November.

"Yoga and the Business World" is an article geared toward the young, active professionals looking to merge their healthy lifestyle with being chained to a desk for eight hours a day. It explores ways to free up the hours surrounding nine to five to allow for a full workout, as well as methods for bringing the relaxation and cleansing techniques of yoga into the office. It also details certain yoga techniques that are effective in ridding yourself of the day's tensions.

As a professional who works in an office and who has also been a yoga instructor for the past ten years, I am well aware of the challenges of balancing a full workout with the time constraints of a fulltime job. I also understand the benefits of using yoga techniques to banish the stress of the office.

Thank you for your time. I look forward to hearing your thoughts.

Best regards,

Jane Smith

editors know this. But why call attention to the rejection of this particular piece if you don't have to? Stay away from any superfluous information in your cover letter, particularly this information.

Follow-Up Queries

What's the best time to pitch an article idea to an editor? How about when you've just delivered—on time and at the assigned length—an article that's exactly what the editor was looking for?

If you were raised in a family where reserved was a positive personality trait and used-car salesmen and other persistent hucksters were frowned upon, this sort of aggressive sales strategy might strike you as a bit rude. "Here's that article you asked for—now how about another assignment?" Shouldn't the well-mannered writer wait a decent interval? Isn't such an approach simply pushy? That's what David A. Fryxell, editor and publisher of *Desert Exposure* magazine thought—until he had it used on him. And he had to confess: It worked.

The follow-up idea has to be right on target, of course, and the "pushy" writer has to deliver precisely what the editor asked for. (Querying for a second assignment when you've just turned the first one in two weeks late and 1,500 words too long is a guaranteed recipe for a rejection slip.) But, as Fryxell notes, writers who've pitched hard on the heels of getting him the goods have indeed caught him softened up and set to say yes again.

This follow-up technique doesn't even require that you make a sale; the same principle applies if you've merely gotten an encouraging response to a query. The bottom line is the same: Don't let too much grass grow between a positive experience with an editor and your next pitch.

In the most extreme example of fast follow-up that Fryxell has seen, a writer actually enclosed his next query with the manuscript of the first assignment to him. While Fryxell wasn't prepared to say yes to the new idea before he'd read the assigned article, the query did get his attention and was put on his to-do list. He felt a certain obligation to give this pitch a look—even before he considered other unaccompanied queries that were piling up in his in-box.

There's a danger to this approach, though. Because the editor is unlikely to say yes to idea No. 2 before at least reading the completed manuscript of idea No. 1, you won't get an immediate yes. Your query could fall through the cracks or get buried in that in-box. By the time the editor returns to your query, the warm glow from your successful accomplishment of idea No. 1 may have worn off. Your once-hot idea may be greeted with, "Who was this guy again?"

An alternate approach is to give the editor a little time to digest your successful submission before pouncing again. Look for an opportunity to start a dialogue with the editor. If she calls to tell you she liked the piece, have another idea in the back of your mind you can pitch briefly on the phone, maybe with a suggestion that you then send in a full-blown query. Or, if you can't come up with a follow-up when the editor calls out of the blue, at least take the opportunity to ask if you can query with another idea—and then do so, fast.

If the editor e-mails a thanks for a job well done, your path is clear: Reply to the e-mail with your follow-up idea. Even if your second idea turns out not to be a winner, you'll have successfully started a conversation about what you might tackle next.

When editors don't take the initiative to tell you that a submission is acceptable, wait a week or so and then follow up. Your first post-submission contact in that case should be a brief e-mail or call to make sure what you sent was indeed on target and to inquire if the editor needs any revisions or additional material from you. Without being a pest, you can demonstrate that you care about your work and about meeting the editor's needs. When the editor replies that your article is okay (or when you've promptly revised it to her satisfaction), you can respond in turn with your fresh query. This is one reason e-mail is probably better than the phone for asking, "Is it okay?"—it opens the door to an e-mail exchange ending in an opportunity for you to query again in writing. E-mail also lets editors respond at their convenience, rather than putting them on the spot; if the editor hasn't gotten around to looking at your article, the "Is it okay?" e-mail gently prods them to do so.

For magazines that send you galleys of your article, returning the galleys makes a perfect excuse to pitch a follow-up idea. The timing couldn't be better: Your article is smoothly sailing toward the printed page, and the decks are clear for the editor to consider something to help fill the next issue or the one thereafter. (Do not, however, return your galleys with a litany of complaints about your copy being butchered or covered with scribbles attempting to undo the editing. Maybe you don't want to write for this editor again and see your work hacked to pieces, and that's understandable. But don't combine complaints about editing with a query to please go through this agony again.)

A follow-up query is also a fine opportunity to upgrade. If you've successfully completed a short item, set your sights for the follow-up pitch a bit higher: Is there a department you can tackle? A short feature?

Don't overreach, though. Even if you've done a bang-up job on that two hundred-word short, the editor will be reluctant to let you leap immediately to an in-depth investigative piece requiring 7,500 words and an unlimited expense account. This isn't mere editorial pigheadedness but simply human nature. Think of the typical father's reaction to a request like, "Gee, Dad, now that I've just gotten my driver's license, how about if my buddies and I make a 3,000-mile road trip to Nova Scotia?"

The careful upgrade follow-up, by contrast, lets you continue to prove yourself without biting off more than you can chew. Get a few successes under your belt, then even if you do drop the ball at some point the editor will be more likely to be forgiving. She'll know that your failure is an aberration—because you'll already have proven yourself several times.

But what if you haven't yet gotten your foot in the door, just an encouraging note with the editor's "no"? The fast follow-up is still a smart tactic. Use that "close but no cigar" from the editor to open a dialogue, just as if you'd actually sold and delivered an article. Again, without becoming a pest, start a conversation with the editor that shows you really listened to his reasons for rejecting your first idea. Make the editor feel he knows you, even that he has an investment in you. Eventually he'll want to give you an assignment to see his investment of time and critiquing pay off.

In this case, your follow-up might even be a downgrade. If you originally pitched a feature and got an encouraging "no thanks," follow up with a query for a shorter, less-ambitious piece. Make it easier for the editor to say yes this time by ratcheting down the risk. If he gives you a five hundred-word assignment, after all, what's the worst that can happen if you turn out to be terrible? Much less than entrusting you with a big feature that leaves a black hole in his lineup if you blow it.

Once you do get to yes, of course, you can start carefully upgrading to the kind of meaty, more lucrative stories you originally wanted to tackle. Just remember to follow up promptly with those pitches and not rest on your laurels. The editor won't think you're pushy—or if he does, he'll secretly admire your chutzpah.

Chapter Three:
Selling Reprints and Rewrites

Selling an article once is a major accomplishment, at least while you're earning your spurs. Selling the same article again and again, or other articles derived from the same research, is utter delight.

First you need to understand the two major means of reselling. The first, called "reprints," is in its simplest form the selling of the same article, as is, repeatedly to different markets. The second, called "rewrites," is the taking of the same facts, quotes, and anecdotes and reshuffling, expanding, and rewriting them into new forms, each a different article using some or much of the same material.

Reprints

A traditional reprint sale follows the original sale of an article to an editor who purchased first rights. That editor bought the right to use your words, that article, in print first. When those words appeared in print, the rights automatically reverted back to you, and your rights relationship with that editor ended. What remained were second rights, which are also called reprint rights. (Second and reprint rights mean the same thing; the terms are interchangeable.)

Once your article has appeared in print from a first-rights sale, you can immediately offer that very same article, without change, to any other editor you think might buy it. It couldn't be more straightforward.

Writer's Market and WritersMarket.com tell you what rights editors buy and whether they buy reprints, or the editor will tell you when you receive a go-ahead to your query.

Who buys second or reprint rights? Mostly editors who pay on publication, plus a few, whose readers would not likely have read your words in the first publication, who pay on acceptance.

How much do they pay? What they can get it for, or normally pay, since editors buying reprints have no idea what you originally received. Alas, those paying on publication often aren't high rollers, and those paying on acceptance for a piece already used will recognize that you will sell it for less (since you've already been paid for putting the research and words in final form), so figure one-third to one-half of what the original purchaser paid, then consider it a boon if you make more.

The best thing about reprints is that through diligent and creative marketing, you can resell the same piece many times. When the final tally is made, you might have earned more money for churning the same winning prose repeatedly than you made for selling the original.

Using dollars to illustrate the point, if the original article took you eight hours to sell, research, and write and paid you $450, that is a gross profit of $56.25 an hour. If you resell the same article three times, each paying $200 and taking forty-five minutes apiece to find the market, prepare a copy of the article, reprint the cover letter, and get it in the mail, that is an additional $600, or $267 an hour. (You can substitute your own prep time and payment rates.)

Mind you, nobody has ever sold a reprint before he sold the original article, so the hard work—the idea finding, market picking, querying, editor studying, researching, writing, editing, rechecking, and submitting—is done first. Reprints sold later are a very tasty dessert to a hard-won meal.

Finding Markets for Your Reprints

So how do you get editors to buy reprints? Sometimes editors feverishly seek you out, begging you to let them reuse a masterpiece you already sold—you name the price. (Or so say writers whose imaginations vastly exceed their credibility.) Yet it does happen, on a far lesser scale. *Reader's Digest* and *Utne Reader* are two well-known magazines that seek high-quality reprints to use (sometimes rewritten in a condensed form) in their pages. You can shorten their searches by sending copies of a particularly strong article with a cover letter suggesting they may wish to consider that recently published work for their pages.

For any other publication that might consider reusing your bought prose, you must find them, approach them in a sensible manner through a reprint cover letter, and include a copy of the article in question and an SASE.

Common sense guides this search. Since you want to sell the reprint without change, look for publications similar to the one that originally printed your article. Check in the same subject category or those with similar readerships. Start with the table of contents. Read carefully about every publication that might even be remotely similar or use a topic like yours, either as is or redirected to a different market or from a different setting.

A good way to keep track of all this is to create two columns on a sheet of paper. In the first column, write the title of every magazine that might use the article exactly as it is.

POSSIBLE REPRINT/REWRITE OPPORTUNITIES

Magazines that Would Use Article As Is	Magazines that Would Use A Rewrite	
NAME OF MAGAZINE	NAME OF MAGAZINE	NEEDED CHANGES

In the second column, write the title of every magazine that might use the subject if you rewrote or redirected it. Next to the name, write down how you would have to rewrite the article to make it buyable: "for women: change examples, approach from female perspective," "wants history, focus on subject in early 1990s," "uses bullets: extract key points, create bullets," "change the setting to France, use French examples."

First focus on column one. You'll most likely want to contact all of these publications, whether they pay on publication or acceptance. Once you've created a master reprint cover letter, computers make it quick to customize the address and salutation and insert a personalized reference in the text. The potential of a resale, even slight, outweighs the small amount of time, copying, and postage required to get your article and letter before a healthy scattering of eyes.

Do not send the reprint cover letter and article copy to those magazine editors paying on acceptance who already rejected your query, or to those major magazines that never buy second rights. Sometimes there are reprint buyers that are flat-out foes of each other. Submit to one first (the most likely to use it or pay the most) and the second if the first says no.

Sending Your Original Article

Once you have identified your target markets, you'll need a clear copy of the article you want to sell as a reprint. If the article is exactly one page long and includes only your copy, great. Copy and send it as is. But when there is adjacent, nonrelated copy next to the text or the prose trickles onto later pages, you'll want to cut your article out and paste it up. Include the photos or illustrations you also wish to sell. If the name of the publication and date of the issue aren't in the copy, add them to every page and number the pages in consecutive order.

Then head to the quick copy shop to have as many copies produced as you will need collated and stapled. Just make certain the final copies you will send to the editors are clear, easy to read, and include everything you want to be seen.

Writing a Reprint Cover Letter

It's not enough just to have names and addresses plus copies of what you want the editor to buy. You must sell the prospective buyer through a one-page cover letter accompanying the reproduced copy of the article.

Your cover letter must do five things:

1. It must make the topic come alive before the editor ever reads a word of the actual article.
2. It must tell what you are offering and the rights involved.
3. It must describe any additional items or services you can provide.
4. It must tell how the manuscript will reach that editor.
5. By far the least important, it might talk a bit about you and your credentials.

Take a look at each of these areas. The editor doesn't know you, already gets too much mail, and has too little time to waste on an unexpected and probably unpromising letter with an article also enclosed. So your first (and probably second) paragraph has to make the subject of the article jump off the page. It has to make the editor say, "Wow!" or, "I'd be a fool not to want to read this article," or, at the least, "Looks interesting. I'd better read this." This is where you show the editor you can write, discuss the topic on which you have focused your obvious talents, and why (by inference or statement) that topic would find high favor with his readers. This gets the editor to pick up the article and read it through.

The next paragraph is short and falls after the point where you've stirred the editor's interest. It tells what you are offering and what rights are available. You must tell who bought the first rights, when the piece was in print, and what rights you are selling. You should get right to the point, since you don't want to dally here: "As you can see by the article attached, first rights were bought by (publication) and appeared in print on (date). I am offering second rights." (You could say reprint rights as well.)

In the following paragraph you will want to tell of other items beyond the words that you are also offering, such as photos. Since photos are almost always bought on a one-time rights basis, you can offer the photos that were in the article or any of the rest that weren't bought. You can offer to send slides or prints for the editor's selection, if interested. There could also be line drawings, charts, graphs, or any other artwork that either appears in the printed article or that you could prepare to add to the piece.

You could also offer a box or sidebar you prepared that wasn't bought by the first editor—or you could produce one specifically for the reprint. (If the text exists, you might send it along with the copy of the article to expedite the sale and show the reprint editor precisely how it reads.)

Somewhere in the reprint cover letter you must tell the editor what format you will be sending the manuscript in. If you say nothing, the editor will assume that you expect the copy of the article to be retyped or scanned, neither exciting prospects. You enhance the reprint sale by offering either to send the original text double-spaced in manuscript form or on a computer disk, mailed, or sent by e-mail. Electronic submissions are by far the most appealing.

As for what to say about yourself, the article alone will speak volumes, and the quality of the reprint cover letter will probably fill in as many gaps as the editor needs. There are three areas you may wish to expand upon, if it isn't done in the bio slug with the article:

1. if you have several publishing credits, particularly in this field
2. if you have a related book in print or are an acknowledged expert in the field
3. if the work described in the article offers some element of original, unique knowledge or research

In other words, inject more biographical information only if it significantly increases the importance of the article or why the editor should use it. Otherwise, the editor knows the most important information already: that another editor thought your writing was good enough to buy and use. The rest the editor can probably deduce from reading the text. If not, supplement.

Finally, don't forget to include either a SASE or self-addressed postcard for a reply. Otherwise you'll never know if the editor didn't want to buy your words or reuse them.

The reprint cover letter is a sales letter, on one exciting page. Spelling, punctuation, and grammar all count. Make the topic come alive and shout to be used on the editor's pages. Keep the rest businesslike, forthright, easy to understand, and compelling. It's a letter from one businessperson to another, one who has space to fill, another with space fillers to sell.

Making Changes to Your Original

What if an editor wants to use your article but insists upon changes? Fine. But is it a reprint or a rewrite? That depends upon how much change the editor wants and who will write it.

If the changes are major, treat it like a rewrite, which will be discussed next. But sometimes an editor just wants to squeeze the piece a bit, dropping a few words here, an example there, or use his own photo. In these cases he will probably make all of the changes. You might ask to see the final copy before it is printed to make sure the changes make sense.

Or the editor may want you to tie the topic to his locale, adding a quote or two, some local examples or a sidebar that offers local specifics, or he may want to use the reprint as the core with modifications by you.

The more labor you put into it, the more you might want to negotiate the price. Find out what the editor intends to pay for the reprint, then try to get that increased to compensate you for the additional research and writing.

Rewrites

A rewrite, in the least complicated terms, is an article based on an earlier article that uses most or all of the first article's information. It is rewritten to create a different article that has its own sales life.

Let's say you write an article about training in long jumping for the Olympics. You follow the usual format: complete a feasibility study, query, receive a go-ahead, do the research, write the text, and edit it. The article is printed. Then you find two other, smaller magazines that pay on publication that are interested in the same topic, so you send their editors a reprint cover letter, a copy of the published article, and a return postcard. One buys a reprint.

But why end there? Why not go back to that first article and see how you

Your Cover Letter

When sending a possible reprint story to an editor, open with a short lead and then provide information about when and where the article was published.

March 1, 2002

Bonnie Krueger
Editor in Chief
Complete Woman
875 N. Michigan Avenue, Ste 3434
Chicago, IL 60611

Dear Ms. Krueger:

Most of us have been bitten by the green-eyed monster at least once. Fortunately you can keep jealousy from threatening—or even destroying—an otherwise satisfying romance. Read "Slay the Green-Eyed Monster: Keep Jealousy From Ruining Your Relationship" and you'll know how to conquer and overcome jealous feelings for good.

Interested in purchasing reprint rights to this story? "Green-Eyed Monster" was originally published in the fall 2000 issue of *For the Bride by Demetrios;* a copy is enclosed.

Thank you for your time and consideration; I look forward to hearing from you soon.

Very truly yours,

Kelly James-Enger
123 Main Street
Anywhere, USA 12345
(333) 444-5565
Enger@email.com

can reuse most or all of your research to create other solid, salable articles? For example, why not an article for the high school athlete called "So You Want to Be in the Olympics?" From the original, you develop a long-range focus and training program for any athlete in any field, perhaps using long jumping as the example—or tying in several examples, including long jumping. Or how about an article based on three or four athletes, each from a different country, showing the paths they followed to the Olympics, with tips from each for the hopeful? Or four U.S. Olympians from widely varying fields, including long jumping, to show their reflections on having competed: Was it worth the effort? What benefits have they received? In retrospect, what would they do differently? What do they advise the readers who are thinking of following their Olympic paths?

By now the process is clear: Extract something from the original article and build on it for a subsequent article. The more you can use from your original research, the less time you need at the feasibility, querying, and researching stages.

Rewrites need their own titles, leads, quotes, and conclusions built around a different frame. You can use the same facts, quotes, and anecdotes but in a different way and for a different purpose. The trick is equally as obvious: You need a clearly different article, one that has its own angle or slant, reason for being, message, and structure.

Looking From the Rights Perspective

Since rewrites have their own legal existence, you can even sell reprints of rewrites. You can even rewrite rewrites, then sell reprints of rewrites of rewrites. That's just a name game. The editor buying a rewrite calls it an article, an original work created for that magazine and its readers. He doesn't want to know, and you don't want to reveal, that it's a spin-off of earlier research. Does it stand on its own merits? If so, the term "rewrite" has sense only to you as part of the developmental chronology and evolution of an idea put to print.

Further discussion of rewrites falls squarely under the general discussion about how you create and sell copy. Since a rewrite is based on an idea that already sold and comes from research that has passed the test of acceptability, it simply has an edge on the competing articles—if it is worth using in its own right.

The difference is best seen from the rights perspective. A reprint is an article sold on a first-rights basis that is being sold again (and again). The original buyer purchased the right to use that article on his pages first. Once used, the rights reverted to the writer. Following the protocol described, the writer then contacts other editors offering the resale of that original piece, on a reprint or second-rights, nonexclusive basis. The copy is the same or includes few changes.

A rewrite is a different article based on a previously written article and all the research that involved. It's a rewrite only in the mind of the writer. To the buyer it must be completely different from the work sold, since first rights to those words have already been purchased and it is not being marketed as second or reprint rights.

Reprints and rewrites require attention to publishing proprieties. If they are done improperly, you can lose more goodwill, and future earnings, than you earn at the outset. The most important element of those proprieties is honesty—defining in your own mind whether the piece is a reprint or a rewrite. If in doubt, discuss it with the interested editors. They don't bite; they just hold their purse strings tightly.

How to Set Yourself Up for a Reprint

If you are interested in selling reprints (and who isn't?), make sure you set yourself up to have that opportunity down the road. Follow these simple steps to maximize your per-story income.

1. **Have a game plan.** Kathryn Lay of Arlington, Texas, has written more than 450 articles and essays—and sold reprints of two-thirds of them. One seasonal piece on how her family has invited people who might otherwise be alone to share their holidays has been reprinted every year for ten years in a variety of religious publications.

Lay said the key is planning ahead. "Whenever I make out a list of places I want to send something, whether it's a query or a full manuscript, I also make a secondary list for reprints. So, when my piece is published, I immediately have a list of places to send it to."

2. **Watch your rights.** If you sign a work-for-hire or all-rights contract, you can't resell the article. If you want to sell reprints, make sure that any agreement you sign leaves you free to do so. Read your contracts carefully—some preclude you from reprinting a story in similar or competing publications.

The best option is selling one-time rights, which leaves you free to resell that story immediately. Keep in mind, though, that if you sell first rights, you can't offer the work elsewhere until it's been published.

"If you think an article topic has reprint potential, try to sell only first North American serial rights," said freelancer Linda Formichelli, who makes about $5,000 a year in reprint sales. "Then, keep track of when your articles become available for resale—some publications buy exclusive rights for a certain amount of time, like three months. I keep a chart that shows the article title, the magazine that originally published it, when it will become available for reprint, and the magazines I send reprint offers to."

3. **Hunt for markets.** Regional newspapers and magazines, small-circulation publications, and trade magazines may all be interested in reprinted material. Web sites are also great places to resell articles. You can sell nonexclusive electronic rights to a story that first appeared in a print magazine. Noncompeting but similar markets may be interested. For example, Lay has sold the same articles to Methodist, Baptist, and Catholic magazines.

Kelly James-Enger uses a similar approach with regional bridal magazines. When she comes across a regional publication, she asks the editor if reprinted material is accepted and explains the types of stories she has available. Enger has found reprint markets for her bridal stories in Boston, Chicago, and San Francisco for $75 to $125 per reprint.

4. **Develop an inventory.** Popular reprint topics include articles on business, technology, health and fitness, parenting, and travel. Evergreen

stories—those pieces that never go out of date—are always good bets.

Finally, when you find a market for your reprints, check in occasionally to keep the editor updated on new stories becoming available. "Following up is also important," self-syndicated writer Mary Dixon Weidler said. "I've had publications print stories but 'forget' to pay, so periodically I will ask if they used anything they had requested, adding, of course, an updated list for them to peruse. Often I don't only get my check and copies—I also make another sale."

While markets tend to pay less for reprint stories than original work, they're a source of income savvy freelancers should consider. Invest time in finding reprint markets—the payoff of "free" paychecks makes it all worthwhile.

Chapter Four:
Finding Markets

One of the keys to getting your queries accepted and your articles published is to find a market in need of writers. Some markets are more open to new writers and some require several clips before they'll give you a chance. Don't be discouraged in your search; everyone has to start somewhere. Give yourself the best chance of getting an editor to say yes to your idea by querying editors who are looking for fresh voices. Get your foot in the door, any door, and more doors will start opening.

Magazines Most Open to New Writers

Some magazines are more receptive to new writers than others. Be on the lookout for these five types of publications that are almost always looking for fresh talent.

1. **New magazines.** Some 700 to 1,000 new magazines are launched each year, according to Samir A. Husni, a University of Mississippi journalism professor who compiles an annual guide to new magazines at www.mrmagazine.com.

New magazines are especially receptive to new writers for a couple of reasons. One, obviously, is that they don't have a vast network of writers in place yet. Another is that new magazines usually don't have the editorial budgets of larger ones, so they're often willing to take a chance on less experienced (in other words, cheaper) writers.

How do you find out about new magazines before they're old magazines? The easiest way is to keep checking both your local newsstand and the supermarket magazine racks for titles you've never seen before and trade magazines that people in the publishing business read.

And never underestimate the value of your own mailbox. What may be mere junk mail to your neighbors could be valuable information to you. Years ago, freelance writer Greg Daugherty received a mailing from *Yankee* magazine announcing a new spin-off called *Collectibles Illustrated*. Daugherty wrote to the editor of the new magazine, enclosed some clippings of articles he'd written, and offered his services in case the editor ever needed a correspondent where he lived. Within weeks Daugherty had an assignment.

2. **Old magazines with new owners.** When a magazine gets a new owner, things tend to change. A new owner almost inevitably means a new team of editors and, sometimes, a new approach to whatever the magazine covers. Any change of that sort means a new opportunity for writers.

The best way to keep track of ownership changes is to read the trade magazines mentioned later in this chapter. Another is to take note when a magazine alters its logo or overall design. A new design may mean a new art director, another near inevitability after an ownership change.

3. **Magazines that are changing frequency.** A magazine expanding from

FINDING NEW MAGAZINES

You should consider carefully the possibilities of getting published in new magazines. On average, twice a day, a new magazine debuts. That's right—twice a day. That means a lot of new opportunities.

To hunt down start-ups and spin-offs, use the same detective skills you already use to find assignments in established publications or to find experts for your articles. Read publications such as *Folio:, Advertising Age, Adweek,* and *Mediaweek* that offer updates on the state of existing and new magazines. *The New York Times, USA Today,* and *The Wall Street Journal* all report on magazine launches as part of their business and marketing coverage. Husni produces an annual book on the topic, *Samir Husni's Guide to New Magazines,* and posts latest developments on his Web site (www.mrmagazine.com). Husni's site doesn't have a search function, but it provides free information on new launches, including title, page count, and price. And of course, *Writer's Market* carries a special designation for new listings in its annual edition, and WritersMarket.com provides online subscribers with recent changes, including magazine launches and demises.

six issues a year to twelve may need twice as much editorial material to fill its pages. Even a magazine going from ten issues a year to twelve may need 20 percent more material. Any frequency boost is likely to mean the magazine is more open to new writers.

4.   Magazines that are changing focus. Sometimes magazines take a new direction even without changing owners. That, too, may spell opportunity, since not all of the magazine's current writers will be right for the new and improved model.

5.   Small magazines. Whether they're under new management or have been run by the same family since the War of 1812, small-circulation magazines tend to be more open to new writers than their giant competitors. Small magazines also tend to have smaller budgets, which means they often have to take talent where they find it. You may never make a living by writing for small magazines, but they can be terrific places to gain some experience and accumulate a few good clips.

A Growing Market

Besides new or changing magazines, there are other ways to find potential markets with plenty of opportunities. One way is to target the increasing population of baby boomers. As the baby boom moves into what has traditionally been thought of as senior citizenry, it will represent a once-in-a-millennium opportunity for writers. Not only are the seventy-six million Americans born between 1946 and 1964 the biggest and richest generation in U.S. history, they are also a generation of readers. And they are facing some tough questions for the very first time.

One place they're likely to turn for help is the magazine rack. Baby boomers grew up with magazines and value them as sources of advice and entertainment. Yesterday's readers of *Famous Monsters* and *Tiger Beat* are today's subscribers to *Forbes* and *Travel Holiday*. And they will be tomorrow's readers of publications as yet unlaunched.

Already there are a handful of magazines targeted at this huge and potentially lucrative market. Among them: *AARP The Magazine* (from the AARP) and *More* (from Meredith Corporation, publisher of *Ladies' Home Journal*).

What will those and other publications want from writers? Two things, and both are important.

The first will be expertise in one or more of the subject areas that are of greatest interest to this age group. That's the easy part, which you'll see in a moment. The trickier part will be understanding and mastering the tone with which these readers want to be addressed.

Many of today's over-fifty readers say they do not want to be called "seniors." They do not want to be called "mature." They do not want to be called "silver" or "golden" or any other precious metal. Nobody knows yet what they do want to be called. There's a big prize awaiting anyone who figures that out.

Above all, they do not want to read anything that condescends to them, that seems to say, "There, there, you poor old thing." This generation is in no rush to trade the Rolling Stones for kidney stones.

How, then, do you speak to these readers? First, be upbeat—but try not to be corny about it. Recognize that, according to any number of studies, the fifties and sixties really are the best decades of life for most people—the times when they are happiest with their jobs, their families, and themselves. Don't wreck it for them.

If you're a baby boomer yourself, you may have a slight edge. You'll know what questions are on your mind and probably the minds of a lot of your peers. That should make it easier to come up with winning article ideas. Plus you already know all the right cultural references, making you unlikely to confuse Herman of the Hermits with Herman of the Munsters, for example. But even if you don't know a Gidget from a widget, never fear: A firm grasp of your subject matter will be the important thing. These, after all, are readers who grew up with the consumer movement and became savvy consumers of magazine articles in the process.

So what subjects will tomorrow's fifty-plus readers be interested in— and where will you as a writer find your greatest opportunities? Here are five areas that are already hot and seem bound to get hotter. Not every magazine will cover all of them, of course, but you're likely to find plenty of markets for any of these topics, starting with the hottest of all:

Health. Even people who have blissfully ignored their health for decades may catch themselves reading nutrition labels on food packages once they turn fifty. Today's baby boomers are still relatively young and healthy, and most seem determined to stay that way as long as possible. That means a potentially huge market for health writers, especially those who know something about nutrition, exercise, and other ways to stay youthful and fend off disease.

Money and retirement advice. With retirement on the horizon for many, baby boomers want to know that they're doing the right things with their money now so they'll have enough of it for the years ahead. If you're the kind of writer who isn't scared off by decimal points and dollar signs, take heed. Best bets in this category: investing, tax tips, and estate planning.

Entertainment and travel. This is a generation that has always taken its fun seriously. Magazines will be there to help readers sort through their endless entertainment options—with book, movie, video, music, and Web site reviews for every conceivable taste. And if you're a travel writer, start packing: People over fifty do more traveling than any other age group.

Family matters. Like health, family seems to become more important to people as they grow older. From happy topics like planning a family reunion or traveling with a grandchild to more difficult ones like caring for a sick parent, readers will look to magazines for advice and encouragement.

Essays and humor. Pieces that speak to the heart are likely to find a wide audience as this generation moves into what's often a more reflective stage of life. If you're an essayist with something to say, especially if you are a member of this generation yourself, here's the time to say it. And, as the people who grew up with Soupy Sales and *Saturday Night Live* look for new laughs, humorists should also find a ready market.

Writing for Local vs. National Publications

When you first decided to write magazine articles, you probably dreamed of being published in your favorite magazine, perhaps a magazine with a circulation in the millions—one that your family, friends, and acquaintances would all know and read every week or month. While it's entirely possible that you will one day be published by one of the major women's or lifestyle magazines, that's not where you will likely get your start.

Most writers begin by writing modest articles for publications with modest circulations. Perhaps you consider yourself better than the average beginner, with some experience and savvy. Even if this is true, without an established track record in magazine article writing, you should consider the advantages to starting small then working your way up to the big leagues.

- **Large magazines rarely, if ever, take a chance on an unproven writer.** They often have a stable of contributing writers and editors—professionals—whom they draw upon again and again. So you should avoid querying the biggest nationals if you're just starting out and lack an arsenal of clips. Small magazines, on the other hand, are more open to beginners and willing to take a chance on an unknown, especially if your query displays professionalism and excellent writing skills.

- **Small magazines—often regional or niche magazines—are easier for beginners to crack.** This is especially true if you've done your homework on the publication. Your query is more likely to be read by a senior editor on the magazine rather than an editorial assistant because smaller magazines have smaller staffs, and often one person wears multiple hats. Your query might be reviewed more quickly and with more careful attention—but don't make the mistake of thinking your query doesn't have to be strong and attention grabbing. You still have to impress and make your writing the best it can be, and if your query succeeds, it will stand out against all the other queries (instead of being mixed in with a thousand others at a large-circulation magazine).

- **Chances are you will be more capable of a successful start with small or regional publications.** This is definitely the case if they focus on a community or interest you already know very well. Let's say you're a lifetime resident of Evansville, Indiana, and intimately familiar with its culture. You might try querying the Evansville city magazine, *Evansville Living*, if you're just starting out because you're more likely to be familiar with the magazine and instinctively know what kinds of articles would interest the magazine's audience.

- **Editors at small magazines are more likely to work with you during the writing process.** They will help build your skills and give you useful feedback. Especially if the publication is less frequent than a monthly, the editor might have more time to spend on the development of a piece. Sometimes, you might even be able to visit with the offices of such publications to further build your relationship with the editors or to discuss your article ideas. Those who work out of New York, at the major magazines, most certainly don't have time for this kind of nurturing, or what they would consider handholding.

Remember, small doesn't mean low quality or unworthy. Many wonderful small and regional magazines are well respected in the industry and win awards for their content and design. Building your skills and expertise through such publications will help you approach the larger ones. Once you understand how the industry works, you'll gain the confidence to approach the national publications with an impressive selection of clips that will make even the most hurried editor pause and read what you have to offer.

Markets to Consider

Countless other markets exist. Let the following list be a springboard to exploring the possibilities and finding the market that best fits with your work.

Women's Magazines

What's not to like about writing for women's magazines? Many pay big bucks—$1 to $2 per word and more—and they get your name in front of millions of readers.

And don't think you have to be a sister yourself to break into the titles collectively known as the six sisters: *Family Circle, Redbook, Good Housekeeping, Ladies' Home Journal, Better Homes and Gardens,* and *Woman's Day.* Freelancer W. Eric Martin has written several pieces for *Woman's Day,* and Pam O'Brien, former executive editor of *Ladies' Home Journal,* said the magazine uses several male writers on a regular basis.

First step: Study the magazines so you'll send just the right idea to just the right person. You'll also learn what not to send editors. "I can't tell you how many poetry submissions I receive," said Cari Wira, *Woman's Day* reader editor. "All of these writers get rejected, not because their writing isn't good, but because we don't ever publish poetry."

Studying a few past issues will give you an idea of the magazine's demographics and the attitudes of its readers. "As a writer, you need to think about who will be reading the article," said Stacey Colino, who's written for about a dozen women's magazines including *Redbook* and *Ladies' Home Journal.* "Do these women have kids? Do they work outside the home? Is their style more suburban soccer mom or urban hip? Factors like these will affect the tone, content, and angle of the article—and these need to be reflected in your query."

For example, when studying *Redbook,* writer Linda Formichelli noticed that writers tended to use short, spunky words like "nix" and "zap," so she used these words when writing her query for (ahem) "The Better Orgasm Diet" to show the editors that she understood the tone they were looking for: "Nix the caffeine for a better sex life" and "Alcohol will zap your sexual energy."

Next, think small. The fastest way to break into women's magazines is to aim for the shorter department pieces. "Unfortunately, many [writers] propose huge features right off the bat before getting their feet wet," said Wira. "My best advice to writers who are just starting off, either in women's writing or writing in general, is to start small. Three hundred and fifty-word pieces for regular columns are tough for editors to brainstorm every issue. To get in the door and cultivate a relationship with an editor, try pitching smaller pieces, which can always lead to larger pieces."

And even unpublished writers have a chance with opinion pieces and essays, since it's standard practice to send in those pieces as complete manuscripts—no clips required.

Compelling real-life stories always stand out in the slush pile. "The best way to break into *Ladies' Home Journal* is through their column called First Person," O'Brien said. "Many of these are as-told-to stories. They need such a steady supply of them and such a variety of them that it's a good opportunity for writers."

All this advice is easy enough to give, but where do you come up with the ideas that will have editors adding you to their favorite writers list?

First, take a look at the magazines and see what they run month after month. These evergreen stories never lose their freshness. In *Ladies'*

Home Journal, for instance, it's the story of an exceptional woman. "They are always looking for stories about women who are doing interesting things," O'Brien said. "Great human interest stories, women who have overcome obstacles—women who both you and I want to read about."

Evergreen topics in *Woman's Day* include finding time for yourself and your family, ways to save money, and learning to love yourself, Wira said. Other good solid standbys for women's publications include how-tos on relationships, parenting issues, health, and saving money. Just be sure to give a tired topic a new twist. For example, Formichelli, who sold articles to *Redbook* and *Family Circle*, broke into *Woman's Day* the same month with an article on not just saving money but unique ways to save money on big-ticket items like appliances, furniture, and cars.

Your life should also be mined for all it's worth. "I draw directly from my life," said Diane Benson Harrington, managing editor of *Freelance Success* (a weekly guide to freelancing opportunities), who has written for *Woman's Day* and *Family Circle*. "Thus, I pitched 'The I-Hate-Housework Guide to Cleaning and Decorating,' which offered tips on how to decorate your house if you hate to clean and [on] how to clean with absolute minimal effort."

Editors are inundated with queries, so it's imperative that yours stand out. A reader-grabbing lead is the way to start. "I don't think it's the length of the query so much as the quality of the idea," O'Brien said. Don't force yourself to write long queries, but be bold enough to include any appealing information, even if it pushes the query over the standard length.

Include in your query the names and credentials of your sources (along with a juicy quote or two from one of them), plus any stats that show why your idea needs to be written. For example, in a recent query on women in martial arts, Formichelli included a statistic that proved women are joining martial arts classes in unprecedented numbers. And women's magazines are sidebar-happy, so be sure to include information on any potential sidebars or boxes you could create.

It's hard to break into women's magazines without related clips, but you can't get clips until you've written for women's magazines. Well, take heart. Formichelli broke into *Woman's Day, Family Circle*, and *Redbook* with clips from health and business magazines. Writer Kathryn Lay sent clips from kids' and religious magazines, and Harrington sent newspaper articles. Clips from Web sites and regional magazines also work. "Even if it's just from a newspaper, any clips you have will help you get your foot in the door," O'Brien said.

Once you land an assignment and get a clip from one woman's magazine, you're in. "Half the editors at every national magazine in the country must have read my first published clip in *Woman's Day*," said Jennifer Nelson, whose publishing credits don't end with *Woman's Day*. "At many places, the doors seemed to open up immediately. Even some magazines that were rejecting my pitches appeared to take a teeny bit of extra time, at least reading them, or responding with a personal rejection."

Trade Journals

Imagine depositing a $1,500 check for an article that had been a breeze to write. Would you care if no one had heard of the publication it appeared in? Trade journals offer writers a chance to publish regularly. They're typically more accessible than consumer publications, and their pay rates occasionally rival those of big-time magazines, even if they are not well known.

Freelancing for the trades seems to be more competitive today, in part because full-time staffers are generating more articles as companies eye the bottom line. On the positive side, the Internet is creating new trade and consumer writing opportunities every day. Many trades want original Web content, and knowledgeable freelancers are in a perfect position to help out.

What is a trade journal? Trade journals focus on particular occupations or industries. Ever heard of *Expansion Management Magazine*? According to *Writer's Market*, its circulation is 45,000. *Trucking Times* pays writers forty cents per word. Also, there are trades devoted to specific passions. Is knitting a hobby? What about *Knitting Digest*? *Dramatics Magazine*? *Antiqueweek*?

Jennifer Juergens, former editor of *Incentive* magazine, said the key for writers is to "have at least a clue about the industry. . . . Once you are known in the industry, publications are going to use you over and over."

John N. Frank, Midwest bureau chief for *PRWeek* magazine, has spent his professional life switch-hitting between freelancing and working as an editor and writer. He's written about everything from beverages to financial markets. When he searches for freelance opportunities, he finds that editors are "very excited I know about their industries."

Before you stop pitching mainstream titles, consider trades' drawbacks. David Leidl, a long-time freelancer and senior editor/writer for *BC Business*, a Canadian business publication, said that at trades, editorial staffers "are often less professional, often resulting in more work for the writer; the work eventually can become utterly boring and you can easily become categorized, making the break into the consumer market much more difficult."

If you want to give trades a shot, what do you need to do? The same things you need to do to be successful in consumer magazines: Write great queries, display a professional, enthusiastic attitude, produce clean, accurate copy, come up with ideas for art and sidebars, and meet deadlines. You should also be up to speed on jargon. For example, if banking publications are your goal, understand that settlement is more than what happens with a divorce.

With trade magazines, you:

1. Select your own area of expertise or interest. Remember the writer's adage: Write what you know.

2. Are relatively certain of a steady income source once you've established yourself in a field and learned about other related publications.

3. Face less competition if you hone in on a field of expertise.

4. Gain some clout and room to grow once you've shown you're a pro. After a few years writing a column for a trade, you may not only be assigned features but the editors may also start to ask for your editorial advice.

But you also must:

1. Know that compensation is likely to be lower initially than with consumer publications. Once your clip file starts to fill and you have developed a long-term, successful liaison with a trade publication, you will receive more steady assignments, and there is room to negotiate on fees.

2. Be prepared to be bored at times, since you'll be writing a lot about the same topics. Also, understand that in the trade magazine business, competition is fierce. Once you write for one, you can't pitch ideas to another. (Most will tell you outright that you can't write for a competing publication.)

3. Understand that trade editor turnover is at least as high as consumer editor turnover, and the subject matter requires time to become an expert. Even as a freelancer, you may at times be helping indirectly to train the new editor.

4. Keep in mind your decision to write for trades could make it more difficult to break into consumer markets. Sending a huge portfolio of trade-only clips won't put you in contention with the writer who sends but a few clips from the consumers.

Writing for the trades may have some downfalls (any market does), but don't exclude them entirely. The trades have plenty of assignments and dollars to offer any writer who is willing to step up to the challenge.

Travel Writing

The Hawaiian resort surpasses every travel fantasy, from the white-sand beach to the gargantuan pool, luxurious marble bathrooms, and doting staff. Too bad while everyone else is reveling in paradise, you're racing around with a notebook, asking questions, and scribbling furiously. You're hot, tired, and cranky.

Welcome to the world of travel writing. You're interviewing a chef when you could be deep into a new mystery at the beach, inspecting the kids' club when you'd rather be playing tennis, or touring hotels when the rest of your family is snorkeling. You rarely daydream by the pool or anywhere else. You interview other pool-goers, skiers waiting in the lift lines, and cruisers filling their plates at lunch.

The good news: You get to go places other people only dream about and meet amazing people. You come home with an entirely different perspective than the average tourist. Even better, you get paid for the privilege. You don't have to begin life wanting to be a travel writer to become one now. Follow the six tips below and you'll be on your way.

1. Start at home. Approach your local newspaper or company newsletter with a story based on a recent trip or one you're planning. Or, query editors elsewhere about a story in your own backyard, whether it's the new restaurant scene in Brooklyn, a runner's guide to Chicago, or the favorite shopping haunts around San Francisco. You can find the names of—and often the e-mail addresses for—feature and travel editors listed on newspaper and magazine Web sites or in *Writer's Market*.

2. Do your homework. Before pitching your story, research the information you need to sell your idea to an editor. Are more people river rafting with kids these days? Is Portugal a new hot destination? Are women opting for ski camps? Are men hitting spas? Most state, regional, or city visitor and convention bureaus have staff assigned to answer reporters' questions. You also can tap sources at resorts, hotel chains, cruise lines, adventure outfitters, and even the National Park Service. Check out the Travel Industry Association of America, which tracks trends, for support for your pitch or to come up with ideas.

Another important part of your homework is understanding what each magazine needs. Travel writer and novelist Shirley Streshinsky said, "Do not, as I once did, suggest a story on Bali to a travel magazine that runs stories exclusively on Europe. And if stories in a given magazine tend to run to 1,500 words, do not turn in a 4,000-word manuscript."

3. Find your niche. It always helps if you've got some expertise on the subject. You could specialize in family travel, snow sports, spas, food or cycling, senior or gay travel. Build on your expertise (or develop one) based on your interests. If you're a gourmet cook, consider writing about new chefs; if you're a golfer, explore golf resorts. Reporting, you'll find, can be a terrific way to learn, whether it's learning about the history of Nantucket, training sled dogs in Minnesota, or hand-painting pottery in Spain. You'll be amazed at how much people will help you, too, sharing their perspectives, talents, and even secrets known only to the locals.

Once you've got your niche, you can explore new angles to travel venues that have inspired reams of copy. Take a lesson from freelance travel writer Eileen Ogintz. In Walt Disney World, she wrote about standing in line and being afraid of roller coasters, not just about the newest rides. In London, rather than writing about the usual tourist haunts, she wrote about exploring London's Portobello Road antique (and junk) markets with her eight-year-old son. Instead of writing about the waterfalls at Yosemite, she wrote about the California families who come to the park every Easter.

4. Be honest. When pitching an editor, be clear about whether you accepted any press discounts for the trip about which you're writing. Some publications won't want your story if you do, while others won't care. Chances are, though, you won't be afforded any great discounts or invited on press-only trips unless you've got an assignment letter from some publication or have published several pieces. Even then, you may not be offered a great deal. But the more travel stories you've done, the more likely you'll get invited along on junkets designed to introduce travel writers to new places, hotels, and cruise ships.

But these organized trips aren't the only way to approach travel writing. Sometimes a more realistic view of each place, exchanging views with locals and other tourists, is better. And when you travel on your own, you're also not tethered to a group itinerary—and agenda.

5. Be realistic. Don't expect an editor to send you to some exotic locale. That rarely happens, especially when you're new to the game. When you're breaking in, you also need to be realistic about what you can sell.

Be ready to write what the publication needs rather than the story you're dying to write. *Travel + Leisure's* research editor Mario Mercado recommends establishing a relationship with a magazine by suggesting several short 200- to 350-word pieces for various departments. "Tenacity has its rewards," he said. "You may start with some short blurbs, but those can develop into two thousand-word assignments."

6. **Keep pitching.** You may pitch dozens of ideas—good ones, you think—that editors don't like. An editor may tell you an idea is overdone. Other editors may like the idea but want to use a writer they know. It's important to realize that rejection often has little to do with your ability or ideas. Perhaps the newspaper you approach about your Alaskan cruise has just published an entire section on the subject. Maybe the magazine you thought would love your story about your bike trip in France just printed a piece about a bike trip along the Oregon Coast.

If one editor turns you down, try another at a different publication. Ask the editors for suggestions. Mercado said he often refers writers to other editors at his magazine or elsewhere. The more clips you have to show—even if you've only published travel stories in your local weekly—the better your chances. The clips not only show that you're serious but that you've been successful.

TRAVEL WRITING RESOURCES

- Travel Industry Association of America (www.tia.org): The trade group offers breaking travel news from the industry's perspective as well as research and trend information.
- World Chamber of Commerce Directory (www.chamberofcommerce.com): The site provides links to more than fifteen thousand chambers of commerce and convention and visitor bureaus worldwide.
- Travelwriters.com (www.travelwriters.com): In addition to information at the site, there's a free electronic newsletter with information on press trips and markets.

Custom Publications

Most magazine writers know that the newsstand can be a fruitful place to look for new markets, but how many would think to head to their favorite clothing store? Or cafe? While most sponsored publications lack the exposure and household cachet of their newsstand siblings, astute writers should take note of several key attributes that make sponsored magazines a potentially viable market for their work.

First, custom magazines need freelancers. While content for some custom titles is prepared in-house or through an advertising agency, many such magazines are farmed out almost entirely to outside writers.

Many publishers work on several titles for different clients, which means they're likely to tap a good writer for more than one project. "If you get in good with an editor for a custom publisher who has a variety of titles, you can get more work from that single source of contact than you potentially could, for example, if you were only talking to the editor of *GQ* or *Cosmopolitan*," said Diana Pohly, president of Boston-based custom publisher Pohly & Partners. Her firm publishes thirteen custom titles for clients including Whole Foods Market, Continental Airlines, and Sotheby's International Realty.

In addition, writing for custom publishers can be lucrative. "It pays better than newspapers and vertical trade publications," said Pohly, who estimates the average pay rate to be $1 per word, a figure other industry sources cite as reasonable.

Still, writers should keep in mind that certain caveats apply. Foremost is the simple fact that the sponsoring client has veto power over editorial content.

"If we're doing a magazine for a fashion retailer," said Louise Sloan, who has experience with G+J Custom Publishing in New York City and American Express Custom Publishing, "we aren't going to be reporting on the latest labor abuses in manufacturing clothes. . . . Journalistic freedom . . . ends if we're going to be badmouthing what our client's trying to sell."

A further difficulty is that unsolicited queries may not be the best way to pitch editors at custom titles. Sloan said, "Since custom magazines are created specifically for the client, we come up with a table of contents for the client. It's all done usually very quickly. We don't have the huge lead time that other magazines have, so we are rarely, rarely able to use any query letters."

Sloan suggested that freelancers submit a résumé and clips to which editors can refer when assigning stories. Clips are especially valuable, she says, because custom publishing's compressed time schedule makes editors wary of unknown talent. Because they only give writers one to two weeks turnaround time, Sloan says they are hesitant to work with new freelancers because there's no time to fix an article if it's not right.

While it may prove initially difficult to develop a relationship with a custom publisher, the rewards for those who persist can be great. Molly Rose Teuke, a freelance writer from Madison, Wisconsin, who has worked on custom titles for several years, offered her experience: "I started doing very short little pieces for one magazine out of a custom house, and within a couple of years I was writing for five magazines out of that same house," she said.

History Magazines

Freelancers with a nose for research and a talent for storytelling can find a rich future in the past.

"The history market began taking off in the 1960s with the centennial of the Civil War, and it's been going gangbusters ever since," said editor Rod Paschall of *MHQ: The Quarterly Journal of Military History.*

The history market is a colorful mosaic of niches encompassing a wide variety of specialty areas. You can choose from a topic as focused as lighthouses (*Lighthouse Digest*) or as broad as Americana (*American Heritage*). You even can pick the war of your choice (*World War II* and *America's Civil War*).

You needn't be an expert or historian to crack these markets. Even at *Air & Space/Smithsonian* magazine, where one in three articles is based on history, editor George C. Larson leans heavily toward writers who have experience in consumer magazines. That's because today's history magazines have shifted away from so-called "footnoters" and "rivet counters" and are seeking good old-fashioned stories about the experiences of real people. Editors want different takes on old stories and material that both entertains and informs while providing readers with new insights into a moment in history.

Getting off the beaten path can also snag a sale, such as an *MHQ* piece on Greek warriors who dressed in drag to gain access to a fortification, or an *Air & Space/Smithsonian* story on a nineteenth-century hoax about the supposed discovery of people on the moon.

History writers do need to be sticklers for detail. Editors look for solid facts that go to the source. "Don't use books for your research," warned *Lighthouse Digest* editor Tim Harrison. "There are too many books out there with inaccuracies. We would prefer to see writers do some in-depth research." That means checking with historical societies, mining old newspapers and documents, and perhaps talking with old-timers who actually lived the history you're writing about.

Sometimes those old-timers aren't so old—what's classified as history varies with each publication. While *World War II* magazine limits its content to the years encompassing that war, *Air & Space/Smithsonian* considers space history to be as recent as ten years ago.

Most editors demand documentation of sources, as well as reference notes. Paschall sounds a common note among history editors: "We want to know who [the writer] is quoting and where he's getting his material, because we just cannot afford to have bogus information in our magazine." Failure to include those reference notes in your submission is a common cause of rejection.

In many cases, you don't need to provide illustrations. But it helps if you can at least offer leads on sources of old photos or perhaps suggest suitable illustrations for your article.

Most history publications are wide open to new contributors and hungry for material. At *MHQ*, for instance, a good 30 to 40 percent of each issue is written by new contributors. Said Larson at *Air & Space/*

Smithsonian, "That's what we thrive on—the constant freshening of material from new sources."

Health Magazines

Squeezed between pressures of daily living and ballooning medical costs, readers turn to health magazines for vital information. "More and more people are really questing for that place in themselves where they feel well in every sense of the word," said Doug Crichton, editor in chief of *Health*.

"Consumers of health services are sick and tired of bad treatment, insurance hassles, [and] the entire health bureaucracy," added Peter Moore, executive editor of *Men's Health*. "They want to take health into their own hands. The boom in health writing and reporting is an outgrowth of that."

But health magazines are extremely niche-oriented, so freelancers must be savvy to each publication's distinctive slant when pitching article ideas. For example, *Health* "is very much about a healthy lifestyle," whereas *Let's Live* is "all about nutrition," and *Men's Health* is definitely a guy thing.

Also, a growing number of publications are devoted to a single health issue. *MAMM* focuses on cancer of the breast and female reproductive organs, while *Diabetes Health* obviously hones in on diabetes. "I think there's a need for information, communication, and community for people who have been diagnosed with life-threatening conditions," said *MAMM* editor in chief Gwen Darien.

Editors look for well-researched, leading-edge health information supported with quotes from medical experts. Many also want the health issue in question to be illustrated with quotes and anecdotes from everyday people. "If you're ready to make the fifty phone calls it takes to provide readers with information that's actionable and that they haven't read a hundred times before," said Moore, "we can use you."

In most cases, you need not be a health-care professional to tap into the health market, and the door is wide open to freelancers. Writers who can interpret scientific studies and make them understandable to laymen "would be worth their weight in gold" to *Let's Live* editor in chief Beth Salmon.

A number of health magazines have Web sites open to freelancers. *Health* magazine's (www.health.com) "is much broader, much deeper, and allows us to do things that the magazine cannot," Crichton said. Along with stand-alone articles, the Web site offers in-depth research and guidelines on specific health issues to complement related articles in the magazine.

Expect a healthy return for health articles. Pay ranges from $50 for short pieces in *MAMM* (that rate goes much higher with longer articles) to a top rate of $5,000 for full-length features in *Men's Health*.

As for the future of the health-writing market, take it from Crichton: "There will always be magazines that are very focused on health, health news, and health-and-medicine."

Home and Garden Magazines

Home and garden magazines cover far more than just sumptuous surroundings. They're into cooking, pool safety, home security, and seasonal lawn care. What's more, they often include consumer-oriented pieces on how to choose outdoor grills, painting products, and range hoods—topics any competent writer can handle.

Therefore, here are a few recommendations:

- **Research first, write later.** Proposing a piece on sofa selection? Check into wood species, craftsmanship, and grades of upholstery. Throw a few knowledgeable tidbits into your query.

- **Collect brochures.** Label according to dealers and store them according to category. Not only will they inform you and later jog your memory, they'll offer possibilities for photo selections. Editors like having something pretty to look at along with something good to read.

"Home decor magazines are all about visuals," said Catherine Yarnovich, former executive managing editor of *Romantic Homes*. "If you've got lovely photographs to go with your query, you've got a better shot at getting an assignment."

While the magazine may send a photographer to reshoot, it's important to give the editors an idea of the visual potential.

- **During interviews, ask questions from a consumer's standpoint.** Why would anyone pay twice as much for a certain washer and dryer? Why does some art look better unframed? Why might buyers prefer stainless steel sinks? Never forget your real audience—the average homeowner with high aspirations.

- **Be aware of trends—and then try to keep up.** Interior design is a living, breathing, ever-changing entity, as fascinating and evolving as human nature itself.

"Be on the lookout for a new take on anything that's on the market," said Yarnovich.

Don't, however, accept company assertions at face value, cautioned Jim Adair, former editor in chief of *Canadian Homes and Cottages*. "Too many writers go with claims that a product is 'the first,' 'the most' or 'the biggest,' when it's really the same as a competitor's."

- **Attend home shows.** Over-the-top is exactly what you need to see—because whatever is cutting-edge bizarre now will probably be routine within five years.

- **Recognize the difference between a do-it-yourself publication and a coffee table display.** Different markets, different subscribers. One deals in reality, the other in fantasy. It sounds obvious, but don't accidentally write for one and then send your piece to another. Also, be aware of geographical differences.

"I get tons of queries from American writers who don't realize that there is a difference between a home magazine for the U.S. market and one for the Canadian," said Gail Johnston Habs, editor in chief of *Style at Home*.

- **Keep it simple.** With everything you're learning, you may be tempted to share with readers the whole history of the coated glass industry. Don't bother; most people want only simple guidelines on choosing windows wisely.

- **Keep readers informed.** Be sure to supply info on costs, said Adair—where and how readers can get products or services. Toll-free numbers and/or Web sites are essential.

- **Vary submissions.** Try submitting queries to city magazines, state magazines, or even local newspapers. Virtually all have home sections and are responsive to fresh ideas.

- **Keep your eyes on the prize.** No, not the money, but an enduring appreciation for the genius of human creativity. Brilliance is everywhere in the home and garden market—in ceiling fans, in patio furniture, in doorknobs, even in plumbing! Feel the romance and enjoy the experience.

In-Flight Magazines

You literally can send your writing higher—say a cruising altitude of thirty-thousand feet—with in-flight magazines from the world's airlines. Every top carrier has a magazine to entertain and inform its passengers.

These magazines often lead their contributors to mainstream writing awards, such as the Lowell Thomas Award for travel writing and the *Folio:* Editorial Excellence Awards. Respect for publications stuffed in next to the airsickness bag? You bet.

Mickey McLean, managing editor of Delta Air Lines' *Sky*, emphasized that the publication is not just a promotional tool for the airline. Elaine Gruy Srnka, editor of American Airlines' *Celebrated Living* also agreed that the inflight magazine is more. "We're not investigative journalism, but we are experts on the needs and wants of the business traveler," she said.

If you've got an out-there idea, a unique voice, or a once-in-a-lifetime experience to relate, an in-flight magazine might be the home for it. In-flight magazines often are regarded as some of the last general-interest magazines around. Many, but not all, of these publications include travel writing. Take a trip and write a story? Sounds easy, but it's not. Randy Johnson, editor of United's *Hemispheres*, explains that the magazine consistently hires a resident of an area—an insider—to write installments in the magazine's prominent "Three Perfect Days" series. "We try to 'let the world speak for itself,' " Johnson said.

Unfortunately, in this market, a blanket query isn't going to work because each of these magazines works to distinguish itself. The airlines are distinct as well. Their customers differ depending on flight schedules, ticket prices, and the locations of airport hubs, and they often serve a unique combination of cities. The magazines, ultimately, are a reflection of these corporations, and that's a sensitivity for writers to keep in mind.

Ethnic Magazines

As the United States rapidly becomes a hyphenated society, the ethnic-magazine market is coming of age. "There's a greater appreciation for ethnic cultures as something more than just a curiosity," said managing editor Daniel Gibson of *Native Peoples Magazine*. "People are realizing there's a lot of value and richness there."

Asian Pages editor in chief Cheryl Weiberg sees the ethnic-magazine industry growing in all different directions in today's global world. One example Vice President of Editorial Nigel Killikelly of *Upscale Magazine* points to is a growing number of African-American publications. According to Samir Husni, in 2003 there were twenty new African-American magazines launched, compared to ten in 1997.

Publishers of ethnic magazines are dedicated niche marketers, but focusing on a specific race, culture, or nationality isn't always enough. *Asian Pages*, whose readers encompass twenty different Asian groups, is one of many publications finding it necessary to micro-focus on divisions within its larger target audience.

Also, *Vista Magazine*, with predominantly Hispanic readers, must keep in mind 2000 census figures showing a growing number of Hispanics who come from Central and South America. According to the census, Hispanics not from Cuba, Puerto Rico, or Mexico jumped from five million in 1990 to ten million in 2000.

Editors across the board welcome submissions from writers outside their ethnic sphere, but you must be prepared to capture the voice, flavor, and spirit of the magazine's audience. "It's important that writers be sensitive to Native issues," said Gibson, "and have some familiarity with Indian culture and history."

If you can take a broad, mainstream issue and show how it applies to a specific ethnic market, you're on the right track. Readers look for tightly targeted ethnic material that touches them on a human level, so emotional content in an article or story can help wring a sale out of an editor. In the case of Weiberg, "If it draws a tear to my eye, it's going to get my readers."

Most ethnic magazines depend heavily on outside contributions. *Upscale Magazine*, more than 90 percent freelance-written, snaps up an estimated 315 freelance articles a year. Some, such as *Native Peoples* and *German Life*, have extensive guidelines for would-be contributors. Studying at least three of the latest issues is particularly important with ethnic publications because they evolve rapidly with the market.

Ethnic magazines are here to stay and primed for growth. Joshua Rolnick, managing editor at *Moment*, said, "There's certainly a strong market for our type of publication."

Children's Magazines

There are hundreds of great children's magazines that need material on a regular basis. And like adult magazines, they run the gamut as far as the audience and subject matter. There are magazines for prereaders such *Babybug*; science magazines like *Odyssey* or *Dolphin Log*; magazines with a religious bent like *Clubhouse* and *Guideposts for Kids*. There are magazines for boys like *Boys' Life* and *Boys' Quest*; and magazines for girls like *Girls' Life* and *American Girl*. There are teen mags like the literary *Cicada* and the mainstream *Seventeen*. Children's magazines publish fiction, nonfiction, poetry, puzzles, recipes, rebuses, mazes, quizzes, and more.

With this much variety, the children's magazine market is a great place for newer writers. But writing short pieces for this audience is not easy, and there is a lot of competition. What can you do to increase the chances of breaking in? Here are eight tips to help you get published.

1. **Study magazines that interest you.** With so many children's magazines out there, it's important for writers to review sample copies of publications they wish to target—don't just read one, go to the library and grab a stack. Read several issues, and note the tone of the magazine, the

word length of the articles, the focus of the pieces, the number of different types of features, etc. Magazine Web sites often offer a few sample articles from the current issues and archives of past features that you can peruse. Also look for writer's guidelines and lists of upcoming themes on the Web sites. Many children's magazines, particularly those focusing on nonfiction, offer theme lists. These can also be acquired by sending an SASE to the publications.

2. **Study theme lists.** Children's magazines' theme lists offer topics that will be covered in upcoming issues and can be a great tool for writers targeting particular magazines. Some themes from a recent list for history magazine *Cobblestone* include "The Electoral College," "Inventions of the 1800s," "Women in the Civil War," and "Russian Americans."

"Theme lists are a great tool for improving the chances of acceptance because you know the subjects an editor is open to receiving," said writer Fiona Bayrock. When Bayrock wants to write for a particular magazine that publishes themed issues, she reviews their theme list and finds a topic she's interested in writing about. "Writing to theme often means seeing my work in print sooner—and building a clip file faster—than writing for nonthemed magazines, which might hold articles for years before publishing them. Usually themes are scheduled for a specific issue, so if a piece for the July/ August issue is accepted, I know it will be published in July."

3. **Consider nonfiction.** When she was putting together the Society of Children's Book Writers and Illustrators (SCBWI) Magazine Market Survey, Pam Zollman found that "100 percent of the children's magazines listed accepted nonfiction. Less than 40 percent of them accepted fiction. And yet, every year editors beg for nonfiction. *Highlights* receives so much fiction that it is sent to a first reader, while nonfiction is sent directly to the editors (no outside readers)."

"Kids' magazines on just about any nonfiction topic you can think of need nonfiction material every month, in addition to the general content magazines that publish a mix of fiction and nonfiction," added Bayrock. "There are far fewer nonfiction writers than fiction writers—it's like several decades ago when a woman going to the North could be married in no time because there were so few women and so many men looking for a wife."

4. **Consider holiday stories.** "After more than fifteen years as a children's market freelancer with 1,600 published articles and reviews, I can say with some authority there is one editorial cry heard often, and above the rest," said Kelly Milner Halls. "The holidays are coming and I need some fresh ideas."

Writers should keep clear of the obvious and come up with new twists for stories related to popular holidays like Christmas, Thanksgiving, and Halloween. When thinking of ideas for a Valentine's Day piece for the *Chicago Tribune KidNews*, for example, Halls wondered about the origin of giving paper hearts on the holiday and found an expert to talk to. "A professor who had spent his whole life studying the subject confessed that the bowels, the spleen, and the heart had each been symbols of love at different moments in history," she said. "So we profiled his research then wondered aloud in banner-sized headlines how modern love songs might change if hearts had given way to spleens and bowels: 'I left my spleen in San Francisco,' 'Stop playing games with my bowels.' " Both kids and editors eat up peculiar stories like this.

5. **Go beyond science and nature for nonfiction ideas.** "While kids love animals and are very interested in them, they also enjoy reading about historical events and places, people, sports, world culture, the arts, and any other topic," said Pam Zollman. When she was editing young nonfiction for *Highlights*, "the vast majority of articles submitted to [her] were about animals. [She] was overwhelmed with articles about birds, bees, and other insects, and all sorts of animals."

6. **Send photos with your article.** While this isn't a requirement, seeing photos can influence an editor's decision on whether or not to accept a piece. "If the article is just okay but the photos are outstanding, an editor might ask for a rewrite instead of sending a rejection," said Zollman. "Nonfiction needs photos. That's what attracts the reader's eye. If you

can't provide photos, give the editor some suggestions of places where the magazine can get them if you can."

7. **Consider crafts or activities, jokes, riddles, and puzzles.** The majority of children's magazines include at least one of these, and editors need a steady stream of them. And puzzle possibilities are virtually limitless. You can create puzzles using codes, logic charts, and mazes, not to mention word games—like opposites, hunts, and scrambles. The key, as with any market, is to find the type of puzzle that best suits your talents. Research the publications, read the submission guidelines, and most importantly, be creative.

According to *Highlights for Children* senior editor Rich Wallace, his magazine looks for originality in addition to age-appropriateness. "It's hard to invent an entirely new type of puzzle, so variations on old standards are okay, too. I want puzzles that a bright seven- or eight-year old will be challenged by but will figure out with a little brainwork," he said.

Highlights has another important requirement—puzzles must be nonconsumable. "It can't rely on kids writing on the page," explained Wallace. This means no crossword puzzles or word finds. Although this policy seems restrictive, it makes sense given that more than one child is often using the magazine. "*Highlights* is found in a high percentage of schools and libraries, so those issues have multiple readers. A lot of families save their issues so younger kids can enjoy them as they get older," said Wallace. "We aren't trendy and have little coverage of current events, so the issues have a long shelf life."

Other magazines don't have such restrictions, however. "Puzzles are probably the most open market for us," said Marilyn Edwards, editor of *Hopscotch, Fun for Kidz,* and *Boys' Quest.* "Although we only use four to eight puzzles in an issue, we are always looking for clever puzzles that fit our themes. We look for a clear, fun puzzle, not something that is like school work," she said. "We have some writers who have sent us puzzles for years, follow our theme list, and know our magazines well. We use these people all the time."

8. Consider Sunday school take-home papers. Because they are weekly they need a large quantity of material on a regular basis. "That doesn't mean they aren't expecting quality," said Kathryn Lay. "And you have to know enough about a denomination to understand any taboos. But a good, moral (not preachy) story with a take-away message has a great chance in this market."

These publications publish nonfiction, short stories, profiles, poetry, crafts, puzzles—you name it. Some use theme lists, "and will continue to send you their lists once you publish with them," said Lay. These are great places to sell material because you can often resell pieces from one denomination to another with few or no changes.

E-Publishing

The growth of Internet media has opened up new opportunities to write about what you want to write about and what you know best. Assume that you are an expert in (insert your favorite topic here). You want to write about your topic and get paid for it. Where do you find Internet publishers who want to buy articles about your topic?

• **Online directories.** Look in the search directories, such as Google, Yahoo!, etc. They're not comprehensive, but they can be your starting point. If the directories don't give you enough ideas for potential online writing venues, spend a little time with an Internet search engine (like www.google.com or www.dogpile.com), a directory service (like www.yahoo.com or www.looksmart.com) or a premium search service (like www.northernlight.com). With a Web search, you'll likely get a huge number of results and a wide variety of leads.

You'll find where articles on your topic have been published on the Web, and if you click through to the articles and look around the site where they reside, you'll find contact information for the editor or site manager.

• *Writer's Online Marketplace.* This book by Debbie Ohi Ridpath (Writer's Digest Books) includes listings of online venues that pay for

Stay Informed on Hot Online Markets

The online marketplace is changing daily, so if you want to make any kind of money or progress, you need to stay current on trends and new opportunities. Here's a list of sites that can help you stay informed and give you leads on hot markets.

MediaBistro—www.mediabistro.com

In its own words, MediaBistro is "dedicated to anyone who creates or works with content." It posts both full-time and freelance jobs and often features interviews with magazine editors—both online and off. You'll also find a daily news feed that tracks movements across the media industry.

Writers Weekly—www.writersweekly.com

This weekly e-newsletter, run by Angela Adair Hoy, is the highest circulation freelance e-zine in the world. It posts new paying freelance gigs (online and off) every week. Not to be missed if you're actively seeking new work.

Absolute Write—www.absolutewrite.com

Run by Jenna Glatzer, this site features a free weekly newsletter on paying markets as well as a special section dedicated to consumer magazines and e-zines.

Journalism Jobs—www.journalismjobs.com

Devotes a special section of its Web site to freelance writing opportunities, both online and off.

Sunoasis Jobs—www.sunoasis.com

This site posts all types of jobs for writers, editors, copyeditors, and copywriters. Special section devoted to online jobs.

Worldwide Freelance Writer—www.worldwidefreelance.com

Find an eclectic selection of writing jobs across the globe.

Writing for Dollars!—www.writingfordollars.com

A twice-monthly e-newsletter alerting you to new opportunities.

The Burry Man Writers Center—www.burryman.com/freelance.html

Posts a wealth of links for people who really like to scour the Web for freelance jobs, 24-7.

freelance writing. It's somewhat akin to an online writer's version of *Writer's Market*. Ridpath gives advice on how to find online venues and presents listings.

- **WritersMarket.com.** As the online subscription-based counterpart to the annual *Writer's Market* (*Writer's Market Deluxe Edition* includes both the print version and online subscription), WritersMarket.com contains more than one hundred online markets, both paying and nonpaying.

- **E-Commerce sites.** Don't limit yourself to considering just the online publications that turn up in your search. You may find that e-commerce sites that sell products related to your topic and also publish related articles. Broaden your notion of whom you might write for.

- **Online jobs sites.** Online employment-matching sites for freelancers are a thriving Internet business. It's worthwhile to watch them for assignments in your topic. For example, go to www.guru.com, www.elance.com, and www.freeagent.com. They all carry notices of writing jobs.

- **Writers' forums.** Participate in online forums or lists frequented by other writers. A discussion list for science or medical writers will be a good forum for sharing tips about science Web sites that buy writing, for instance.

As you can see, there are many easy ways to find online venues that buy freelance writing—and a wide variety of content buyers. But to find them all, you'll have to look beyond the directories.

CHAPTER FIVE:
RESEARCHING

Once you sell your article to your targeted market, it's time to write the article. In most cases, your article will require some amount of research and interviewing. In some cases, you will already be an expert on your topic, but sometimes you will know very little about the subject. In either case, it is essential that you do the necessary work to get accurate information.

There are ways to research and interview efficiently and effectively in order to spend as little time as possible to get what you need. Even though research is essential, it doesn't have to consume all of your time—in fact it shouldn't. Make sure you leave time to actually write. Take your researching and interviewing seriously, but also enjoy it. After all, if you are interested in writing, you are interested in learning new things and finding answers to questions.

Editors don't want and can't use the same details found in other publications. They need fresh ideas, freshly stated. Study what is already in print, then focus your research and interviews on details the other articles have overlooked. The same goes for sources who have been quoted everywhere. While you're looking for overlooked details, keep an eye out for important sources other writers have ignored.

Tackling Any Topic

Write what you know? While it seems perfectly sound on one level, living by this mantra can limit and even deter your career. In order to grow as professionals, writers should be taught: Write what you don't know.

Why take on work in this manner? For one, it builds your repertoire. Second, editors want all-around writers that they can send on any assignment. Third, it opens doors to other opportunities. If you can research and write about an unfamiliar subject, you bring to the table a fresh perspective. Editors always need new ideas—even new takes on old topics.

You might ask, "Can I understand everything about a subject?" The honest answer is, "No." If you try to know every tiny detail you'll never stay within your deadline. But you must gain a good working knowledge, concentrate on finding key points, get your facts straight (which you undoubtedly will be extra-inclined to do in foreign territory), and talk with the right people.

After hours of research and interviewing, you'll notice when you start to write that your words have a depth, an authority. Suddenly you'll discover that you're a legitimate source of information; in short, you'll have become a kind of expert.

Here's how to get up to speed on any subject:

1. **Cruise the information superhighway.** Read, study, and print out pertinent Web pages. You may have some intense reading to do the night before a big interview, but it'll be worth it.

2. **Read all about it.** Buy magazines related to your subject. Pick up the jargon, trends, leads, and ideas.

3. **Use multimedia sources.** Documentaries and CD-ROMs are fun and quick ways to soak up facts and build a foundation.

4. **Ask and you shall receive.** If you're not sure of something, ask an expert. Always double-check with an authority if you are not sure. It's the safest and quickest way to get information, and it will save work later.

5. **Let it breathe.** Give yourself time to nail inconsistencies in your story.

6. **Use organizations and associations.** Almost every subject or topic is associated with some professional organization. Many organizations have resources online or people who can help you fill in the gaps.

While these steps won't make you a certified expert, they will help you write about even the most foreign of topics. Don't underestimate yourself: With a little legwork, you can tackle any topic.

Finding Experts

One of the most important steps in your research is finding the sources you need for the story. If you've written about this topic before, you should have some good ideas about where to start searching for the people you'll need to interview.

When approaching a new topic, a good place to start is with two online services that are free of charge for working journalists: ProfNet (www.prof net.com), sponsored by PR Newswire, and ExpertSource (www.business wire.com), backed by Business Wire. Each allows you to enter queries for experts on a topic of your choice. You type in an inquiry and even can set a deadline for responses. You also can scan each service's expert list to find people who have listed the topic you might be searching for. The lists include academics, consultants, and pretty much every public relations agency in the country, which means if the sources you're searching for have PR people (and who doesn't these days?), you should be able to find them.

Writers constantly face the challenge of finding people to share information that will make their work believable, entertaining, and accurate. Not only must you find someone to talk to, you must try to find the right someone.

With any project, the first thing to ask is whether you need an expert or just someone to give you background on, say, hunting. The guy at the local sporting goods store may be fine for that. But when you need more authority, here are some ways to track down the right experts.

1. **Remember the source.** Ideas often come from something you've seen or read elsewhere, a conversation or the experience of an acquaintance. Whose quote in the story started you thinking? With whom was your

conversation? Who had the interesting experience? Often these people will have useful information and can get you started.

2. **Play telephone.** Your local yellow pages are a convenient source of experts. They're full of professionals of every stripe. Don't overlook them. The directories available on the Web can broaden your search nationally or even internationally.

3. **Ask other writers.** One of the best sources you can tap is your network of other writers who may have worked on a related story. Online communities are often the best for this kind of inquiry. For example, freelancer Timothy Perrin posted a request for stories about finding experts to the discussion groups of the American Society of Journalists and Authors and the Periodical Writers Association of Canada. Many of his online writer friends sent their tales and advice, which he incorporated into an article. If you want to cast a broader net, Internet newsgroups and e-mail lists are good options.

4. **Use a professional.** If you are looking for a particular kind of expertise, professional organizations can steer you in the right direction. For example, the American Medical Association and the American Bar Association maintain lists of experts in particular topics and can often point you to a qualified person in your area. The AMA even has a Doctor Finder database that will find a specialist in your own backyard (www.ama-assn.org). If you need someone from a less obvious profession—say chicken farmers—check the *Encyclopedia of Associations* at your local library for the right group.

5. **Remember PR.** Believe it or not, there are people who make their livings finding experts just for you. You'll find them in any public relations office. Start with your local college or university. The PR department will likely have a list of faculty members and their areas of expertise. Some, like the University of Southern California, have online databases of experts (http://uscnews.usc.edu/experts/index.html).

Some companies are in the business of finding experts for journalists. ProfNet has a searchable database of experts and will send your inquiry to more than six thousand colleges, universities, and corporations. News-wise (www.newswise.com) is a similar service that also provides you with weekly tip sheets of story ideas from its clients. Guestfinder (www.g uestfinder.com) can also point you to people with particular areas of expertise.

6. Read your Rolodex. Make a list of experts and resources. For some articles, you may spend a day or more looking for that one perfect indus-try expert or analyst. Why let that person end up buried in your archives?

Create a list of experts, analysts, and industry insiders—indexed by category—which you can turn to when a specific topic arises in the fu-ture. This can be as simple as opening a Word document or creating a category in your contact management software or Rolodex. Editors hire freelancers for the information they have—including the industry con-tacts they've amassed.

Part of your expertise as a writer is your little black book of contacts. "I have a Rolodex of experts," said Maxine Rock, Atlanta-based freelancer and former ASJA board member, "cross-listed as to name and subject, plus little notes on them, such as 'Jones, John. ABC Research Facility, Atlanta. Heads gorilla research studies on speech; also expert on fly-fishing.' This person is under his last name, gorillas, and fly-fishing."

And don't forget to ask those experts for other experts. "At the end of every interview," said Monterey, California writer Heather Millar, "I close with, 'Do you know of anyone else I should call about this?' I've found tremendous sources with that very simple question."

7. Cast a wide network. Never miss an opportunity to meet new people. Edmonton, Alberta resident Richard Sherbaniuk, techno-thriller and nonfiction writer, recently joined the board of directors for the various museums at the University of Alberta. He quickly found his expertise being put to work as editor of the quarterly newsletter.

"As a result of talking with these professors I have more ideas than I know what to do with," he said. "An art professor told me in detail how to forge a Rembrandt, including the precise formula for grinding seven-

RESEARCHING TIPS TO SAVE TIME

Time is an endangered resource to writers: time to query, time to write, time to research. The last seems to be the scarcest and yet is the most important for creating salable prose. The three Rs of conservation apply to writing research, not just the environment: Save time by reducing, reusing, and recycling your research.

You easily can cut back on the amount of research you perform without hiring an assistant. How? When qualified, professional people volunteer to look up information for you, take them up on the offer. Even if you don't need the facts right now, you should tuck the info away in your files. Set up categorical tidbit files, grouped in a way that will help you remember what was put where.

For instance, the next time you're booking a flight for a pleasure trip to central New York, and the travel agent asks if you want any information on the area's attractions, take her up on it. Before you know it, you'll have a mound of Web site printouts, brochures, and maps on your desk. Once you snap a few photographs and tackle the prose, most of the research on places to visit and the nitty-gritty facts will already be done for you. You could sell two articles or more from the same research.

Small-business owners and industry experts often are eager to talk shop and sometimes see the possible benefit for themselves—free media exposure. An article by Deborah Meyers about vintage car upholstering for *Classic Auto Restorer* was based solely on picking the brain of a seasoned upholsterer and shop owner who also happened to be a classic car fancier. To show her thanks, Meyers included a sidebar listing his shop's number and address, and he received calls from several readers who wanted further information.

You'll get most of your article ideas by meeting people—not by trying to scramble around and find people who you can interview and thus support your article idea. By truly listening to your spouse's boss, your hair stylist, your child's teacher, and their fascinating lives, you can spark article ideas that would be of interest to a particular audience.

Librarians and their high-tech counterpart, the Internet, are also terrific resources. Just make sure you know what you want when you talk with librarians, and know roughly how to find what you're seeking on the Internet, or you may not save time.

When using real people, don't ask for too much or ask so often that they flee the next time they see you coming.

Save only the information that you know is 100 percent reliable. If you're not sure it is, crosscheck with a second source. Be sure to document sources in case you need to verify facts later or if you need to reference sources in the piece.

Never, ever throw away your research notes. Even if you think you'll never write about Holstein dairy cows' milk again, keep those notes in your files. Even old statistical information can be useful if it is compared with present-day stats. Plus, you may be able to reuse the research in an article on the same topic targeting a different market. When you do so, be sure the two articles are substantially different in tone, wording, slant, illustration, and content. This ensures that you're not selling a reprint as new material. These kinds of timesaving efforts will help you squeeze more out of your research.

teenth century paints, a biologist explained in fantastic detail how the common stickleback, a kind of fish, is an environmental lightning rod, and a forensic chemist told me an infallible way of committing arson without being caught."

A final caveat: When you've identified your experts, make sure you know their background—and agenda. On rare occasions, you will run into people who are more interested in selling a book or a point of view than they are in providing information. Ask all your sources how they came to know about their subject matter, what their experience is in the field, and what degrees they have and from what schools.

Also, ask about the people you've already interviewed. What's their standing in the community of experts? In the course of half a dozen interviews on a story, you'll quickly find out who's who. Most fields are pretty closed shops and everyone knows everyone else.

Finding experts can be challenging, but once you learn how to do it, it becomes perhaps the most rewarding part of writing. At each stop, you'll talk to the best and brightest people who will want to share just what you need to know.

Making Your Research Go the Distance

When researching, plan multiple articles from the get-go. Donna Poole, a Michigan-based writer, interviewed a missionary to the Pemon Islands and used the information in a book, a nonfiction article, and a children's fiction story. With a little careful planning, you can ask enough questions in the same interview to get the information you need for several pieces. Ask questions that represent the various angles you will present. For example, Poole asked questions about the games the children play on the Pemon Islands and what school is like for the kids who live there. She asked questions centered on the spiritual and physical needs of the people and how mission work can meet those needs. By covering a broad scope of interest in her questions, Poole was able to use the interview for three different articles.

Not only will these efforts save you time, but they will help you sell more stories, and the best part is that you will expend little extra effort doing it.

Organizing Information

If you have been collecting and recycling information and stockpiling contacts, then the next step is to organize everything so you can in fact use it when you need it. If you have scads of files filled with useful information, but don't look in these vast resources until after you file an article with which they might have helped, then your organization and research is useless. All is lost because your system doesn't have an initiator. In other words, your reference and tickler files need to have a tickler.

Freelance writers often lack the resources of a publication's editorial research department. Editors and writers just send a message to their publication's reference librarian, and—viola!—some of the latest articles or numbers on some hot trend magically appear in their inbox.

Most freelancers don't have such resources at hand. But they do pride themselves on having a bevy of world-class information that makes them specialists in their chosen areas. Whether they're reading an in-flight magazine, flipping through the Sunday newspaper, or even taking notice of a piece of mail, they clip and stash with what would appear to be scientific precision.

Until, that is, it's time to reach into the precious storehouse and pull up that ditty of data that would make all the difference in an article. Then they trip up and render it as useless and empty as Al Capone's infamous vault.

"The key is in making a decision," said organizational expert Greg Vetter. In other words, decide what you're going to keep and where you're going to keep it—and remember to make the filing system part of your professional life so you don't re-create the research wheel every time you need a pithy piece of insight.

Here are four tips for turning vast stockpiles of otherwise latent research and data into user-friendly, actionable, and powerful snippets for your stories or leads for future pieces.

1. Index your past work. If you specialize in a certain area, create an index of past articles so they can be reused, or at least accessed, for information. This way, you'll have all your work—by topic, date, subject, etc.—at your fingertips.

Just open a Word document or Excel file and start to log your work. Include the date the article was created, the file name, a brief note about the story, and whom it was written for. This also will help you track resales of your articles in the future. An important point here: Archiving must be done regularly or it will become daunting to go back and enter months of articles—and a potentially powerful tool will become useless.

2. Develop a "topical" tips file. When editors come calling for story ideas to take into their editorial meetings, grab the hanging file you should have filled with potential leads and clips and type up some ideas from it. Central to being an expert scribe on a topic is knowing what the trends are and having plenty of story ideas to pursue. This is especially important if you write a recurring feature or column and have to think up stories with regularity.

3. Revisit your file cabinet. It's great to have a powerful, insightful, and deep research archive—only if you use it. Every few months, browse through the folders, both those online and in the file cabinet, as well as your Web bookmarks. This will refresh your memory about the data you've amassed—and the variety of topics covered.

4. Cull your files—selectively and efficiently. Files bulging with years-old clips or reports burden potentially useful reference information with aged, useless data.

Every few months, go through your desktop files, file cabinet, and even your e-mail inbox to weed out useless information. Before you toss that fax, report, or e-mail, scan it for any person or organization's name that might be helpful down the road. Transfer that information to your contact management system of choice.

It's important to have a filing system that fits your personal information needs, but it's more important to live that system. Stay up-to-date with your data, files, and categories. You may find that one category should be broken down into several more to aid in retrieval of useful information.

Researching is an essential part of writing, but it doesn't have to be tedious or difficult. Planning ahead and staying organized can make any daunting research task much easier. Enjoy the research phase of your writing; just don't get so caught up in it that you postpone the actual writing part of the process.

Chapter Six:
Interviewing

In many cases, your writing assignment is going to rely on some amount of material gained from interviews. If you are writing a profile, the interview will be tantamount to the success of your article. In other articles, you may only need to quote an expert to support an argument. Sometimes you may need to interview a big shot or celebrity, and other times it will be your neighbor. No matter what, you don't want to be unprepared to meet the needs of your article and publication, and you don't want to waste your interviewee's or your own time. You need to know how to find a subject, how to contact him, and how to conduct a successful interview. As with research, preparation and organization can carry you a long way in the art of interviewing.

Interviewing Strategy

In order to know whom you need to call, you must have an interviewing strategy. Think of the interview process like following the circles a stone makes when it's thrown into a lake.

If you're standing on a shore, the first thing you're likely to see are the circles radiating out from the submerged stone. If you follow from the outermost circle back to the center, you'll know where the stone is even if you hadn't seen it land in the water to begin with.

Organize your interviews like those circles. Start with experts farthest from the story's center. For example, if you're profiling a company for a business publication, you would start with academic sources or consultants who know the industry.

The next circle would be people more familiar with the company you're writing about, perhaps ex-officials, suppliers, or others who have had direct contact. Stock analysts could be in this circle as well.

The next circle would be executives at the company, and the center of the story—the stone—likely would be the CEO or chairman. As you work your way through the circles, you gather more and more information, so by the time you reach your key interview you should be knowledgeable enough to conduct a good interview and get some solid answers to your well-thought-out questions.

Scheduling Interviews

When your writing depends on interviews, it is good to know what to say to whom. If you are working on a piece in which you'll need to do interviews with high-level people, you may wonder, "How do I get through to these people?"

The glib answer is, "Ask to speak to them." While that's true, the confidence to ask the questions doesn't come from writing. Use the skills from the previous chapter to learn what you can about your topic before the first interview. Determine from previously published articles which analysts or company executives are open to interviews. Call them first and then move on to their referrals. If you're writing an article about the declining market for widgets, read background material before interviewing the experts. You're more likely to gain access if you exhibit a grasp of the issues.

Gatekeepers aren't your enemies, but you need to be ready for the secretaries and assistants who control access to the important people. Consider writing a short script, which might go something like this: "Hello. My name is F. Lance Writer. I am writing on assignment for XYZ publication. I was hoping to speak with Ms. Big about her views on widgets. I know that she would add greatly to this piece, and I am sure she would be interested in hearing about the research I have done. I am on deadline. I hope you can help me."

If you have been referred to Ms. Big by someone else, this is the time to mention it. Saying that you have a go-ahead from a publication gives you authority, confidence, and a strong reason for people to speak with you.

If you have never been published or have not written on a particular subject area, be more cautious. You might say: "I'm a freelancer writing on widgets. I am pitching my article to a number of publications and hope you'll give me an interview once I receive the go-ahead."

Then, when you do query, mention that you have contacted two to three experts about interviews. Never, however, lie to an editor about whether someone has agreed to be interviewed by you.

Robert B. Tucker, president of The Innovation Resource in Santa Barbara, California, is a futurist, speaker, and author of *Managing the Future* and three other books. He believes that a writer can land the big interviews by being enthusiastic. "You play off the fact that people want to help." "Be comfortable with who you are. You need to sound like you know what you are talking about," said Tucker. "You have to know what you are up against. Preparation is everything."

"You need to understand that you are bringing something of value to them. You have to show this in the opening presentation. Give before you receive," said Ray Cech, freelance writer and president of Dunhill Executive Search of Los Angeles. He suggests starting at the top. "You can get through to anybody as long as your first call is to the president. You have to understand that the president has the brightest, sharpest person in the company working for them. If the presentation is good enough, he or she would not dare *not* to tell the president." Once you have interviewed the president of an organization, you will be able to get referrals right down the line.

Vicki Cox of Lebanon, Missouri, author of *Diana: Princess of Wales* (Chelsea House) and *Rising Stars and Ozark Constellations* (Skyward) always sends a letter and a sample of her work to a prospective interviewee before calling. "Most everybody is very gracious and interested," she said. "I tell them where I am going to send the story. I can't think of a person who has turned me down."

Remember, you have the right to speak with anyone. You are giving people free publicity, so call with confidence. But once you do make the call and schedule the interview, make sure you have a plan to ensure you are successful the rest of the way.

Always prepare questions in advance. Here, too, start with general questions to put a source at ease, and then work to more specifics. But if time is short, start with the key questions. Number your questions by importance so you know which you have to get answers to. Keep your interview focused. Many people like to ramble or avoid tough questions. It's your job to keep the subject on topic and on time for your timetable.

Try to set up interview times in advance so you don't have to waste time calling back again and again. E-mail is a convenient way to set up interview times. Make use of it when possible, but try to avoid doing e-mail-only interviews—in general, they're flat and dull and don't give you a chance to pounce on unexpected answers.

Keep an interview log sheet with names, phone numbers, and e-mails on a single sheet of paper. Attach this to a file folder you create for whatever information you gather for the story. This will save you time looking up numbers again when you need to call someone back.

You'll have to call more people than you eventually interview; many people simply don't return calls or know nothing about your topic. But don't over-interview. When you start hearing the same answers again and again, chances are you've done enough interviewing.

Conducting the Interview

It's been said that a good interview is just like a good conversation. That's not so. In a good conversation, it's polite for the folks involved to ask questions of each other and to listen with equal interest to the answers. It's a time for mutual discovery and communication.

But an interview is a lopsided interaction. The interviewee probably doesn't care about the person popping the questions, and the interviewer is doing more than simply enjoying himself. Interviewing is work. It shouldn't feel like work, however, and that's what the interviews-are-conversations theory is all about. If a person being interviewed feels as if she is talking to an old friend, the interview is more likely to produce powerful anecdotes, colorful quotes, and revealing information. Yet for a source to feel comfortable with an interviewer, the interviewer has to relax—a tough trick for beginners.

Nothing will relax you more than feeling prepared, and for feeling prepared, nothing can take the place of doing your homework before an interview. There's no excuse for asking someone who's just been awarded the Pulitzer Prize whether she's won any awards lately. Before doing the interview, head to the library or go online and look up background information on the topic and your interview subject. Research also helps to point out the controversies in a topic, and, importantly, helps you devise appropriate and engaging questions.

Don't think you have to know everything about the topic prior to interviewing someone. It's perfectly okay to tell a source that you've read his latest report on wastewater treatment options but you need him to explain the finer details. (In fact, sometimes, playing dumb is the best way to get people to open up to you.) Most people are grateful that an interviewer has taken time to try to understand their business, and many enjoy assuming the role of a teacher to an interested pupil. Still, the more you learn about the topic the less likely you are to be confused by a source's statements or bamboozled by someone who wants to evade controversial issues.

Don't overwhelm the source with questions. You want the source to do much more talking than you. Just ask questions and allow him to do the talking. Former anchor Bob Edwards, of National Public Radio's Morning Edition, once told a journalism professor that his two favorite interview questions were "Oh?" and "No!"

Jot down a list of questions that pertain specifically to your topic before the interview. You will probably need to ask closed-ended questions designed to gather information or provide verification ("Did the dress really cost $10,000?") as well as open-ended questions designed to encourage the source to describe events, processes, thoughts, and emotions ("How did you know she was the woman for you?"). Start with the easy-to-answer questions and end with the explosive ones. That way, if the source ends the interview after the touchy question, at least you'll have something in your notes to write about.

A lot of interview prep work goes into coming up with the right questions. As was stressed earlier, research is crucial in helping you form smart and revealing questions. If they're available, read previous interviews your subject has done so you can get a feel for how he will respond to certain questions and what his stock answers might be. This way, if you get one of those stock answers, you'll recognize it and know that you'll need to dig a little deeper to get something fresh for your piece. But it's important to recognize that research alone isn't enough to pull off a successful interview. By exploring different types of questions, phraseology, and sources you can come up with the right questions for any interview.

Who is the foremost question in the sextet of journalistic queries, followed by *what, when, where, why*, and *how*. When you write profiles, *who* is paramount, along with *what* that person does/did. However, finding out more about who you're interviewing is quite useful for many other types of stories. It's often a good idea to observe, as well as ask questions, to gather color to add to your stories.

Few sources volunteer all the details you will need to make readers see and feel as if they are in your story. You'll have to prompt them with follow-up questions. You'll have to make a point to look for the telling details. Because these questions can become pesky, it's a good idea to let sources know what you're up to by stating first, "I'd like to know about that in much more detail because it's so interesting. Let me ask you some specific questions."

The peerless follow-up question to so many answers is, of course, *why*. But the problem with asking why is that its single syllable can seem abrupt and provoking. It can jab the source like a poke in the ribs, inducing defensiveness. Try softening the thrust of this necessary monosyllable by cushioning it inside other words: "Do you remember why you made that plan?" or "What an interesting idea. Why do you say so?" All those words really mean one: Why? They just sound nicer.

Even though you might know the right questions to ask, sometimes you need to know the right way to ask them. Some television journalists have rightly earned contempt for pushing a microphone in the face of a grieving parent of a dead child and asking, "How does it feel?" Yet our emotions tie us together; they draw readers deeply into stories and books through a rush of recognition and understanding.

Observation and description can be better than quotes in conveying emotions in your writing. It's more powerful to write that tears trickled into the wrinkles in the elderly woman's face and dripped steadily on the bedclothes of her comatose husband than to quote her saying, "I felt sad." But if you're not there at the moment of turmoil, you'll have to ask how it felt. When you do, show respect for your sources who have experienced pain, and ask your questions gently.

Besides the emotional details of a situation, you will also rely on your interviewees to give you concrete information. Often, the substance of the story can be elicited by addressing four issues, suggested some years ago by LaRue Gilleland, a professor and former director of the University of Nevada's School of Journalism. They go by the acronym GOSS, for goals, obstacles, solutions, and start over.

- What were your (or your organization's) goals?
- What obstacles did you face?
- How did you find solutions to those obstacles?

The last S means that you often need to start over and probe for details and background. Ken Metzler, author of *Creative Interviewing* (Pearson Education), suggests adding EY to the GOSS formula: E to ask the source to evaluate the information and Y as a reminder to ask why. Using these questions as the scaffolding, it's easy to sprinkle your own probes among them.

Often, interviews help you discover new story ideas. If you find yourself finished with an interview for one story, and your source is friendly and willing, try fishing for a few other possible ideas that might translate into additional stories. As mentioned in chapter three, this will help you earn more money for the same amount of work.

Interviewing can be the most fun part of the writing process, as you're free to approach people you never could hope to meet under ordinary circumstances. So bring your notebook, pen, and/or tape recorder, and leave your antacid tablets at home.

Handling Difficult Interviews

What if you are organized and prepared but your interviewee is not being as cooperative as you had hoped? What if you are stumped by the silent source or run into the interviewee who talks so much that you spend more in cassette tapes than you make on the article? Even the most hard-boiled journalist breaks into a cold sweat when faced with interviews like this. So take these tips from four talented writers who are masters at the craft of talking up their sources to find out how to handle the interviewee from the Ninth Circle of Hell.

1. **Run-On Ralph.** You may have an interviewee who, when asked about the health benefits of carrots, launches into a half-hour monologue about how his mother used to force him to eat carrots when he was young, even

though he hated them, and ever since then he can't tolerate the color orange, and now Halloween decorations cause him to hyperventilate, and . . .

Stop! Here are some tactics for keeping the Run-On Ralph on topic:

Set a time. Let your source know up front how much time you've set aside for the interview so he can time his answers accordingly. Also, "I let the source know that this is an article I have to turn around in forty-eight hours—even if it's due in a month," said Myatt Murphy, a former fitness editor for *Men's Health* and a freelance writer who has written for *Cosmopolitan, Prevention, Esquire,* and others. If the interviewee has a sense of urgency, he tends to focus a lot faster.

Flatter him. If your source still runs off at the mouth and over his allotted time, appeal to his vanity: "This information is so interesting, and I wish I had more time to interview you, but I have five more questions I need to ask and I don't want to use up all your valuable time."

Do your research. Chances are someone has already covered what you're about to write, and you can find this info online. "From this, you can get a general sense of what principle things you want to discuss," said Murphy. "That will help you focus the interview."

Take it online. Tell the interviewee that you're very sorry, but you misjudged the amount of time the interview would take—and would he mind if you e-mailed him the remaining questions?

Cut it short. "I try to politely cut them off," said Monique Cuvelier, who has written for such magazines as *Family Circle, Portable Computing,* and *Psychology Today.* "When they get off track, I interject a lot of 'Uh huh' and 'Yes' so that when I do interrupt with a question, it's not out of the blue." She then steers the interview back on track with a relevant question.

2. The Wrong Guy. You're in the middle of an interview and you realize that the person you're talking to is completely inappropriate for your article. The source's PR rep told you that she was a nutrition expert, but you discover that she actually sells herbal remedies over the Internet. Here's how to ditch the dud:

Let her down easy. Cuvelier usually says, " 'I'm so sorry, but I think

I misunderstood what your expertise is. I'm afraid I just wasted part of your morning.' I take the responsibility on myself," she explained. "They're not my boss, so I'm not concerned about being self-deprecating in front of them."

Say "buh-bye." If the source is actually trying to sneak her way into an article she knows she's not appropriate for (it happens), she may not let you go so easily. In that case, as soon as you realize that the source is a no-go for your article, it's best to tell her that she's answered all your questions, thank you very much. Then give her a disclaimer: "I have to let you know that just because I do an interview, it doesn't guarantee that you'll be quoted in the article, though I'll try my best."

3. The Product Plugger. No matter what question you ask, the Product Plugger manages to turn the answer into an ad for his product, service, or company. "What should small business owners do to attract talented employees?" "Well, if you have a great product like our automatic peach defuzzer, which retails for the low, low price of $19.95, the employees will come flocking to your door." "How should small business owners price their products?" "They should price them low, like our automatic peach defuzzer, which retails at the low, low price of $19.95." Here's how to deprogram the Product Plugger:

Boost his ego. Say something like, "Your peach defuzzer is so wonderful and successful, you must have done a lot of research into the market. Do you have any insider comments on X?" That way, you've already gotten the product plug out of the way so the source can answer your question minus the self-promotion.

Blame the editor. "What I say is, 'Look, this will never make it past my editor,' " said Juliet Pennington, a reporter for *The Sun-Chronicle* of Attleboro, Massachusetts. Tell the source that you'll be sure to mention his product, but blatant pitches will be cut by the editor. If he wants his quotes to appear at all, he'll have to tone it down.

Paraphrase. If all else fails, do what Cuvelier does to salvage the interview and paraphrase your source's answers. "I present the quote to them:

'Would you agree that X, Y, and Z?' " she said. "Then if I use a quote, I look for punchy two- or three-word phrases."

4. The Blow-Off. If a person agreed to an interview, you'd expect that when you called she'd be there panting with anticipation—right? Sources get called away on emergencies, or they forget to record the interview in their personal digital assistants, or sometimes they're just not that interested in being interviewed. Follow this advice to corral a source who flakes out on you:

Commit her. When Jennifer Lawler, author of more than twenty books, including *Dojo Wisdom for Writers: 100 Simple Ways to Become a More Inspired, Disciplined, and Fearless Writer* (Penguin Compass), was stymied by a no-show source, she changed her approach. "The next time I had to interview a source, I got her to answer a question or two during my first contact [to set up the interview]," she said. Not only does this tactic give you an idea of whether the source is truly interested in being interviewed, but it also makes the source feel invested in the scheduled interview. "They feel like they know me a little more, and it's harder to blow me off," Lawler said. You can ask your preliminary questions either via phone or e-mail.

Diversify. If you have just one source and she blows you off, you're up the creek. Try to have one source for every five hundred words plus one extra for good measure. So a 1,500-word article will have four sources. Even if one of them ends up being a no-show, you're still in good shape.

5. The Monosyllabic Marvel. This is the source who can't or won't respond to your questions, grunting "Yes" or "No" to every query or dancing around your questions without actually spitting out an answer. Use these tips to get the words flowing:

Descarify it. When Cuvelier schedules an interview, she doesn't call it an interview, which can conjure up scary images of Barbara Walters peppering sources with incriminating questions. Instead, she calls it a "chat." And when she's doing the interview—er, chat—she doesn't say things like, "Okay, question number five . . ." or "My next question is . . ." She transitions into her questions naturally to keep the conversation flowing. One good way to do that is to say, "That's so interesting. And what about X?"

Warm him up. Try starting with some warm-up questions that will help ease the source into the interview. Some good ones are, "How's the weather where you are?" and "How about those Knicks?" If you have anything in common with the source—maybe you both have teenage daughters or you recently visited his hometown—bring it up. Once he starts feeling more relaxed, you can hit him with the more relevant questions, like, "Is it true that your company is dumping chemicals into the public water supply?"

Go virtual. If you sense that the interviewee is uncomfortable being interviewed, you can do what Lawler does and ask if she'd feel better doing an e-mail interview. "Some people really are more comfortable responding in print," Lawler said.

Be quiet. "A lot of people, like me with my Type-A personality, have trouble with silence," said Pennington. "Sometimes someone is just formulating their thoughts, but you're already onto the next thing because there was a two-second pause." So maybe your interviewee isn't reticent—you just aren't giving give him a chance to respond.

Prep him. For some articles, you can send the source the questions ahead of time so he can prepare himself.

Be humble. "My philosophy is that the source doesn't have to be talking to me," said Cuvelier. "So I'm humble, and I think that takes me pretty far. I thank the source profusely and try to remember how busy these people are and how nice it is for them to be taking this time out of their day."

6. The Expert. You've scored an interview with the foremost expert on your topic. But when you interview her, she talks so far over your head that she might as well be speaking Farsi. Here's how to bring the expert down to your—and your readers'—level:

Explain your readers. Tell the expert that the audience you're writing for doesn't understand the topic as well as she does. Ask her, "If you had to simplify this for a patient/client/child, how would you explain it?"

Spell it out. If the expert hits you with a word like "tetrahydrodipicoli-nate," don't fake it—ask her to spell it for you.

Say it again, Sam. "When they throw out a word you don't know, repeat it," said Murphy. "Sometimes you have interviews where you listen to the tape and you've coughed halfway through the word and you have no idea what they said." If you repeat it, then you've heard the word a couple of times—and the expert can correct you if you get it wrong.

Don't let a difficult interviewee get in the way of the success of your article. By using the right tactics, you can walk away from any interview with the information you need to write your article.

E-Interviews

Once touted as convenient and inexpensive, the e-mail interview has lost favor with editors and writers. The biggest concerns surrounding the e-mail interview are:

- **Fabricated quotations.** Writers can never be sure that publicists aren't doctoring or inventing quotations for the interviewees.
- **Artificial quotations.** Writers cannot characterize sources according to voice tone, inflection, and colloquialism, which e-mail routinely sanitizes.
- **Missed opportunities.** Writers miss out on off-the-record remarks and other aspects of on-site interviews, including descriptions of people and places.

Still, there are times and occasions for electronic quotations. Knowing the five Ws and one H of e-mail interviews, you can gather quotes from a variety of sources or put elusive ones on record.

- **Whom to interview via e-mail.** Writers call them VEEPs—very electronic elusive people. These are the Bill Gateses of the world—CEOs, celebrities, famous authors, and other public figures who routinely turn down telephone or face-to-face interviews or who have publicists sanitize or invent quotations. Some such sources are just plain secretive.

Mickey McLean, managing editor of Delta's *Sky* magazine, allows e-mail interviews for a regular column called Mystery Guest, which features a book excerpt of a current mystery or thriller accompanied by a question and answer interview with the author.

In the November 2001 issue, *Sky* ran an excerpt from Charles Todd's fifth novel, *Watchers of Time* (Bantam), along with an interview done via e-mail—the only way the magazine could put the author on record.

The problem, said McLean in a telephone interview, was "Charles Todd" is a pen name for an elusive mother-and-son writing team. E-mail protected that guise.

Sky ran the interview by writer Lynn Coulter, noting the Q&A was done via e-mail and informing readers that Todd was a nom de plume for a writing team. "Some mystery authors are hard to pin down," McLean said. "Some submit to interviews only if done by e-mail." *Sky* generally permits the practice as long as the writer informs the editorial staff or acknowledges use of e-mail in an attribution or editor's note.

"Face-to-face interviews are best," McLean said. "Telephone interviews are second best."

- **When to interview via e-mail.** Most VEEPs check e-mail before or after their workday schedules take hold. Sending interview requests between 9 A.M. and noon may be optimum. Sources who check e-mail at noon or night may respond to questions that very day, and a morning source may see your message first in his queue the next day.

Some sources check e-mail throughout the day. One such VEEP is Mark Shapiro, general manager of the Cleveland Indians. Justice B. Hill, senior writer for MLB.com—the official site for Major League Baseball—dislikes e-mail interviews but may message Shapiro electronically with a specific question when he has been unable to contact him by telephone "and when his publicist is at the stadium."

"I know Mark's computer is always on," said Hill in a telephone interview. "His responses come back too quickly to be sanitized by anyone."

Robert Glidden, former president of Ohio University, responds to e-mail interviews "early in the morning, every morning, usually during midday if possible, and always in the late afternoon or before the evening's activities. "I try to be sure that no message goes unattended for more than twenty-four hours, even if I'm out of the country," Glidden added in an e-mail interview.

In that sense, e-mail is a distinct advantage for writers on deadline. Otherwise, they may wait weeks to slate on-site or phone interviews.

- **What to interview via e-mail.** E-mail interviews work well for roundups—stories that focus on a multitude of perceptions about an issue or incident. (For instance, the opinions on e-interviews gathered for the sidebar "The Writing World Weighs In" on page 113 were collected via e-mail.)

The general rule is to use e-mail if the individual source is less important than the topic or theme being documented.

Susan Porter, editor of *Scripps Howard News* magazine, said in a telephone interview that use of e-mail can be effective "when you need a number of opinions on a topic."

Porter cautions that if you want something spontaneous, don't do it on e-mail, especially in investigative work. "You can tip off your hand," she said, with your e-mail being sent to others. "There goes your exclusive!"

In any case, Porter noted, writers who interview via e-mail should ask sources if they would be willing to do a telephone or face-to-face follow-up interview.

- **Where to do e-mail interviews.** Because e-mail is mobile, from laptop to cell phone, the impulse is to do electronic interviews (or check for responses) wherever the technology is available. That can lead to problems.

Successful writers frame questions based on fact and/or background research. Usually those files are found at a primary workstation. Do not compose your questions without those references on hand. You also want to download all interviews into one computer at that station rather than leave them languishing at various locations: at work, the home office, the portable laptop, your pocket cell phone, etc. This decreases the chances of technological glitches and lost text.

- **Why do an e-mail interview.** Before you do an e-mail interview, ask "Why?" If the answer is your convenience, consider doing a telephone or face-to-face interview.

For that reason, Jennifer Pavlasek, associate editor of *Ohio Magazine*, is wary of e-mail interviews. "Part of being a writer is being able to capture a subject and convey it for an interesting read. Human interaction just can't happen naturally in cyberspace." Hill agreed. "One of the things that doesn't come through e-mail is sarcasm or inflection. People tend to be more colorful in their personal conversations than in their writing. E-mail lacks color."

Color includes authentic quotations garnered from face-to-face interviews, replete with sensory data—sound, sight, taste, etc.—and other important details and descriptions. A source's physical surroundings say a lot about the person's lifestyle and priorities. Moreover, writers usually can photograph sources or surroundings, enhancing the visual aspects of their manuscripts and increasing chances for a sale.

- **How to do an e-mail interview.** The cardinal rule in setting up e-mail interviews is to be brief: Quickly introduce yourself, the topic and your assignment, followed by a maximum of three quick questions. All should fit on one computer screen:

Dear John Wilson, President and CEO:

I am a nationally published freelance writer (*Forbes, Business Week, Wall Street Journal*) doing a story for *Widget News* on the planned corporate merger between Wilson Widget and Acme Services.

Would you please respond to the following:

According to my research, the planned merger may negatively affect Wilson Widget stock, at least in the short term. Why do you believe the merger eventually will benefit your current stockholders?

Thank you for your time. I hope you can respond before 5 P.M. Friday so I can meet my deadline.

The Writing World Weighs In

Freelancers, editors, and authors offer up their two cents on the pros and cons of e-mail interviews.

"E-mail interviews can be a fast and effective way of gathering information and quotes, but they're not appropriate for every article. They work best when, for example, you need a little bit of information from a lot of people, or if your subject is quite technical. But it's hard to write a good personality profile based on e-mail interviews, because you don't get a sense of what the person is really like."

David A. Fryxell, editor and publisher, *Desert Exposure*

"E-mail interviews should be used only as a last resort with sources you absolutely have to get some comment from for a story. The e-mail interview gives all the power to the interview subject since it leaves little or no room for follow-up or for pressing for answers to tough questions."

John Frank, Midwest bureau chief, *PRWeek* magazine

"I'm shy on the phone, so I love doing interviews by e-mail. . . . There's also virtually no chance of misquoting someone when you have his or her words written out for you. I also prefer being interviewed by e-mail, because I have time to think about my answers."

Jenna Glatzer, author and editor in chief, AbsoluteWrite.com

"I find it is more expedient to send my questions to someone I'm trying to reach via e-mail. Rather than playing phone tag, my 'source' can answer my questions in time to meet my deadline. . . . The drawback is obvious, however: You might not accurately grasp the person's tone or feelings from an e-mail as you would from a conversation."

Eileen Ogintz, syndicated newspaper columnist

If possible, give your source a week to reply. The day before your stated deadline, send a reminder: "Just to let you know I look forward to receiving your responses on the Wilson-Acme merger by tomorrow at 5 P.M."

In your original or reminder e-mail, you also might include a caution to ward off publicists: "Would you kindly let me know if you collaborated with an associate who supplied answers or altered quotes? Lacking such a note, I will assume that your responses came verbatim from you."

Such a disclaimer may put off sources accustomed to having handlers respond to interviews. In those cases, you still might want to go ahead with the e-mail interview, but treat the responses as an official statement rather than as verbatim remarks. Otherwise, you will be less than honest with your editor and readers. When readers see words in quotations, they believe that those words were uttered verbatim. That much has not changed.

Putting It All Together

When you've done all your interviews, it's time to write. But first, you need to organize your notes; otherwise you'll spend more time looking for key quotes, facts, and figures than you will writing.

Go through all your interviews and make notes on your notes—short summaries of what each source told you. Circle key quotes you might want to use in the story and number them so you can find them quickly later. Put sticky notes with the source's name at the start of each interview on your notepad so you can quickly get to the place you need to find a quote or fact for later.

Taking notes on your notes is like studying for a test. Once done, you should have a pretty good idea of what your story is going to say.

Chapter Seven:
Avoiding Problems

In addition to knowing how to research and conduct interviews, another critical factor in the process is knowing how to use the information you've gathered without breaking any spoken or unspoken laws. You must have a system for taking notes and collecting information that guarantees you will be able to attribute any direct quotes or information to the sources they came from. Mistakes in the realm of plagiarism or inaccuracy can ruin your reputation faster than anything else. So be meticulous and thorough to avoid problems.

Foolproofing Your Process

The editors of *Vanity Fair* were probably thrilled to get a personal letter from actress Julia Roberts following writer Ned Zeman's summer profile of her. Thrilled, that is, until they saw she was writing to correct a major error from the article. "My late father was born Walter Roberts, not Walter Motes, and his children carry the name proudly," Roberts wrote.

The journalism adage, "If your mother tells you she loves you, check it out," suggests a lot about how inaccuracies get into print. Too often, writers make assumptions about information, trust their sources (even dear old Mom) too much, swear they got that number right the first time, or chalk a notion from their imperfect memories up to "common knowledge." It's easy to get wrapped up in a beautifully told anecdote, an engaging lead, or a stylish ending. "Once you get it written, it seems right," said Mary Best Ellis, former editor of the regional monthly *Our State: Down Home in North Carolina*. "Remember to question yourself."

Why should you bother? Because editors are going to question you. Every magazine editor evaluates an article for accuracy. At some magazines—generally those with a small staff or tight deadlines—this evaluation is kept simple: a double check on the names and phone numbers, a review of past clips about the topic, and a call to the writer to clarify a confusing or contentious point.

At the most thorough publications—generally those with a larger budget and staff or lengthy production times—fact checkers comb through your text to verify every sentence. They'll retrace your research steps by calling your sources, going back to the books you mention, visiting pertinent Web pages, consulting a reference librarian, or even running your article past an independent expert. Depending on the topic, it may even be reviewed by a publisher's lawyer.

Amazed? You shouldn't be, say editors. Mistakes, misquotes, or misinterpretations can result in more than mild embarrassment. "We don't have a place for corrections," said Martha Miller, health and fitness editor of *Better Homes and Gardens.* "It's life-and-death stuff and you can't be wrong. It has to be the right advice."

Ashley Arthur of *Southern Living* explained that credibility is important no matter what the topic: "To me the most important thing is the facts. If readers can't trust us, they won't buy the magazine."

How do you keep in the running? The best approach is really the same no matter how much (or how little) effort the magazine you're writing for puts into fact checking. If the editors trust you to have done a professional job, you must make sure your research is reliable. And if they check on your every move, you want your work to pass that test.

Improving your accuracy is not about taking a magic perfection pill. It's about technique. Here is more expert advice from editors:

• **Ask about the process.** Not every magazine checks articles the same way. The editors' expectations may be outlined in your contract or assignment letter.

Miller requires writers to provide an annotated copy of their manuscripts—footnoted like a high school research paper—so she can match information in the article to the list of sources as she fact checks.

- **Go in with the right attitude.** Fact checking isn't about attacking your work or saying that your editor doesn't trust you. Writers should appreciate knowing that someone is backing them up. At most magazines, every writer's work gets equal treatment—newcomers, longtime contributors, staff members, or Pulitzer Prize winners.

- **Be a pack rat.** While you're researching, gather business cards, brochures, ticket stubs, menus, maps, corporate annual reports, magazine or newspaper clippings, articles from professional journals, Web page printouts, library books, and photos. Consider tape-recording interviews.

  By the time you're done, you'll have a bulging folder to rely on as you sit down to write and a paper trail to pass on to the magazine staff or refer to when the editor calls with a question.

- **Beware of shaky sources.** Information and experts are plentiful, but not all sources are reliable. If you've got a choice between a Whitney Houston Web site designed by her recording label, said former *Ebony* senior editor Charles Whitaker, and a Whitney Houston Web site designed by a teen fan in Michigan, pick the recording label site as your source.

  The same criteria apply for selecting interviewees. Yes, a family doctor in Florida will tell you everything he knows about hypothermia, but when was the last time he actually treated a patient for it? "You need to speak to people who are leaders in their field," is the advice Miller gives her health writers. As double verification, she asks experts from organizations such as the American Cancer Society or the Juvenile Diabetes Foundation to read stories to spot errors.

- **Listen to your gut.** You've researched your story carefully, written it, and rewritten the tough parts. Frankly, you're sick of working with it. Put it down for a bit so you can go back and identify the parts that may still be problematic. Call up your sources again or check a reference, said Whitaker, "whenever there's a nagging sensation that something's wrong." It will never be a waste of your time or your source's time.

Avoiding Plagiarism

Plagiarism is the act of using another's words as if they were your own. Even the pros can have problems with plagiarism.

Popular historians Stephen Ambrose—late author of *Band of Brothers* and *Citizen Soldiers*—and Doris Kearns Goodwin—author *of The Fitzgeralds and the Kennedys*—in early 2002 acknowledged they failed to properly credit the work of other scholars. Ambrose blamed the errors, in part, on the fast pace with which he turned out books. Goodwin likewise said that "sloppy" note keeping had caused her errors. The safest way for you to avoid plagiarism is to keep accurate notes. For that, you need a system that is organized, simple, and consistent.

To many writers, this sounds like the enemy of creativity. But being organized and consistent as you take your notes can free you up for big creative bursts while writing your first draft.

- **The paper method.** If you take notes by hand, start a new sheet of paper for each resource. At the top, write all the information you need for citations: author name, book title, publisher, and year of publication. Then number the page in the top right corner and draw a big circle around it.

Start every subsequent page with the author's name, publication date, and a big page number—the minimum you need to keep your notes in sequence and identify the source.

Write on one side of the page only. This allows you to read over your notes later and jot down ideas on the back.

- **The computer method.** Some powerful database programs can be used to cross-reference source material, tag it with keywords, and theoretically make life much easier. But the simplest way to keep notes on a computer is to open a new document for each source or theme. Name the file something obvious and store it in a folder you use for that project.

You may want to create subfolders for different themes or types of resources. Don't forget to include page numbers, quotation marks, and comments to identify the author of a particular note or quote. If you choose to take notes via computer, you can record bibliographical information for each quote using your word processor's footnotes feature. When the quote is cut from your notes file and pasted into your manuscript file, the footnote tags along. The comments feature also allows you to link comments to each quote, keeping them visually separate. In Microsoft Word, for example, these comments are preceded by your initials, further limiting the chances of confusion.

To easily find your information later, make use of the properties feature, which allows you to attribute keywords and notes to each document. These notes do not show up in the text of your document but allow you to search for all documents containing certain keywords or comments.

Working via computer also lets you preserve sources in their original forms. E-mail interviews can be saved and the interviewee quoted error-free with a simple copy and paste. Articles published online can be stored for later reference, and again, the copy-and-paste function allows you to reproduce quotes accurately.

A word of caution on technology, however—copying and pasting from electronic documents is very easy. Too easy. Be sure that you are not falling foul of copyright and fair use restrictions.

No matter how you store your notes, here are some easy tips to follow:

1. Always put quotation marks around any string of words taken from the text. Always—even if it is only three words. This way, you will always know that these are the author's actual words. Never combine quoted material, your comments, and paraphrases in the same paragraph. If you do not want to include the whole paragraph of the author's text, use ellipses (. . .) to indicate the missing sections.

2. Add the source's page number in the margin beside each quote. Even if two quotes come from the same page, write the page number for each. By doing it every time you develop a habit and therefore always have a page number handy for each footnote. On a separate line, write any comments—identified in the margin by your initials.

3. Try to quote rather than paraphrase. Even if you paraphrase in the final draft, you need to know exactly what the author said to avoid accidentally duplicating those words. If you do paraphrase in your notes, make sure you identify it by jotting a quick note (such as "para") in the margin.

Whatever method you develop, the cardinal rule is to be consistent. You need to be sure of the source of every scribble.

Every writer should scrupulously check the last draft of his work against the original source material. But it is also dangerous to rely on this final read to identify plagiarized passages or omissions. If a section is not in quotation marks, you probably wouldn't check it against a source. You may accidentally lift a whole passage or, as Goodwin found, become so familiar with a passage that you think it's your own wording. That won't happen if your original notes are clear. Develop an organized, simple, and consistent method of note-keeping now and avoid the whole plagiarism mess later.

Libel

Another legal issue for writers is libel. You are guilty of libel if you publish a false statement that is damaging to another living person's reputation. The false statement can be unintentional and still be ruled libelous in court, which is why the law requires writers to take every reasonable step to check for accuracy. While it is up to the plaintiff to prove falsehood, it is up to you to prove that you made every reasonable effort to be accurate.

Few writers would knowingly publish falsehoods, yet the pitfalls for writers are numerous. You can accurately print what you have been told and still commit libel—if the person giving you the information was wrong in her facts. Many writers get in trouble simply by failing to check minor facts, which is why you must double-check and triple-check information—even when you believe it is correct.

Misspell someone's name while writing about a crime and you can implicate an innocent person in wrongdoing. That's libel. You can be held just as libelous if you falsely state someone has died. The "lucky living" have won such cases on claims of undue hardship and emotional distress. Errors in something as innocent as a high school sports story have even resulted in libel suits. While such instances are rare, the important point is that nearly any form of writing can put you at risk of libel. The only way to be safe is to always be 100 percent certain of your facts.

Freelance writers have some special issues of concern with libel. First, keep in mind that you aren't necessarily going to be defended by the publisher if your work prompts a libel suit. If the publisher alone is sued and loses, it could come after you for damages.

To protect yourself from groundless suits, it's good to have tapes of your interviews. Bear in mind, however, that taping phone conversations is illegal in some states unless the other party is aware he is being taped.

Not all libel suits may stem from anything you did. Bad editing can cause errors that result in a suit. The best protection is to see a proof of the edited version, including headlines and photo captions. For your own protection keep a hard copy of all manuscripts you send to a publisher.

Rules for Quoting

Quoting a person accurately is another one of the most sacred rules of magazine nonfiction. When you put quotations around words and attribute them to a source, you are telling the reader that those words were actually spoken in front of you.

Fabricating dialogue may be legitimate in fiction or public relations (as long as the practitioner clears the quote with the client or source). In magazine nonfiction, however, quote-making is called "invention." And it's taboo.

Because of e-mail and the Internet, many writers are becoming lax about the sanctity of direct quotations. Dialogue these days passes as "chat," typed on keyboards (rather than spoken) and transmitted electronically anywhere on the globe.

Before home computers, most writers felt obliged to inform readers that a quote was said "in a telephone interview." Otherwise, they feared, the audience would incorrectly assume that the quotation was made face-to-face. Fewer writers are making these fine distinctions—much to the concern of editors in newsrooms across the country.

"I feel the sanctity of quotations is absolute," said Peter Copeland, editor and general manager of Scripps Howard News Service, in a telephone interview. "Readers have the expectation that things in direct quotations are 'preserved under glass'—that they have a special place in the text." Magazine writers must uphold the same standard, he said.

You can do that by learning these rules of direct quotations:

1. **Don't "invent" quotations.** Your job is to put your sources on record—not put words into their mouths. If a source refuses or is unable to give you the quote you need, go back for another interview or go to another source.

2. **Don't lift quotations.** The Internet makes it easy to locate sources with nifty things to say. If they didn't say those things to you, you can't pass them off as your own . . . or even verify that the quotations are authentic.

3. **Don't pretend.** Don't excerpt passages and cast them as actual quotations. You can access all kinds of documents online, including speeches, court proceedings, testimonials, and minutes of meetings. You can cite them as such, but you can't reprint them as quotations, pretending that the source said the excerpt to you in an interview.

4. **Do go live when possible.** As mentioned in chapter six, good magazine writing relies on "sensory data"—descriptive passages that appeal to the five senses or convey motion. You can't always convey that doing telephone interviews, which may suffice for a quick expert quotation but seldom for a biography or an article.

There are also some gray areas regarding quotes. They include:

- **Maybe you can correct grammar and syntax.** Purists will argue that you can't fix such common errors as wrong verb tense or idiom, noun-pronoun disagreement, or run-on sentences. When you get such quotes, purists believe, you should make them indirect. Realists believe you can make minor corrections that typically involve a word or two. Your goal is to quote sources, realists say, not embarrass them. Bottom line: If you change meaning when you change a word, you can't use a direct quotation.

- **Maybe you can do e-mail interviews.** Purists argue that e-mail is typed, not spoken, and lets sources invent their own quotations rather than participate in spontaneous exchanges with the writer. Thus, purists claim, e-mail interviews are bogus. Realists believe that e-mail is speech and more accurate. Better still, the writer has a transcript when a source denies that she said something. Bottom line: When you use an e-mail interview, note it as such in the attribution.

- **Maybe you can let sources see their quotations in advance.** Purists argue that your job is to quote sources accurately—not to ensure that they are comfortable with what they said. Realists believe that writers sometimes misquote sources, especially when information is technical. Bottom line: If you let your sources see their quotations in advance of publication, advise them that they cannot change meaning—only inform you of any mistakes.

How you quote sources reflects your standards, especially in an electronic age that emphasizes convenience rather than legwork. If you take shortcuts with quotations, you can lose more than assignments. You can lose your reputation.

A Final Check

To avoid inaccuracy, plagiarism, libel suits, and misquotes, do you ever want your interview subject to review an article before publication? Sometimes. Do journalists and editors shiver when you suggest this? Usually.

The Society of Professional Journalists recommends writers "distinguish news from advertising and shun hybrids that blur the lines between the two." Well, when you're just starting out as a freelancer, "shunning" isn't always an option.

Some of Wendy Hart Beckman's first assignments were "promotional writing"—not ads, but very one-sided. The subjects, who would portray themselves in the best light, provided the material. She accepted these assignments with misgiving but, as the writer, she still assumed "primary responsibility for truth and accuracy" as prescribed by the American Society of Journalists and Authors. The subject had to approve Beckman's article before publication. Sometimes the caliber of the changes requested by the subject compelled her to tell the editor to remove her byline because the article no longer met her personal standards. The National Writers Union recommends you reserve the right to do so if a dis-

ANOTHER OPINION

- "That I can remember, I've never shown an article to a source for an advanced read. Why? Because I should be smart enough and diligent enough to get it right on my own." Steve Yahn, former executive editor, *Editor & Publisher.*

- "An advance look at your article is an ethical no-no for freelancers and staff writers—in most cases. However, I will read back a source's own quotes, but that's all—and only if he or she specifically asks. I never volunteer to do it.

  " . . . The exception: When you write for an in-house publication and the article quotes or deals with the company, organization, staff, or executives. In those situations, it's standard for the higher-ups to review the article before it appears in an official publication." Eric Freedman, Pulitzer Prize-winning reporter and Michigan State University journalism professor.

- "I've never shown an article to a source before publication. What I have done and would do is show the source how I plan to use their quotes or material, essentially to check for accuracy, but not grant editorial control. But I would not show the entire article to the source before publication unless I'd previously discussed it with my editor and gotten their concurrence." Paul D. McCarthy, president, McCarthy Creative Services; author of books, articles, and essays; former senior editor at HarperCollins and Simon & Schuster.

pute arises so "you will have a legal way to disassociate yourself from the piece and still get paid."

An advantage to having your subject review the article is to verify technical accuracy. One researcher Beckman interviewed said a television station once embarrassed him by drawing inaccurate conclusions from an interview with him. "The important thing to me was being allowed to have input into the design of the article," he told her after the interview. "It is difficult addressing the reconciliation of understanding of topic between the person writing the article—who has limited knowledge—and the person being interviewed—who has a lot of specialized knowledge."

Many times it boils down to the writer's comfort. This can vary depending on the topic, the genre, or the experience of the writer. If most of your writing is not controversial, or even critical, you may feel comfortable asking your subject to review the material. For example, your note-taking skills aren't perfect, so you may want to fax one page of the article to the subject and ask him to check the information. The subject may be surprised you offered, but this will help you maintain your quality standard, and your subject will appreciate it.

Ask yourself who needs to be in control of the article: the writer, the editor, the subject, or a combination? Beyond the requirements of the situation, it is your own comfort level and morals as the writer that will dictate your actions.

Chapter Eight:
Writing Techniques and Revision

Novelist John Irving once said, "Know the story—the whole story, if possible—before you fall in love with your first sentence, not to mention your first chapter. If you don't know the story before you begin the story, what kind of storyteller are you? Just an ordinary kind—making it up as you go along, like a common liar."

What's your story about? That seems like a simple question. But the search for its answer challenges writers in all communication disciplines: journalism, creative writing, screenwriting, speechwriting, advertising, marketing, and public relations. Whether you're using terms like nut graf, dramatic premise, or unique selling proposition (USP), the goals are the same: to understand and synthesize material in order to convey a message, promote a concept, or tell a story.

The Overview

Put your notes aside. Think about how you'd describe the story to a friend. Do it in one sentence, boiling down all the information you've collected into one coherent statement. This helps you deal with information overload when learning about a new topic. It strips away the jargon and points of view and gets to the essence of what you want to say.

Once you have that sentence, it should become clear how to organize the story. If it doesn't, try creating an outline. Group information about a given topic together and arrange your topics in an order that will be logical to the reader.

Next, try writing the start of your story. If you're doing a two thousand-word feature, write the first five hundred words, summarizing key points you're going to convey and hopefully encouraging the reader to read on. The next 1,200 words or so, expand on that summary, fleshing out key points with quotes, facts, figures, whatever is needed. Look at the notes on your notes to find the information, and make more notes to yourself if there's any information you think you should double-check or look up. Use the last three hundred words to sum up, draw conclusions, look ahead, or look back, as the story dictates.

Once finished, put the story aside for a while—at least overnight if you have the time. That allows you to come back and edit it with a fresh eye. When you do so, cut extra verbiage and try not to end up with a piece that's a lot longer than your assigned length.

Focus and Structure—In Depth

In *The Editorial Eye*, author Jane Harrigan states, "For writers, determining focus is the first prewriting step. Next they have to find a structure." Harrigan says writers need to first ask, "What am I trying to say?" The question of organization comes next: "How do I want to say it?"

Answer those questions correctly and consistently, and you'll become a stronger, more confident writer.

Step 1: Find your focus. Many writers can't see the story through the trees of their material. They mistakenly believe that their focus is the same as their topic. They also may not realize how important it is to sum up their story in a simple conversational sentence early in the process.

Differentiating between topic and focus is critical to clearer writing. Topic refers to the subject matter. Focus goes much deeper. It is what the story is about, its theme or dramatic premise.

For example: A feature on campus crime, such as a tale of a student who survived an assault, isn't merely about the facts of the case. That's the topic. The focus goes to the heart of the story, such as how the crime changed this student's life and those of her family, friends, and associates.

In *Editor & Publisher*, Jack Hart, managing editor of the *Oregonian* newspaper, wrote about the importance of story focus using the nut graf or essential theme of the story. He said a "carefully crafted nut helps focus the writing, draws the reader into the content, and makes reading more meaningful."

Two examples reveal the subtle power of a clear nut graf. In February 2000, *The Washington Post* ran a feature on the late cartoonist Charles Schulz. Henry Allen's touching 1,200-word story contained this focus after the first 200 words: ". . . Charles Schulz redeemed the ordinary, lonely, forgettable, hopeful person at the core of all of us by invoking the kind of laughter that comes when you realize you're caught between the rock and the hard place of fame, existence, whatever."

USA Today sportswriter Tom Pedulla wrote a compelling piece in 1999 about former NFL star Darryl Stingley, who had been paralyzed in a game twenty years before, and his son Derek, an Arena Football League player. So what's this story about? Football? Think again. Wrote Pedulla: "But this story is not so much about loss. It is about how a courageous father and son have grown through tragedy." The nut graf sums up this chronicle of human transcendence and the timeless love of a father and son.

What are some techniques to help you find your story focus? Start by interviewing yourself. Is there a single image, detail, or quote that conveys your central message? Why would someone want to read what you've written? Will they be informed, enlightened, or emotionally affected by your words? What's your story's conflict or complication? (Remember English 101: person vs. person, person vs. nature, person vs. himself?)

A logical way to begin is to list the important actions taking place in the story. Who is doing what to whom with what result? You can answer that by listing the information under three headings: subject (noun), action (verb), and impact (object). To construct such an action or scene list you also might use the headings problem/solution or goal/result. What you list depends on your material and your intended story format.

For a more creative story genesis, writing coaches like Donald Murray (*Writing for Your Readers*, Globe Pequot Press) recommend stress-free brainstorming or mapping exercises. On a blank sheet of paper, write a single word in the center. Circle it. Then draw branches from this circle as more thoughts occur. Don't stop to edit yourself. Start new branches when a new idea appears. Write steadily for five minutes, and you'll end up with several potential focus statements.

Grope drafts (writing without looking at notes) help writers discover their focus during the prewriting stages. It may take you several drafts before your main theme or dramatic premise presents itself, but this drafting stage is key not only to finding your focus but structuring your story as well.

Step 2: Organize your story. You need to patiently sift through your drafts if you hope to find narrative gold. What points are you trying to make? What messages keep recurring in your copy? What themes exist? Use your rough draft to craft a jot outline—a preliminary listing of statements that are central to your story. Order and reorder these statements until a fluid structure appears. Fluid is a key word because your story organization likely will shift as you continue to draft.

Once you have the jot outline, review your notes and draft again. Whether you're producing a work of fiction or nonfiction, you need to analyze your sentences and paragraphs. Each sentence and paragraph should serve a single purpose. Remember: If you can't sum up or label a paragraph in less than six words, you're likely trying to cover too much territory. Labeling paragraphs will help you organize your story by linking similar blocks of text.

Models can enable you to craft stories in the same way machinists make parts using product molds or dies. In hard newswriting, reporters still rely on the inverted pyramid model to organize a story from most important to least important information. A classic feature story model is the three-part diamond structure: lead, nut graf, and story. Scene-by-scene construction is the appropriate model for a dramatic narrative. Profiles rely on the proper ordering of anecdotes and quotes. Other story models include the conventional or modified (e.g., use of flashbacks) chronology, cause and effect, pro and con, and comparison and contrast.

If you are comparing/contrasting two individuals, organizations, or issues, you may opt for a (1) point-by-point or (2) block-by-block approach to story structure. In the first approach, the criteria are selected and the material proceeds with the comparison or contrast of each side on a particular point. In the second approach, the story is structured with the complete criteria presented separately and thoroughly for each side. This point-by-point or block-by-block model is ideal, for example, when examining two candidates' platforms.

Once the major building blocks of your story are in place, other organizational devices should be implemented. Transition words such as "in addition," "besides," "however," "despite," "though," "regardless," and "consequently," are necessary to clearly and coherently join sentences, paragraphs, and entire sections of a story.

End your sentences with words that emphasize. This will hold reader interest and promote smoother segues as you begin new sentences. Whenever possible, close your story with a quote from—or some reference to—the person, place, or subject that first appeared in your lead.

How to Craft a Successful Lead

Comedians say the first joke of a set is the most critical. You can either sink or swim with that initial punch line. As a writer, your audience of overworked editors and distracted readers can be just as flighty and cruel if you don't grab their attention from the get-go.

The lead of an article is no less crucial than an opening stunt, enticing people to the edge of their seats or out the back door. When a reader picks up a magazine, he has more than a dozen different articles to choose from, so if he stops to peruse yours, you better give him an immediate and convincing reason not to flip the page.

Writing is informative, but it is also entertainment, and in order to be successful and guarantee your readers stick around for at least another paragraph you need to treat your lead like a fifty-yard dash. If you're tying your shoes or busy looking behind you, the competition will leave you in the dust. And there's no catching up in a sprint.

But how do you get their attention?

- **Cut to the chase.** You don't need to start from the beginning. Background information is important and necessary, but don't bore your readers with statistics and setups that seem superfluous until you've told them *why* you are writing this article and, more importantly, why they are reading it.

The structure of an article is not like that of the traditional novel—beginning, middle, and end. Tell the climax first. As Annie Dillard encourages in *The Writing Life* (Perennial): "Spend it all, shoot it, play it, lose it, all, right away, every time. Do not hoard what seems good for a later place in the book (or article). The impulse to save something good for a better place is the signal to spend it now."

The lead is like an audition. An aspiring Broadway actress sings her best ten bars on stage, hoping she'll be asked back for a second round. It's only ten bars, but they're the first and only notes the director will hear if she doesn't knock his socks off. Similarly, writers need to present their very best information in those opening ten words in order to get "called back" by their readers *before* they can get to the research and the details.

Let your opening line be the carrot dangling at the end of your reader's nose. *Then* in subsequent paragraphs you can explain why the carrot is orange and if it's indigenous to North America.

Take a look at *The New York Times*, *Newsweek*, or any other successful publication you respect. Read the headlines and recognize the power a good headline has to catch your eye. Now read the lead that follows and notice that it has filled in a few of the holes but still maintains the same urgency and significance as the headline.

Headline: Ohio Cleric Arrested; Terror Link Is Cited

Lead: A leading Islamic cleric who runs Ohio's largest mosque was arrested Tuesday on charges that he concealed his ties to terrorist causes when applying for U.S. citizenship (*The New York Times*, January 2004).

The details of how the event unfolded and background leading up to the perpetrator's arrest are very essential but must follow the initial hook of your article. Set your bait first. You can't reel in fish that aren't biting.

No-frills newspaper-like leads or "summary leads" are very effective and a good base when beginning any article. The summary lead, as shown above, is most often used for news stories because it is concise and condenses a large amount of information into the fewest words possible. In a summary lead, you compress the entire article into the opening lines. The trimmings can always be added later, but make sure you've got the *why* in there first to avoid having your readers ask the dreaded question: *So what?*

Who, what, when, why, how? These are the questions you want an audience to ask. Answer a few in your lead and leave some to be revealed—then your audience is hooked. Otherwise, they'll turn the page and the race is over before it even began.

- **Webster's, eat your heart out.** Beginning your article with a definition is about as exciting as a root canal. If your reader wanted Webster's opinion, they would have read the dictionary, not your article.

> Mackinac State Historic Park is one of Michigan's most prized landmarks, as it is home to preserved battlegrounds of the War of 1812 and the French and Indian War.

Are you asleep yet? Tell them something they *don't* know. Answer the question, why is this relevant right now at this point in time? And get that big clunky proper noun out of the first line.

> Clues to the 1812 British invasion of Fort Mackinac unravel as forensic expert Sandra Anderson and her specially trained police dog sniff out hidden trenches and mass burial grounds beneath what is now a golf course for summer tourists.

Maybe they never cared about the War of 1812, but the rewriting of history will catch many readers' attentions. Present your story in a way that lets your audience play detective with you. Everyone loves a good mystery.

- **Tell a story.** Narrative leads are often used for feature articles, as they take you into the mind of the character. Telling the story from the main person's perspective raises the emotional bar and can be a great way to paint a scene for your readers. *Time* reporter Terry McCarthy implemented this technique in his 2004 "Gang Buster" article:

> William Bratton strides into evening roll call at the police station in the Rampart section of LA, and the fifty officers in the room break into applause. The police chief cracks a smile. It is the week before Christmas, murders in Los Angeles are down 22 percent, and the man whose crime-busting tactics cut New York City's homicide rate almost a decade ago is once again being hailed as a savior.

The setting and characters come alive on the page. Before even realizing it, readers are sucked into the story and want to keep reading.

- **Can I quote you on that?** If used well, a quote can be a very effective and eye-opening way to begin an article. If your article is lighthearted, let your quote be funny and clever. However, more serious articles call for a quote that creates tension, keeping your audience on the edge of their seats.

"We've got him" was the opening line to a *New York Times* article reporting the capture of Saddam Hussein (January 2004.) An article in a young adult magazine discussing teenage pregnancy and birth control might begin by quoting a fourteen-year-old girl: " 'What my mother doesn't know won't hurt her,' claimed high school freshman Lauren Quinn."

It's a safe bet that every girl who reads that opening line won't skip right to the horoscopes before finding out what it is the mother doesn't know. This is a powerful and provocative tool—use it.

- **A lead needs a metaphor like a fish needs a bicycle.** Not true. Metaphors are definitely attention-getters and very effective. They generate immediate visual images that scoop the reader up and into the text. Use them to get your story rolling, but remember less is more.

You may have noticed the repeated use of metaphors in this section— the comedian, the actress, the runner, the carrot, the fishing bait . . . do you get the point? Though effective and creative, these too can be over-done. Pick one or two of the most visual and let them carry you through the article.

- **Credibility counts.** Your readers are smart and their patience is thin, so don't over-dramatize. Clever is allowed, but cutesy is not. Just as an actress can overact, so too can a writer outdo herself on the page. This refers to made-for-TV-movie metaphors, exclamation points, and *fire-in-the-house!* openings. Recognize the different volumes of ringing alarms and set yours to the appropriate level. You aren't doing yourself any favors by misleading your audience, because more than anything, readers want to trust the voice on the page. Exaggeration is suspect:

> Throw your treadmills to the curb, reports say. With the help of Dr. Atkins' New Diet Revolution, the whole world seems to be dropping pants' sizes and eating all the McDonald's hamburgers they want!

Credibility is key:

> Trading off low-fat yogurt and diet shakes for red meat and blocks of cheese, Americans are losing a considerable amount of weight on the Atkins diet, reports FDA official Tom Brown.

No matter what kind of lead you use, don't become so invested in your own words that you are unable to throw them out when necessary or at the very least find new places for them. Writing one lead may not be enough or it may just direct you to an even better one. Write five or ten. Let some of them be off-the-wall and others cut and dry; then see if you can blend them. Pitching a few different leads to an editor to show flexibility is never a bad idea.

Be concise. The more a reader trips over your words, the less effective your point is and the less likely he is to keep reading. Lead sentences that extend more than a few lines and require taking lunch or bathroom breaks are *too* long. Remember, the lead is a fifty-yard dash; the mile is still to come.

Write to Grab Readers' Attention

Once your have your focus, structure, and lead, you need to think of other elements to make your story command attention. You want something shocking! Incredible! Amazing! Reading the supermarket tabloids may actually help you find the tools you need to be a better writer.

Some mainstream journalists and writers look down their noses at *The National Enquirer, Star*, and *Globe*. But they shouldn't. These publications, owned by American Media, sell three million copies a week. *The New York Times* and ABC-TV's Ted Koppel are among the mainstream news organizations and commentators who have praised the tabloids, so they must be doing something right. Rather than writing long and windy pieces to win awards, tabloids feature short and sensational stories to win readers. These ten tabloid tips will help you jazz up any type of writing.

1. **Never be boring.** Boring is the cardinal sin of tabloids. Take this non-celebrity story from *The National Enquirer* about a man who constructed a canine house of worship. Rather than do it straight, the author wrote:

> Cats may have nine lives—but dogs go to heaven! Just ask Stephen Huneck, who spent $200,000 building a church for dogs . . .

This is your basic tabloid lead.

You start your story with the commonly known statement about cats having nine lives, then set up tension with the dash and finish with the kicker that dogs go to heaven, a play on the movie *All Dogs Go to Heaven*. This statement then leads you into what the story is about.

2. **Find the "Hey Martha."** It's the amazing amount of money spent or the incredible feat accomplished that makes the reader turn to his wife and say, "Hey, Martha, get a load of this." It's not just that Huneck built a church for dogs; it's that he spent $200,000 to do it.

3. **Use your best shot.** Tabloids tell the whole story in the lead. Lots of writers want to save the most fascinating aspect of a story as a payoff, but most readers are not going to wait around that long.

The *Globe* began a review of Kirk Douglas' autobiography, *My Stroke of Luck*, like this:

> Kirk Douglas put a pistol in his mouth determined to kill himself and only an accident of fate prevented him from pulling the trigger.

That's the most shocking element of the book and that's why the *Globe* started the story with it. The scene immediately engages the reader and makes him want to find out how Douglas got to that point of desperation. Make sure the rest of the explanation is just as engaging.

4. Make a long story short. That is the essence of tabloid writing—to take ten pages of notes and distill them into one page of copy packed with fascinating details, illuminating background, and hard-hitting action. Check out this pithy description of Queen Elizabeth for a *Star* story about feuding among the royals:

> The Queen, seventy-five, has been on the throne for fifty years and married to a grumpy husband for fifty-four. Even palace insiders admit she shows more affection to her beloved pet corgis than to her dysfunctional family. Personal fortune of $2 billion has not bought her happiness.

5. Use effective transitions. When you write tightly, the transitions that take the reader from one aspect of a story to another are crucial.

Here's a moving transition from a story about the heroes of the September 11 tragedies on Flight 93. After Todd Beamer said, "Let's roll!" and Jeremy Glick and others rushed the terrorists in the cockpit of the doomed aircraft, the *Star* used the transition, "Glick and the other heroes stormed from their seats and into history."

6. Pace yourself. Vary your story with longer and shorter sentences to avoid monotony. For the most part, your paragraphs should be short and so should your sentences—three typewritten lines for a sentence is the max. This creates the breathless feel of an exciting read.

7. **Keep it simple.** Write to express first, impress second. Write simply and directly. The reader shouldn't have to work to understand what you are saying.

8. **Use active verbs.** It's more exciting to write (and read), "Cops busted Robert Downey Jr. for drugs," than "Robert Downey Jr. was taken into custody by police for the possession of an illegal substance."

9. **Have fun with puns.** Journalism doesn't have to be deadly serious. In entertainment and offbeat news stories, it's okay to have a little fun. In a story about sixty-year-old actor Harrison Ford dating a much younger woman, the *Star* referred to him as "Raider of the Lost Cradle."

10. **Give it a top and tail.** This tip comes from the *Globe*'s veteran tabloid man and editor in chief, Tony Frost. What he means is that the story should be almost circular in construction, returning to the lead at the end of the story. Many newspapers use an inverted pyramid structure and cut to fit from the bottom. But a story shouldn't just trail off at the end.

In a story about *Survivor IV* contestant Gina Crews, the *Star* began by saying she was already a survivor for having endured a terrifying bout with a stalker. And a friend was quoted who said that ability would serve her well on the show. After describing her ordeal, the piece came back to that thought at the end. "She's pretty good at seeing a situation and finding a way to deal with it," said the friend. "I think TV viewers will be impressed with her."

And readers will be impressed with you if you write tightly, brightly, and pump up your stories with exciting details.

Using Anecdotes

Adding anecdotes is another way you can entice readers and give them interesting, personal details. Effective anecdotes aren't like red sprinkles on top of sugar cookies, adding bits of glitz but no flavor or substance. Anecdotes are like raisins in oatmeal cookies. Sure, you can eat the cookies without them, but you'll miss out on the added flavor, contrasting texture, and enhanced nutrition.

For the nonfiction writer, anecdotes are tools that bring generalities to life and help readers see and hear rather than simply be told. Think of them as ministories, as this anecdote from William Goldman's *New York* magazine article about the former wrestler-turned-film-star Andre the Giant illustrates:

> He was very strong. I was talking to an actor who was shooting a movie in Mexico. What you had to know about Andre was that if he asked you to dinner, he paid, but when you asked him, he also paid. This actor, after several free meals, invited Andre to dinner and, late in the meal, snuck into the kitchen to give his credit card to the maitre d'. As he was about to do this, he felt himself being lifted up in the air. The actor, it so happens, was Arnold Schwarzenegger, who remembers, "When he had me up in the air, he turned me so I was facing him, and he said, 'I pay.' Then he carried me back to the table, where he set me down in my chair like a little boy." Oh, yes, Andre was very strong. When Arnold Schwarzenegger tells me someone is very strong, I'll go along with it.

Effective anecdotes rarely fall onto your manuscript like manna from heaven. Instead, you must search for them while doing that research and interviewing discussed earlier. Listen carefully for hints of an anecdote lurking below the surface. Elicit more than dates, places, formalized statements, dollars-and-cents statistics, and opinions. The way to draw out the ministories you need is through open-ended questions such as, "Tell me what happened when . . ." or "What did you do that day?" or "Describe what you saw when . . ."

As you have learned, the personal nature of face-to-face interviews makes them more productive than phone interviews in mining anecdotal material. And when you interview, be sensitive and attuned to cultural distinctions and nuances, whether the subjects live down the road or thousands of miles away.

Your own experiences and observations may give birth to anecdotes. During her research trips for her book *Headwraps: A Global Journey (Public Affairs/Perseus)*, Georgia Scott wrote a column for Essence.com, the online version of *Essence* magazine. She recounted her deportation from India to Nepal after her travel agent botched her visa arrangements. The anecdote recounted the night she spent in custody with a guard sleeping in the same room and the bathroom door bolted so she couldn't escape.

Don't ignore documents as sources for anecdotes. Eric Freedman's book *Pioneering Michigan* (A&M Publishing) drew heavily on diaries, family histories, and letters to bring life to the women, men, and children who settled in frontier-era Michigan. Instead of merely stating that Jefferson Gage Thurber acted bravely in the midst of widespread panic during the 1832 cholera epidemic in Detroit, Freedman used a letter to his New England relatives:

> I was a daily attendant in the hospitals, both of the Army and the citizens. From the fact of not having it, I concluded it was not contagious. The panic at that time exceeded anything I ever imagined. The timidity of our border settlers from sudden incursions of the Indians forms but a faint comparison. I have no doubt from what little experience and observation I have had that fear has killed as many as the cholera.

Those same kinds of sources provided Freedman with details of how horses broke through the frozen crust of a snow-covered route and how a pregnant wolf kept in a family's shanty provided its owners with a $5 bounty on the pups.

Finding a potentially worthwhile anecdote isn't enough. You must also use the raw material wisely. First, where does an anecdote go? Most are placed in the heart of an article, like the Schwarzenegger one, but the correct answer is: anywhere it fits. The lead may be an ideal place, especially for profiles or trend stories. Steve Wilson launched his *Folio:* magazine profile of a boating magazine owner with this anecdote:

> One evening in 1973, Bob Bitchin, future editor and publisher of *Latitudes & Attitudes*, pulled his chopper up to a stoplight on the Sunset Strip in Los Angeles. He made eye contact with a man in a fur coat behind the wheel of a Ferrari. When the light turned green, they raced. The driver (who won) turned out to be Evel Knievel, and their late night of partying and entanglement with the law later made it into a *Rolling Stone* article.

Or wrap up with an anecdote, leaving a ministory in the readers' minds. Douglas Preston does so in the evocative ending to his *National Geographic* piece on Cambodia. Preston told how he touched an ancestor stone, then:

> . . . ran my finger into the cool groove of a carved lotus. Here, broken soldiers from an Angkor temple had been put in the service of an even more ancient religion. One of our soldiers, a skinny, barefoot teenager with an AK-47 slung over his shoulder, stopped at the shrine, placed his hands together and bowed deeply in an act of veneration. A gecko called twice, and then the forest fell silent in the stifling noonday heat. Life went on in this strange, timeless land.

You can even split an anecdote between your lead and your ending. Profiling an athlete, for example, you may open with an anecdote about a key basketball game and, in a few sentences, draw readers up to the buzzer when your subject shoots the make-it-or-break-it basket. Then wind up with the ball arching toward the basket as fans hold their breaths, and tell your readers the result.

To make your anecdotes effective additions to your article, remember to do these two things:

- **Write tightly.** Remember, the anecdote isn't the point of your article—it's merely a device to make or emphasize a point. Not all details are important. An overly long, overly wordy anecdote detours readers. The length of an article also helps dictate the desirable length of an anecdote. In a 1,000-word article, a 350-word anecdote is apt to be out of proportion and won't leave you enough space to cover everything else.

- **Think fiction.** Even though you're writing nonfiction, use literary devices that characterize fiction, including plot, dialogue, characterization, sharp words, and description. Something should happen. If people talk, they should sound conversational rather than stilted, but don't distort the meaning of what they actually said. If a person—or even an animal or machine—is the focus of the anecdote, readers should gain a personality insight. Choose vivid words conducive to the tone of the piece, and weave in description or color to help readers visualize what's unfolding.

The Evel Knievel anecdote conveys a sense of Bitchin's love for action and adventure. There's no dialogue but plenty of plot, characterization, power words, and description—in fewer than a hundred words.

If you've done your interviewing, observation, and research well, you'll have more than enough anecdotal material for your project. The question becomes how best to pick and choose from your riches.

For impact, an anecdote must be more than a window dressing or a way to boast how clever or lucky you were to snag this treasured tale from your sources. No matter how entertaining, omit those that fail to bolster a relevant point. Also skip those that are repetitive or clash with the mood you're striving to create. For example, the Schwarzenegger-in-the-restaurant incident illuminates the writer's observation about Andre the Giant's insistent generosity toward his friends. The writer may have heard other stories about Schwarzenegger and Andre that were less on point, and a second ministory about generosity would have been superfluous.

Finally, don't think of unused anecdotes as junk or regret the time you spent unearthing them. Keep them on file because they may tell just the right minitale in a future project.

Ending Your Article

Your lead strikes the perfect chord. Your body copy follows with flawless rhythm. You're sitting at your desk, pages of linguistic brilliance before you, and only one thing stands between your article draft and your editor: a grand finale.

A well-written lead grabs your readers' attention, and an effective ending is the return on the investment of that attention. No matter how you approach it, the ideal close should make your readers feel rewarded for the time they spent reading your piece. Specifically, it should do *at least one* of three things: leave your readers feeling they've learned something or gained some new insight; show your readers how this information impacts or relates to their own lives; and/or encourage your readers to explore the topic further.

The appropriate style for your conclusion is largely dependent on the type of publication, your audience, and the subject and tone of your article. A brief informational piece will not afford you the opportunity for extensive quotations or anecdotes, so you must rely on concentrated language. Conversely, you might leave your audience feeling cheated if you use a "just the facts, ma'am" approach to wrap up a human-interest feature story.

In addition to selecting the perfect closing strategy, you must also use propriety in your language. Choose powerful words and images that appeal to your readers' emotions, but steer clear of melodramatic descriptions, saccharine adjectives, and clichés. Your ending should be memorable, not ridiculous or trite. If you suspect something you've written might be toeing the oh-brother line, read it out loud to someone else. If she wrinkles her forehead or rolls her eyes, there's your answer.

Once you have a general idea about the purpose and style of your conclusion, consider some of these possible approaches.

- **Go to your sources.** One of the most effective ways to end your article is to use a quotation. Not just any quote will do, however; you must choose one that is definitive. Search your interview notes for a statement that sums up the issue at hand and adds an element of pathos.

Consider ending your article with something like this:

> Despite resistance from the city's gaming commission, Dr. Ellen Parker and other ecologists continue to search for a safe home for the endangered birds because they believe each creature plays a vital role in our ecosystem.
>
> "If this species were to disappear, it would cause an explosion in the insect population and that could have a disastrous effect on local agriculture," Parker said. "Then it's not just about the birds. The problem will affect all of us."

Not only do the experts' words underscore the critical nature of the situation, they also connect the subject of the story to the reader: *This is not just about birds; it's about the food you eat. It's about the livelihood of you or someone you know.* The final line leaves the reader with a new, personal insight.

- **Have the last word.** You can also pack an emotional punch by responding briefly to an ending quotation. Limit yourself to one or two lines. This is especially effective if you have an interrogative or controversial statement from one of your sources. For example:

> Professional baseball players and franchise owners remain deadlocked over the issue of salary.
>
> "As long as there is a misdistribution of wealth among the teams, high-priced players will flock to those few cities that can afford them. The less wealthy teams lose their talent, and with the talent goes their post-season prospects," says baseball historian Anthony Davidson. "They become annual losers."
>
> And as the number of basement-dwelling teams with no hope of redemption increases, the true "annual losers" are the fans.

An ending such as this adds a new dimension (the fans) to an already sticky situation in baseball. This also has potential to "include" your readers in the story. Even if individual members of your audience are not fans, per se, chances are they live in a city that supports a baseball team or have a family member who loves the game.

- **Bring it full circle.** Choosing the appropriate ending often depends on your lead. The "bookend" approach revisits a word, phrase, or idea from your introduction—often in a different or humorous way. This reminds the reader why he started reading, bringing your article full circle.

Here's an example from a concert preview by Lauren Mosko in the *Louisville Eccentric Observer*:

The Lead

The Rudyard Kipling: It's a restaurant, it's a bar, it's a playhouse, it's a musical venue, it's a . . . garage? You're out of luck if you're looking for an oil change, but if it's garage *rock* you're seeking, then you've come to the right place. Three groups of shaggy-headed boys—French Kicks, The Walkmen, and The Deathray Davies—are converging on The Rud this Saturday to play some rock 'n' roll and look retro-cool doing it.

The End

Three bands, three chords (give or take a few), one night. It may sound like a garage, but if you're not there by nine, don't expect to find a decent parking space.

In this set, the author is playing with the meaning of the term "garage rock," a genre influenced by the sounds of the late sixties and recently repopularized. By playing with this genre jargon, she's identifying herself as an insider. *Of course* she knows garage bands don't literally play in garages; she's just poking fun at a terminology that she and her audience share. Revisiting the joke in the last line reminds the readers of her authority and their initial identification with her. You can get really creative with this method, but if the subject or tone of the article doesn't lend itself to this sort of conclusion, don't force it.

- **Reach a higher ground.** Take the idea in your final paragraph to the next level by introducing a provocative statement or question that has not been explored and is probably out of the scope of your article. The new information will plant a seed of curiosity in the reader's mind, encouraging her to seek out more information on the subject or to think about the topic more critically. An article on music therapy and autism could end like this:

> Dr. Jonathan Edwards' research suggests that music therapy stimulates new neural pathways in the brains of children diagnosed with autism spectrum disorder, allowing them to better connect sensation and language. While this is a spectacular accomplishment for the research team, it is minor compared to the accomplishment each parent of a child with ASD will feel the first time they hear "That song makes me feel happy." To hear the child independently express himself outside of the therapy session portends his new socio-linguistic potential.

Because this piece is focused on the research of the music therapists, the reactions of parents of children with ASD and projections about the future of this science are topics that go beyond the article's boundaries. The conclusion ends on a positive, hopeful emotional note, while encouraging the reader to pursue further.

- **Speak common language.** Sometimes the mark of a clever writer is her ability to break the rules and do it well. The subject of your article may just be begging for wordplay based on a maxim or proverb, such as "The early bird gets the worm" or a common cultural idea like "Diamonds are a girl's best friend." Rather than use these figures of speech in your lead where they risk being seen as weak or unimaginative, try putting them in your closing paragraph. Use of these devices can be tricky and fall just shy of the dreaded cliché, but they can also serve to unite your audience because a colloquialism is part of our collective knowledge bank. The trick is not *what* you use but *how* you use it.

Remember the first national press blackout in U.S. history, which occurred during the 1991 Gulf War? An article addressing that situation could have ended like this:

> And so for twenty-four hours, the country received absolutely *no news* on the conflict. Whoever said that's *good news* couldn't have been a journalist. Or the parent of a soldier.

"No news is good news" is a pretty tired maxim, but in an unusual context with the right emotional spin, it works.

• **Trust your gut.** Don't be afraid to end your article at a logical place. Forcing it to conform to some smart device or tacking on an extra quotation can sometimes ruin your article instead of enhancing it. The push in magazine writing these days is brevity—your readers are busy—and if you've said what you needed to say, end it.

Here's a no-nonsense way to close a news piece about a new downtown high-rise:

> Despite their disagreement over materials, designers for the building project expect to have their formal proposal, including an approximate budget, submitted to city council by the end of the month.

Profiles often lend themselves to these types of natural endings, too:

> Refusing to rest on the laurels of the success of his story collection, J.R. Bates is back in New York City and hard at work. His new novel, yet untitled, is forthcoming from University Press.

The chronology of these conclusions makes them reasonable. You've told your audience all you know at the moment and now you will all wait together to see what happens next.

Of course, this is not an exhaustive list of ways to end your magazine article. If none of these approaches feel right for your piece, grab your favorite magazine and read the conclusions to articles that are similar in length and tone to your own to get some inspiration. If you're still stuck, try writing draft paragraphs based on several different methods and read them aloud to yourself or have a fellow writer help you choose which one works best. Again, trust your instinct. When you've found a concordant ending, you'll know.

Revising Before Submitting

After you've written your article, complete with the perfect lead, close, and everything in between, you'll come to realize it's not so perfect after all, and you'll have to revise it before it's ready for submission.

In one memorable episode of the popular television show *The Simpsons*, Marge Simpson decides to write her first novel. Having already taken a brownie break and written her "thank you" page, she finally sits down to write. Upon completion of her first paragraph, she spellchecks her work.

Wrong! Marge shows how truly basic a writer she is in her lack of knowledge of one of the Commandments for Writers: Thou Shalt Separate Thy Editing From Thy Writing.

When you are writing, or especially when you're prewriting, you want to turn off your internal editor. Period. Let it flow; get everything on the page. There will be plenty of time for revision later. If you let that inner critic creep in, it will stifle your voice and your creativity.

When you have that first draft of your article done, then revision begins. Get ready to roll up your sleeves, because this is the real work and often, the real fun. The first step in this process is to take a break. What? What about rolling up your sleeves? Well, taking a break is not always easy, but it is crucial. You want to get right in and start tinkering. But the best thing you can do is to take a day or two to step away and build up a bit of fresh perspective. If you have another writing project, work on it. Or work out in the garden. But leave that article draft alone for twenty-four to forty-eight hours.

Then, it's time to get to work, to sit down and *critically* reread your article. But it's more than rereading: You have to read the piece as if you are not the one who wrote it, as if you are reading it for the first time.

That's not always easy, but to revise effectively, it must be done.

What exactly is revision? It's a lot more than spellchecking. It's even more than looking for misplaced or missing commas. That comes later. The most important thing to know about the revision process is that it is just that: a process. It is not a "once over." It is a reseeing of what you have written. And there are some logical steps to follow which will make your writing stronger—and more salable. This can be broken down into four key components: focus, organization, style, and grammar.

- **Focus.** As you reread your article draft the first time, ask yourself, "What is the major impression I want my article to make on my reader?" and as you reread it, see if your article succeeds. Try to read it as if you are reading it for the first time. This is easier said than done, but unless you have a qualified second reader available at your beck and call, you'd better start practicing.

See if you can summarize your article in one or two sentences. If you cannot, then you are probably trying to cover too much ground.

Don't skip this part; having a clear focus is one of the most important parts of article writing. Make sure that everything in your article relates to your primary focus. If it doesn't, find a way to make it fit or get rid of it.

- **Organization.** Once you have done this, reread the article again, this time concentrating on organization. Does the piece flow? Are the various components presented in a logical fashion? Do you have transitions linking your major points or topics?

While you're rereading the article this time, also check for places where you may not have enough information or places where you may have too much. Tell the reader what he needs to know, but don't include anything that is irrelevant or repetitive.

When you do these first two rereads of your article, print your article and read it from a hard copy. It may be helpful to read it aloud. That way, you can both hear and see what you've actually written, which will increase your comprehension as well as help you get more of an "outside reader" perspective.

- **Style.** Style is one of the most important—and elusive—parts of good article writing. Remember, your readers are looking for information that is both interesting and easily read. Style is something that is hard to teach; it must be developed, largely on your own, as you write more and more and find your own voice. But there are some key questions you can ask yourself as you revise that will help you rise to the top of the slush pile:

Is my lead interesting? If your lead doesn't engage your reader, your reader will turn the page. Hook them from the beginning with an anecdote, quotation, fact, or other lead that makes them want to read more. Don't feel the need to summarize every point you will make right at the top.

Do my paragraphs flow? In other words, make sure your article reads like one cohesive whole. Look for transitions where it sounds disjointed or jumps from subtopic to subtopic with no rhyme or reason.

Does my ending bring everything together and leave the reader feeling satisfied? Too often when reading a magazine article, readers get to the end and say "that's it?" While it's good to leave your reader wanting more, make sure that you don't leave your reader hanging.

Does my style fit the market I'm writing for? Shakespeare may have written, "To thine own self be true," but when you're a freelance writer, your mantra should be "To thine editor and market be true." Of course, you have studied and familiarized yourself with the content, style, and tone of the market. And of course, you've carefully read their writer's guidelines. When you revise, keep these specs in mind, and ask yourself if you're adhering to them. Pay special attention to length: If a market asks for features of no more than 1,500 words, don't go over that mark, especially if you have not previously landed an assignment for that market.

- **Grammar.** Once you have made sure that your article is making the point you want to make, and that it is organized and flows well, you can move on to proofreading. This should always be your last step; there's no point in searching for errant commas if you're going to be substantially rewriting your piece. This phase of self-editing can be broken into four steps:

Verbs. You've probably read before that strong verbs make strong writing. This is so true. Yet you'll be amazed when you reread your own writing how often weak verbs can creep in without you even realizing it.

The first thing to do is check for passive voice. One easy way to do this is to do a search on your word processor for phrases like "it is," "there is," and "there are." Sometimes these are the best phrases for the job, but most of the time you can reword the sentence and make it stronger—and often shorter—by using a stronger verb construction in place of "there is," etc.

Next, search for nouns that you can strengthen by turning them into verbs. The main culprits here are verbals ending in "ing." You can search for "ing space" to find them; then reread the sentence, and see if you can strengthen it by eliminating the "ing."

You can also search for all forms of "to be," though this is a little more time consuming. Look for "is," "are," "was," "were," "be," "been," "being," etc. See if you can rewrite the sentence without the "to be" form. The more active verbs you can use, the stronger your writing will be.

Lastly, look for any adverbs in your writing. Most of these can, and should, be eliminated, especially if the adverb is used to modify a verb. One way to catch a number of adverbs (but not all) is to search your document for "ly space" occurrences. This will catch your "quickly," "loudly," etc. Nine times out of ten, you can replace a weak verb and an adverb with a strong verb, making your writing stronger and tighter at the same time.

Nouns. Next to verbs, nouns are the key to strong writing. Use as specific of nouns as possible. As you reread your piece, look for adjectives/noun pairs. See if you can replace these with a better, stronger noun. As with verbs and adverbs, you can strengthen your writing and lower your word count by eliminating unnecessary adjectives.

Tense and point of view. When you revise, check to make sure you are using the same verb tense throughout. Also, make sure you keep your point of view consistent. If, for example, you are writing a how-to article using second person ("you"), watch for places that you may slip into third person ("he/she"). This requires painstaking attention to detail, but it's worth it in the end.

Punctuation. This can be one of the hardest areas to self-edit. If you find you have trouble in this area, make yourself a checklist of mistakes you commonly make. When you proofread for punctuation, review this list first, and keep it handy as you reread. Also, get a good grammar reference to keep at your desk to help you with any tricky punctuation you're uncertain about.

The nitty-gritty. No matter how many times you reread and revise, it is still easy to miss careless errors. Your eyes tend to read what the brain thinks should be there, especially if you've been reading and rereading the same piece over and over. One good way to catch these errors is to read your article backwards, sentence by sentence. This way, you are forced to take a little more time and work a little harder.

This is also a good way to catch repetition. Sometimes on the first (or third) draft, writers have the tendency to use certain words over . . . and over. This is fine for a first draft when you're just getting thoughts on paper. But using the same word twice too close is usually not a good idea. If you find you overuse certain transition words or phrases like "moreover" or "it is interesting" when you're drafting, keep a list of "my overused words" and search for them when you're revising. As often as possible, try to eliminate the repetition.

This can also happen with jargon specific to your topic area, and sometimes there is not a good substitute word. If so, try to substitute a pronoun.

When you proofread the final, printed version of your article, check for smudges or blemishes on the page. Editors don't want to waste their time trying to figure out what letters are under that peanut butter smudge.

This may sound like a lot of work—and it is. But as you write and revise more articles, a lot of it will become second nature. For what doesn't, make a cheat sheet or checklist.

Rewriting Your Article

You've revised your piece and submitted a polished draft. But what happens if your editor calls and the piece you thought was terrific needs some major surgery? Can editors make you do that? Darn right. Only attorneys get paid to rewrite the drafts they've mucked up.

Chin up. A do-over doesn't mean your career is trashed. Consider it an opportunity to give the magazine exactly what it wants. Just mount your white horse and deliver the goods.

Want to snivel a bit? Sure, go ahead—then get over it. The editor called you to finish the collaboration you two started, not to shatter your ego. What does that editor know? Plenty. Because editors have less energy invested in a story than you do, they read with unbiased eyes, said *Saturday Evening Post* travel editor Holly Miller. Since freelancers typically write for many publications, they can't anticipate a magazine's needs the way its editor does.

Plus, it doesn't pay to get nasty about this if you want to maintain a relationship with the publication. "Writers who are intractable and fight with us probably won't get another assignment," warned former *OnHealth* senior editor Kathleen Donnelly.

Fortunately, total rewrites are rare—if only because the story needs to go back fast to make deadline. More often, you'll find tons of copy in your original article you can save.

Before pecking away aimlessly at the computer, rethink the piece. Start by ruthlessly rereading your query, assignment letter, and article, advised *Kiwanis* magazine's former managing editor Chuck Jonak. Many times a writer forgets what sold the editor on the piece in the first place.

Did you overshoot your word count? (If you ran short, that's really bad, because you might not have the time or capability to get what's missing.) Did you fail to respect the magazine's lead time, writing news that has appeared elsewhere? Did you interview too few sources or conduct superficial, garbage-in/garbage-out interviews? Consider what you've learned, then work with the editor to save your story.

Sometimes you'll do a job exactly as assigned, but an editor will ask that it be revamped. That do-over probably isn't arbitrary. Occasionally the article fights something else running in a particular issue or mimics too closely what's appeared or about to appear in a competitor's pages.

Or perhaps you and an articles editor saw the story one way, but the editor in chief wants it done another way.

A piece may need restructuring simply because a writer interviewed the same experts that another writer used in a second story. Once again, the advice is simple: Get over it. Editors are human with quirks and prejudices, said James Wiggins, a book publisher and former editor in chief of *Dynamic Years*, an AARP magazine. A freelancer's job is to help the editors carry out their vision for the magazine, not quarrel with that vision.

What if the writing itself is the problem? Say you've got the wrong tone or maybe you're underwriting or overwriting the piece for the intended audience. In that case, deconstruct the piece coldly. Drop all defensiveness and solicit your editor's help if anything confuses you. If you stay objective, problems jump from the page that once hid between the lines. If you're resentful, you'll go into deep-dish denial, failing to correct the problems.

But what if you rewrite the copy and flounder? Donnelly believes asking an editor to rework just one paragraph often helps. She said most writers are able to follow a model.

Working thoughtfully keeps the revision from coming back—or worse, being killed. To turn do-overs into done deals you need patience, persistence, and adherence to procedures. Unless you live near the magazine, your editor will ask you to go over the manuscript by phone or e-mail. Some editors prefer the phoning method because writers can keep a manuscript handy to jot changes and new directions. Others see the phone as time-consuming and prefer to rely on e-mail or a faxed manuscript.

When you get the article back, make sure that new material duplicates the tone of the version you received, said *Indianapolis Monthly* senior editor Brian Smith. "Some writers worry so much about getting individual facts straight that they don't hear the flow and what it does to the cadence of the story."

Whatever you do, don't rewrite the editor's rewrite. You won't be regarded as a hero on a white horse but rather a portion of that horse's anatomy.

TIPS FOR REWRITES

1. Don't be soft on sources. If you get the full picture, you're more likely not to have to call them back on rewrite because you'll have the answers to the editor's questions. It is always better to have to much information than not enough; it will save you time later and will impress your editor.

2. Don't use copy and quotes from a press release, said Jennifer Oxley, former associate editor at *OnHealth*. If the editors wanted a public relations piece, they wouldn't have assigned you the story.

3. Do make a checklist of everything your editor will require: a source list with phone numbers, sidebars, highlighted pull quotes, and notations if a proper noun has an unusual spelling. Make sure you turn in all those elements with your article. Freelancers tally up good-guy points when they are thorough and logical.

4. Do e-mail an outline to your editor, if time permits, before writing the whole article, says former *New Choices* editor in chief Greg Daugherty. Structurally, you'll both start on the same page. If your subsequent research uncovers something that changes the piece, inform the editor.

When a piece comes in long, often it's overloaded with chaff. Good candidates for the delete key include qualifiers, digressions, unnecessary prepositional phrases, and too many quotes or passages reinforcing a point already made.

For example, here's a passage in a magazine story Hank Nuwer wrote on octogenarian book collector Fraser Drew. He likes to think his readers are grateful for the change. Originally it said: "He is like the survivor of an automobile accident. He is safe for the moment but aware of the red lights and clatter outside the patrol car in which he sits."

Here is the rewrite: "He is like the survivor of a bad accident, warm in an idling patrol car but aware of wreckage nearby."

When Nuwer was a magazine editor in chief, he wanted writers to speak up if his criticisms would lead to inconsistencies or inaccuracies. As a writer, you've got rights, too. Extra expenses should be compensated unless your editor can show you squandered an earlier advance. If you need to make additional calls or an additional trip, the magazine should cover these costs.

Most pros stop at three rewrites. Insist on a contract that protects you from reprising Bill Murray's role in *Groundhog Day*, or you'll end up writing the same piece over and over. It also makes sense to establish up front that you need to see the work before it's published, whether you've been given a rewrite or not. Watch out for editors who chop your piece without even sending you a galley.

If that happens, compare your original manuscript with the version that actually runs. Note the changes and learn from them. If you don't understand them, ask the editor for an explanation so next time you can turn in better copy—and avoid a do-over.

Writing for Digital Media

As readers move from paper to new digital devices, writers must adopt styles that are different from those in print.

One of the biggest challenges in the publishing industry is the new requirement to distribute content to multiple formats. For a magazine, newspaper or newsletter, content often is prepared not only for a print edition but also the Web, e-mail delivery, handheld devices, portable e-book reading devices, Internet-enabled mobile phones, and digital audio players.

The trend toward portable digital devices is especially intriguing because content often will be in audio form. Think of the magazine of the future. It will come in traditional print, of course, but you'll also be able to read a magazine on the screen of a portable digital device. Or, if you prefer, you'll hear the content read to you via the device's audio jack or perhaps its built-in speaker.

What does this have to do with writing? A lot, because writing must adjust to the new media forms that tomorrow's consumers increasingly will use. If the article you wrote for a print magazine also will be published on small digital devices, the form and style that you wrote it in won't be optimal. Even when published on the Web, a print-original article often must be tweaked to work online (where users have shorter attention spans than print readers).

Some of your audience will read your article on personal digital assistants with small screens. For them, a condensed version of the article is best. Others might prefer to get the article in audio format. (The book industry has long had books on tape as a print alternative. Today, companies like Audible.com are selling subscriptions to condensed, audio versions of newspapers and magazines.) Audio versions must be significantly condensed and written in a conversational tone.

This trend offers good news and bad news for writers. The bad news first: You may be asked by your publisher to turn in multiple forms of an article because it will be published to a variety of media. The good news: There's opportunity for writers to command additional fees for this work.

Here are some tips for writing with new forms of digital media in mind:

- **Write short.** If your audience will be reading your words on small devices, don't expect them to read all two thousand words of your magazine piece. It's hard work reading that much on a small electronic screen. The same goes for the Web because it's harder on the eyes to read on a computer screen than on a piece of paper—so online users tend to read less.

- **Write for the presentation medium.** Sometimes long is okay, even when writing for digital media. E-book readers are getting closer to becoming mainstream, but these devices aren't just for reading digital versions of books. Increasingly, they will be used for reading magazine and newspaper content. Because they have large screens, the reading experience is similar to print. If your prose is destined for consumption on e-book readers, printlike style and length are appropriate.

- **Get to the point fast.** This applies to most digital media—especially the Web and small portable devices. Don't dilly-dally with your wording. Get to the main point of your article—why a reader should care enough to continue on—as quickly as possible. In a Web article, try to present your main point within the first screen—so it's read without the reader having to scroll down the page. Do the same when your readers have portable reading devices, but get down to business even faster. On PDAs, for instance, smaller screens mean there's even less space to state your main point and keep it on the first screen.

- **Write a great headline.** When your writing appears on small digital devices, there's no room for ambiguity. Funny but obtuse headlines don't work as well in enticing readers to scroll on. Use clear ones that quickly explain what an article is about. Summary or deck headlines that sit below a main headline are a good technique for making the main point in ten or so words. They'll tell a reader whether or not to keep reading.

- **Speak to them.** Clearly, digital devices will offer more and more content in audio form. It's not that text publications are going anywhere— only that tomorrow's consumers will choose whether they wish to read articles and publications themselves or listen to them. Therefore, tomorrow's writers are advised to get to know how to write for spoken presentation.

Writing for broadcast is a discipline not easily explained in a single paragraph. The best quick advice is to read up on writing for broadcast, and read your words aloud so you can hear if they work in spoken form. And follow the earlier advice: Keep your stories succinct.

Foremost, recognize that the publishing world is changing rapidly. If you're only writing for print, you're ignoring the part of your audience that has moved from paper to digital reading (and listening). Your writing style should keep up with them.

Chapter Nine:
How to Write
Common Articles

As you saw in chapter eight, there are general writing techniques for all magazine articles. But if you want to show an editor how good you really are, you must also learn the specific techniques for certain types of articles. Staple articles exist in every magazine, and each one requires a unique approach. If you are writing a profile, you would not go about it the same way you would a how-to article. Many of these skills come with practice and experience, but it doesn't hurt to be aware of them when you're first starting out.

Writing Profiles

More and more publications are buying profiles of successful or intriguing people. The subjects don't necessarily have to be famous, just interesting. Here are six profile-writing techniques that work.

1. Let the story come to you. Why go in search of interesting people when they already come to you? Watch for lecturers at local colleges, nationally known comedians performing at nightclubs, bands stopping by on concert tours, singers visiting coffee shops, bookstore signings by best-selling authors, or other special events.

Look online to find out who is coming, when the person will be in town, and where he will be appearing. Then, contact your local radio station or arena to find out the name of the road manager for upcoming events. That's the person who'll set up your interview time. Then, contact the road manager. Explain that you're a writer working on a story for (whatever) magazine and be sure to say, "I'd like to mention Joe Famousguy's new book, CD, video, and so on," so she realizes how the person will benefit from spending time with you. Do be honest; if you don't have the assignment but plan to write a profile to submit to the magazine on speculation, say so.

Be polite, professional, and persistent. Many times the person you'd like to interview is pleasant and willing to talk; it's just tricky getting through all the gatekeepers.

Be sure to ask for a press kit. The publicist will send you free products (books, CDs, and so on) and lots of background information that will cut down on your research time. Read earlier interviews online or at the library.

And remember, Joe Famousguy is doing you a favor by granting this interview. His time is a gift to you, so be gracious.

2. **Ask the right questions.** All good stories need conflict, so structure your interview questions to bring out the conflicts or struggles in your subject's life. For example:

- "What's the biggest setback you've had?"
- "What dreams do you have? What obstacles do you foresee? How will you handle them?"
- "Some people criticize you for. . . . How do you respond?"
- "It must to be tough dealing with life on the road. What keeps you going? What makes it all worthwhile?"
- "What special memories do you have? What regrets do you have?"
- "How did you get started? What kinds of struggles did you face?"

Most people in the media spotlight hear the same questions and repeat the same pat answers over and over. You'll find out which questions those are during your preinterview research. Look instead for the passion that drives that person, and ask questions that reveal the story behind the story.

3. **Target your article.** Think of profiles as falling into one of three categories. Before you pitch a story idea to an editor (even before you craft your article), decide the type of profile you'll be writing because the selling angle differs for each one.

A. Profiles of the rich and famous: Let's be honest, profiles of famous people sell well. Editors want stories about the people their readers have heard of and admire. The key to selling this type of profile is timing— you want your article to land on the editor's desk just as she is thinking about that person.

To do that, you'll need to keep your finger on the pulse of the magazines to which you're interested in submitting. If you interview a rock band for a college magazine, the editors might like the profile, but if that band isn't very popular with their readers, you won't be able to sell that story to them. Always take the time to really get to know a magazine's readers. To sell a profile of someone famous, tell your editor, "Your readers have already heard of Joe Famousguy and want the inside scoop about him. I'll give it to you!"

B. Profiles of up-and-comers: These are the people making waves and breakthroughs in their fields. Or they're the people quietly changing the world through great ideas, innovations, or inventions. The introverted billionaire who lives just down the street. The Internet pioneer. The reclusive writer. The talented young actor who is on his way up but isn't well known yet.

When a tennis coach friend of writer Steven James mentioned that the thirteen-year-old girl he was training was ranked internationally, James started asking himself if there were any teen magazines he wrote for that might want to publish a profile on her.

After choosing one, James told the girl the magazine's name, and she said, "Oh, cool! I get that magazine!" She was an up-and-comer and a subscriber! Of course, he mentioned that when he pitched the story to the editors. The result? A few months later, her profile ran as the cover story.

Here your selling angle is that the readers should know about this person but for some reason don't. When you pitch this type of profile, emphasize the surprise: "None of your readers have heard of Joe Notsofamousguy yet, but they should have! You won't believe what he has accomplished!"

C. Profiles of unsung heroes: It isn't always the famous people who have the interesting stories. You can sell stories about the guy who owns the restaurant down the road, your grandmother, missionaries in southern Mexico, or even the choir at your church.

Keep your eyes open. Look for those amazing true stories of real-life heroes. Lifeguards. Firefighters. Police officers. Survivors. Overcomers. Great men and women of the past. Fame or no fame, there are heroes among us. Their profiles show us examples of courage, virtue, integrity, and heroism.

When pitching this type of profile, emphasize the drama of the story rather than appealing to the person's popularity. Tell your editor, "Your readers will be inspired by the incredible story of Joe Hero!"

4. Tell a good story. The biggest secret to writing a quick-selling profile is telling a good story. A great profile doesn't just repeat the facts; it tells an engaging story about an interesting person in a unique way. Don't just overwhelm readers with details of your subject's history; focus on telling a gripping story.

Once, James interviewed a Grammy® Award-winning singer. She'd sold her first album when she was a young teenager and had been appearing on the cover of magazines ever since. When he asked the editor of a parenting magazine if he'd like to include her profile in an upcoming issue, he said, "Only if you have information no one else has already written." Like any good freelancer James said, "Of course I do!" Then he hung up the phone and scoured his notes for something—anything—unique.

He had to quickly restructure the article to get away from the typical information about her recording success and focus instead on her answer to his question, "What's the one message you're trying to get across to teens?" The profile touched on the singer's true passion and, because of the strong message of hope, the editor bought the article.

The more famous someone is, the more tempting it'll be to repeat what others have already written. Decide from the start that you're going to tell people what they don't already know.

5. Open with an image. Instead of spouting facts, start with a specific image that contributes to your story: a tour bus rambling down the dirt road . . . a blazing fire in an ornate fireplace . . . the cruelly curved barbed wire fence of the prison. You can start profiles with an image and use it to shape an article's structure.

Take a cue from fiction writers and grab your readers' attention in the opening paragraph. Use action-packed, mysterious, or dramatic openings. Often, your opening image can serve as a "bookend" that you can refer back to in the closing paragraph.

6. Look for contrasts. Another great way to structure your profile is by pointing out the incongruities in your subject's life. James has written profiles that begin by telling about a rodeo star who is now paralyzed, a multi-platinum Christian band that plays in bars on the weekends, and a missionary who can't speak the language of the people to whom he's been sent to preach.

Look for things that don't seem to fit. They make strong openers for profiles. Paradox also gives you a great angle for your profile because you can show how two seemingly contradictory traits come together in this intriguing person. Listen for those contrasting images during the interview.

To sum it up: Let the story come to you, ask questions that reveal struggles and discoveries, carefully target your article, and focus on crafting a good story with vivid images and intriguing contrasts. Follow these steps and you'll be well on your way to selling more of the profiles you write.

Writing the Roundup Article

The roundup article presents a unique challenge to its author: You must manipulate information from several different sources into a piece that reads as though the people you surveyed sat down in a room together, perhaps over coffee, and had a discussion about your topic. Basically, your job is to turn raw data from a poll of experts into an intriguing, informative article.

As-Told-To Articles

An as-told-to article is a story written in first person by a writer about a subject. Instead of a writer doing an interview and a third-person profile, he interviews a subject and then writes the story as if the subject were telling it himself. What is the benefit in this type of story? Why not just write a profile or ghostwrite for someone?

Many times, a person has a great story to tell but doesn't have the writing know-how to do it on her own. That's when a writer can step in and get the subject's story on paper for her. Writing the story as an as-told-to allows for a more intimate telling. Often, these stories have some dramatic or emotional component that loses much of its immediacy if told in third person. In order to give readers the full effect and draw them in, the first person is needed to help make the connection. As-told-to stories also credit both the subject and the writer, whereas ghostwritten pieces don't mention the writer at all. In an as-told-to article, the byline usually looks something like this: "by Suzy Subject as told to William Writer."

As-told-to articles are a great way to break into many publications that need an endless supply of such stories. Many women's magazines are always looking for first-person stories of women who have accomplished something great or overcome some obstacle. Many religious magazines, like *Guideposts for Kids,* use as-told-tos, and a selection of magazines from almost any market needs as-told-to pieces.

Stories worth telling can be found almost anywhere. If you read a newspaper or magazine article about a dramatic incident that happened to someone from your hometown, you may want to contact that person to see if she wants to tell her entire story. In your day-to-day interactions with people, you may also come across a person with a story to tell. The two of you might form a mutually beneficial relationship: He has a story you want to sell, and you are a means for him to get his story heard. It can be a very satisfying experience for both of you.

There are a few key points to remember when writing an as-told-to. Keep these things in mind for a story that editors will want for their publication.

- You must tell the story in first person, as if you were that person. That means you must be able to see things from the point of view of your subject without projecting any of your own thoughts into the story. In essence, you must become your subject

Continued next page

while you are writing. In order to do this, you have to include the details that the subject might not think to tell you. Ask questions that help him reveal the specifics that will make the story more personal.

- You must be an editor as well as a writer. Part of the reason the subject is not writing her own story is because she lacks the skills of a professional writer. You must take her story and craft it into a salable piece, which means you may have to tell the story in a different order than she tells you. Make sure you put the pieces together in a coherent way that will make the most sense for readers and keep them reading.

- Finally, don't forget to show your story to your subject for his final approval. While you don't need to check your story with a profile subject, it is important to have an as-told-to subject approve the final story. His name will be associated with the piece, as well as yours, so he should have the right to suggest changes, add details, or revise statements. In fact, it is probably best to have a form that the subject can sign after he approves the article so you have proof that he is okay with what you are submitting.

As-told-tos are a great way to get your foot in the door at magazines and can be a personally satisfying experience. Consider writing an as-told-to if the perfect opportunity presents itself, or actively seek out people with stories that need to be told.

For example, say you decide to write a roundup article on how the rise of malpractice suits has affected the medical field. Before you begin to write, there are several things you must decide. Who will you interview? How will you find them? What will be the slant of the article, your unique approach to the material? How will you organize your data to ensure the easiest conversion from survey to interesting article?

But before you go any further . . .what, exactly, is a roundup article?

A roundup article is exactly what it sounds like—a roundup of expert opinions on a certain topic. The roundup article is extremely versatile. A publication like *Newsweek* could find the top four botanists in the world and interview them on what they think about certain pesticides and their effect on crops, and a magazine like *People* could ask several celebrities what they think about the new spring fashions.

Roundup articles are a very effective way for a writer to explore a topic, because many expert opinions lend instant authority to your piece. They are used frequently for just this reason—readers feel as though they've gotten an entire overview of a problem without having to read more than one article.

Though the roundup article inevitably starts with a survey of some sort, the best ends up a cohesive, well-rounded argument incorporating all the varying conceptions of the people you have interviewed. The quotes you have compiled supply the industry research you need for credibility, but it's your writing that will make a cohesive argument and draw the conclusion.

For example, in a roundup article written for WritersMarket.com, Erin Nevius interviewed four publicists on the difference between staff and independent publicists, and whether or not an author needs both. The four professionals she interviewed were very insightful, giving her plenty of great quotes, all of which she tried to use so readers could hear the experts' opinions in their own voices. However, as the writer, it was Nevius's job to reflect on what they were saying and distill it to the major point.

> Whether you decide to use your staff publicist, contract an independent, or do both, it's important to recognize that publicists are an indispensable part of being an author in the twenty-first century. With over 150,000 books being published a year, all your hard work could languish on a clearance shelf somewhere if you don't find someone who pinpoints the unique, fascinating aspect that only your book possesses and tells it to the world.

Obviously, who you interview is entirely dependent on your topic. You want to find experts in the industry you're covering, and you want to find people from a broad range of experience and locales. This ensures a wide survey of your topic and enough difference of opinion to make it interesting.

If you were assigned an article on gourmet chefs in New York City and their favorite ingredient to work with, you would not want to interview five men who work in Italian restaurants. You would want to find a few men and a few women who cover all sorts of different cooking, from Italian to Japanese to Indian. This way, every reader can find something they like or relate to in the piece, and you'll have a brief cultural overview of the restaurants in New York. It is unlikely chefs from such different backgrounds would share the same favorite ingredient.

The challenge, of course, will be finding the thread that ties them all together. Maybe, "New York Chefs Take a Walk on the Wild Side" if they all choose off-the-wall ingredients, or "Chefs From All Specialties Spice Up Your Life" if they all seem to like spicy foods.

Finding your experts is a lot easier than it sounds for two main reasons. First, it's easy publicity for whomever you ask to be in your article. To continue with the chef example, each of them would have to answer a few questions that would only take a few minutes of their time, and each would get to see a plug for their restaurant in a magazine. Secondly, experts in a field all tend to know each other. Find one, get him to agree to an interview, and ask who else would be a good fit. More likely than not, he'll have a sizable list of people and their contact information.

And of course, the Internet goes a long way to ease the process of finding interesting, informative people from a variety of backgrounds. Suppose your assignment on gourmet chefs was not specific to one area. A quick search of the Internet and you could have expert opinions from New York, Los Angeles, London, and Paris.

Now, take heed to this unorthodox piece of advice regarding interviews. The roundup article interview differs from most others in one crucial area: It is the only type of article where it is easier and almost more informative to conduct the interview over e-mail instead of over the phone or face-to-face. When you're only interviewing one person, it's very important to follow her lead. You may have a set list of questions when you begin to talk to her and by the end you've asked only three or four of them, but you've compiled a ton of interesting information you didn't see coming. In an article focusing on one viewpoint, it's best to let the subject shape the focus.

However, with a roundup article, the focus is your own—the people you are interviewing are there to supply industry expertise to support your thesis or round out your topic. By compiling a list of maybe ten questions and e-mailing them to three, four, five, or six people of your choice, you can both control the direction of the article from an early stage and have the answers written down in front of you when you start to write.

Not only does this help in the development of your piece, it makes the organization of it a breeze. When you receive the answers from your experts, try making a chart with the names and businesses of the people you interviewed running across the top and the questions you asked down the left side. Copy and paste your answers into the correct slots, print it out, and voila! You have an instant diagram of each contrasting and agreeing answer right next to each other. Pull out the quotes you like as you need them to make your point, and you'll be done in no time.

An example of the charts used for the article on staff vs. independent publicists is on page 168.

Using this formula, you are able to see all the answers and opinions at once, get a feel for each one, and develop the hypothesis that their information will prove: No matter whether you use a staff or an independent publicist, they're an indispensable part of today's publishing world. The opinions of these heavyweights in the industry give authority and weight to that idea.

Writing Templates

When owners of art supply stores wanted to learn how to find a new lawyer, freelance writer Eric Freedman told them how. When antique dealers wanted to learn how to find a new lawyer, he told them as well. He also told sign industry managers, dance studio operators, photo lab owners, and other types of businesspeople—all through a process called templating.

For woodworkers and artisans, templates are precut patterns used to make precise copies. For writers, however, they're blueprints used to customize an otherwise standardized article for individual magazines.

Noncompeting trade magazines form the primary markets for tem-

Staff Publicist Questions	Answers from John P. Koizi, St. Anthony Messenger Press	Answers from Alexis Burling, Scholastic Press
1.		
2.		
3.		

Independent Publicist Questions	Answers from Erin Saxton, The Idea Network	Answers from Regina Lynch-Hudson, The Write Publicist & Co.
1.		
2.		
3.		

plated articles. Their readers expect practical advice to help make more money, avoid financial and legal problems, handle employees more smoothly, and operate efficiently. For instance, managers of shoe stores, auto body shops, and wineries all need to know how antidiscrimination rules, tax law changes, and job safety regulations affect them, their employees, and their customers.

Templating is a lot more than filling in blanks. Instead, it blends expert advice applicable to a variety of businesses or industries with anecdotes, examples, and quotes tailored to each magazine's readership. The key is making each version sound fresh and relevant. Think of it as a four-step search-tell-and-show process:

- **Pinpoint a topic.** Narrow is best—"how to use noncash incentives to improve employee morale," not "how to improve employee morale."
- **Use *Writer's Market* and other resources.** These can help you identify prospective markets and prepare query letters to appropriate editors.
- **Tell readers about overall concepts, problems, and solutions.** That's where your generic experts come in.
- **Give examples.** Show how people in their field apply those generic concepts to solve specific problems.

Consider Freedman's templated article, "Do You Need a New Lawyer?" He uses essentially the same lead, theme paragraphs, and ending, slightly massaged, for each new assignment. Here's part of the version published in *Dance Teacher Now*:

> Your lawyer has been a faithful advisor since you started in business. You call when the city inspector issues a noise citation at your building, when the IRS questions your tax return, when a client is injured, when a costume shipment fails to arrive on time for a recital. He has a sympathetic ear, constructive suggestions, and even sends a holiday card.
>
> But as times change, your legal needs do, too. Society is more litigious, consumer activism more evident, government regulations more complex, zoning concerns more visible, employee rights more pervasive, financial decisions more risky. From ERISA to OSHA, an alphabet soup of rules, regulations, and laws confronts American businesses.

From there, the article weaves generic and customized advice. For the generic, Freedman interviewed the head of business law at the State Bar of Michigan and the president of a small-business consultancy. He also inserted other research and his own knowledge of legal affairs.

To customize, he interviewed six dance studio and dance company experts from across the country. They included the owner of a California fitness and dance center, the director of a nonprofit ballet company in Texas, and the artistic director of the State Ballet of Rhode Island.

To succeed with editors and readers, you must create a feeling that the article is written just for them. That means identifying knowledgeable and articulate sources, then interviewing them to make the article relevant to the audience's needs.

"There's a concerted effort to make sure everything . . . is industry-specific," said Chris Sanford, former executive editor of *Cleaning and Maintenance Management*. "Familiarize yourself with the industry you're writing for. The writer has to show me that what he or she is using—which may be applicable to other industries—fits."

Not all trade publication editors welcome templated stories, concerned they'll appear mass-produced or canned. Others are more receptive. Your queries don't need to mention that the article will be templated. Instead, explain your plan to interview both general experts and professionals in their field. However, if previous pieces have been published, it may help sell the proposal if you tell an editor, "My articles on finding a new lawyer have appeared in A, B, and C."

When a freelancing accountant first submitted his articles on tax topics to *Fitness Management*, editor Ronale Tucker Rhodes rejected them. However, "as time progressed, his submissions showed that he was taking more time to understand how the generic information applied to our industry. Rather than substitute the words 'health/fitness industry' every couple of paragraphs, he began to make more specific references to the health club business."

Brian Alm, editor of *Rental Management*, uses templated articles in his trade magazine for the equipment rental industry. When inserting industry-specific examples and references, he advised, "It's important not to overdo it or do it too gratuitously so it looks phony, but in small doses in the right places it adds the right amount of authenticity."

Templating offers several major benefits for freelancers:

First: It's time-efficient and lets you maximize your background research.

Second: It allows you to reuse effective, polished leads, transitions, endings, graphics, and sidebars.

Third: Given what many magazines pay for articles, it may not be cost-effective to interview a new group of generic experts for each version. Templating lets you concentrate on finding people in each field with on-point stories to tell, case histories to share, and lessons to teach.

Finally: You can build on what you learn from each templating experience. The information you pick up from each interview can open doors to more assignments and more templating opportunities.

How to Write How-To Articles

Imagine the following scenario:

> The bomb was set to detonate in five minutes. Officer Wilson, the first to arrive on the scene, knew he faced a fiendishly clever device as he examined the complex array of wires and circuits. But the bomb expert guiding him over the radio knew just what to do. "Cut the green wire," the expert commanded. The officer gingerly took the green wire between the jaws of his cutters and, squinting through the sweat that poured down his brow, began to squeeze. As the cutters bit through the insulation, the bomb expert's voice crackled over the handset: "But first . . ."

A fundamental mistake in how-to writing is giving instructions out of order. Not only should you write steps in order, but the reader must know the instructions are in order. Words such as when, then, now, and next give him these cues (but don't overdo it). But there's more to it than making sure step one comes before step two. Consider Mr. Birdhouse Builder, reader of *Birdhouse Monthly*. Your article has just instructed him to nail the shutters onto his sparrow house—but you forgot to mention how long the nails should be. Mr. Builder has now created a miniature iron maiden.

While it's unlikely that the how-to articles (a.k.a. service pieces) you write are going to create life-or-death consequences, you don't want to tick off any readers, either. Ticked-off readers mean ticked-off editors. In addition to getting first things first, a good how-to writer will:

- write with authority
- summarize information as the project progresses
- give the reader a sense of what the project entails before she begins
- provide a practical list of tools and materials
- write succinct captions for photos or illustrations, if applicable

How-to articles are a mainstay at many magazines (not to mention newspaper lifestyle sections), so developing a skill and flair for writing them can be a ticket to repeat assignments. Remember that you're not writing for the ages here. The objective is clarity.

Beware of unstated assumptions. Take this example from an issue of *Brio*, a magazine for teen girls. In an article on pressing and framing flowers, the author instructed readers to gather some old books (to press the petals) and take them to a field. So far, so good. The girls are in the field, and the writer has provided great step-by-step instructions for what to do after picking the flowers. But she forgot a key point. See if you can spot it:

> Turn the book sideways and start by placing the flowers in rows, with the stems pointing toward the outside edge. Gently close the book and place a heavy object on top. A couple of bricks will do. It will take up to two weeks for the pressing to be done.

As written, readers have to lug bricks to the field with them and wait there for two weeks until the flowers are ready. An alert editor caught this problem and corrected it to read this way:

> Gently close the book. When you get back home, place a heavy object on top. Even a couple of bricks will work. Now leave the flowers alone—don't even peek! The pressing will take two weeks.

Lesson: Put yourself physically in the picture to make sure you don't tell readers to do something unnecessary or have them commit an irreversible step in the wrong order.

Assume the proper stance. You're the expert, and readers have turned to you for advice. Give it to them! Write in the imperative voice. Instead of saying, "You should grasp the stem," say, "Grasp the stem and pull it out."

From time to time you'll have to explain why something needs to be done: "Shake the colander until all water is drained from the pasta," for example. This not only tells the reader what to do but why to do it. You wouldn't want her standing there all day shaking her spaghetti.

Include appropriate warnings or alert the reader to wait a certain time before proceeding with the next step: "Do this in a well-ventilated room" or "Wait until the paint is completely dry before continuing." Also, define terms that might be unfamiliar to readers, ideally in the narrative flow of a sentence: "Be sure to clean all paint from the ferrule, the metal clamp that fastens the bristles to the brush." And use adjectives and adverbs sparingly, for when they're important: "Grasp it tightly or else it will snap back at you."

To keep how-to copy from getting dull, have a little fun with your approach. Consider this example from Cindy Jacobs' "Showdown at Clutter Corral," an article from *Single-Parent Family* magazine. The goal is to tell readers how to unclutter their houses, but she establishes the scenario first using imagery from the Wild West:

> At the break of dawn, me and the boys faced the enemy head-on. . . . It was time for a showdown.
>
> I faced the closed door and swallowed hard. My gang stood behind me, ready for action. . . . Tucked in the stillness of the dark closet, I faced the enemy. I was up to my eyeballs in clutter.

As she moves into the heart of the article, Jacobs follows the rules of strong how-to writing. Notice the strong verbs, easy-to-follow steps and, again, a touch of humor—just to make sure you're paying attention:

To find your clutter, grab a notebook and take a tour of your home. Step inside the door of each room and write down all the distracting, disorganized areas. Then write down drawers, closets, and other areas hiding debris that you want to organize. Since you will be referring to this notebook periodically, make a point not to add it to one of the piles.

Provide a guiding hand. You can slip out of the imperative voice every so often to give the reader an update on the state of his project: "By now, the two sides of the frame should be aligned at a perfect ninety-degree angle," or "You should now have three complete rows of blocks." If the reader realizes he has only one side of the picture frame finished or his blocks form only two rows, he knows he's messed up and can go back to correct it.

Help the reader out in other ways, too. For instance, let her know what the project entails. "This project requires you to thread a needle three dozen times," or "Before you're finished, you'll have painted 150 figurines." She might say, "Forget that. It's too much work." If nothing else, you've provided fair warning. You'll also need to provide a complete and detailed tools and materials list when appropriate. If you think such a list should be the first thing you do when writing a how-to article, think again. It's better to wait until you've already written the body of the article so you can consider exactly what the project involves. As you mentally walk through your article and draw up an outline, you might realize that only a three-sided widget puller will work for a particular step. That might not have occurred to you if you'd already thrown together a list of what you thought was necessary.

It's safe to assume that most readers have or can easily get something as common as a screwdriver or pair of scissors. But use your judgment and err on the side of telling too much. As for the three-sided widget puller, not only should you tell the reader what this is but also where he can get one.

Some things are pretty difficult to explain in words only, so it's a good idea to provide illustration suggestions to the editor as you write the article. This isn't as easy as it sounds, though. If done incorrectly, you'll confuse the reader more than if you'd used words alone.

In a craft article for *Clubhouse Jr.* magazine (for kids ages four to eight), the writer provides instructions for making a "woodsy" vase as a gift for Mom. (It involves fastening sticks to an empty jar and decorating the jar with raffia, corn, and small seeds.) One photo illustrates Step 3 in the project. The caption could've been written like this:

> Tuck sticks under both rubber bands, placing each stick as close as possible to its neighbors.
>
> [Photo shows child's hands placing a stick between rubber bands. A few sticks are already in place. Show other materials such as raffia, corn, or seeds on the tabletop next to the jar.]

If you write captions for illustrations, they can repeat information contained in the body, but they'll probably have to be short and to the point. As a rule of thumb, the first sentence of the caption should explain the action in the illustration. The only possible exception is to use the illustration to show actions that are too difficult to sum up in words.

Now that the reader has learned how to do something new, your ending can offer a pat on the back and remind her why this was a project worth undertaking. If you've framed the piece with some kind of metaphor (such as the "clutter corral" piece), come back to it to tie the story up neatly. Remember, nobody's going to blow up if you write your how-to piece incorrectly. But with a smart plan up front, you can spare yourself the torture of wriggling out of a self-created writing trap.

Service Journalism

Service journalism is much more than just "how-to." Communication research theory indicates that people use the media either for entertainment (and that includes escape) or for utility. Utility, yes—but don't forget the entertainment part. Try to present useful information in the most entertaining way. The three most important words of service journalism are useful, usable, and used.

- **Useful.** You can write interesting articles about many topics. The trick is to give those topics a useful slant or at least indicate to readers how they can use the information.

  Travel stories have the most obvious examples. Tell how to get there, where to stay, where to eat, what it costs, and how to get a deal. But even profile stories can offer a list of tips that led to the subject's success. You can write about a wonderful art exhibit in your area, but perhaps what will get your readers there is parking information.

- **Usable.** Somewhere, some years ago, it was said that information should be presented in such a way that people will clip it out and stick it on their refrigerators—refrigerator journalism. That's why boxes are so useful. Boxes get attention. If you put something into a box, you have an excellent chance of getting it read. Some readers will even cut it out if you put something usable in it.

- **Used.** The reason it's so important that people post the information on refrigerators or bulletin boards is that there's a good chance they will do what you tell them to do. Why should you care about that? Well, magazines care. They know that people stop subscribing to publications when they never do any of the things they read about. They also know that advertisers want proof that subscribers are active. Smart editors want smart writers who use devices that get readers to do things.

  Service journalism has four underlying principles: Think time, think engagement, think new or news, and think money.

- **Think time.** What people don't have is time. You serve people best when you respect their lack of time and when you show them how to save time. Start by cutting your article by at least a third. Perhaps the most important consideration of service journalism is this: Have I presented this information concisely?

- **Think engagement.** Find ways to involve your readers. First, help them find you by including your e-mail address. Point them to other sources. Asking readers to respond in various ways makes great sense.

Again, publishers impress advertisers with the numbers of readers who respond to the magazine.

- **Think new or news.** Sometimes we forget that the important part of news is "new." New is a magic word, and readers are always looking for new ways to do things and new things to do. Advertisers and direct-mail experts know the power of the word "new." There may be nothing new under the sun, but find a new way to say it, a new way to present it, a new way to use it, or a new way to think about it.

- **Think money.** Articles about how to make money or how other people made money are irresistible. People want to save money; that is, they want a deal, a discount. Think about it. People live for sales, they travel to outlet stores, and they cut out coupons. And the only thing people want more than to make or save money is to get something free. This guarantees attention. The value of your service journalism article increases with the number of reader hooks.

- **Lists.** Lists get better attention, comprehension, retention, and action. What's more, you can cut so much copy with a list because you don't need to write sentences. Former *Good Housekeeping* editor in chief John Mack Carter said that you must not only list the benefits of something but quantify the benefits. List the advantages and disadvantages of the program or project in your article. Give a dos and don'ts list about that camping trip.

- **Questions and answers.** This format serves readers well because they can skip the questions they know the answers to or are not interested in. You may be pleasantly surprised how many magazines will accept a well-crafted Q&A piece. Too many times we think only of celebrities or interviews for Q&As. They are also excellent for delivering practical information on such topics as health, nutrition, and exercise.

- **Subheads.** Readers enter your article when they find something useful. Write subheads to create entry points. This will also help you organize your piece (but know that an editor may adjust them).

- **Blurbs.** Write a summary/benefit/contents blurb to go under the title of your piece. Readers should not have to read the entire article to find out what they will learn from it. How often have you found yourself drawn into a magazine article by a blurb and "cheating" by trying to find where the blurb is discussed in the copy?

- **Sidebars and boxes.** Breaking up articles is important. Readers are not attracted to long columns of gray. Writing in chunks gets more readers and aids their comprehension and retention. Here are some boxes to consider:

Glossary box: For that somewhat technical article, don't stop and define words some readers might not understand. Put them in a box. Indicate they are in the glossary with italics or color.

Reference box: The Internet has spoiled people by connecting them to other sources. When you wrote papers in college, you wrote footnotes and bibliographies. Shouldn't you now connect people to your sources and tell them where to find more information?

Biography box: For that profile, why not put biographical information in a separate box so it doesn't interrupt the flow of your article?

Note box: Remember when you used note cards to cram for an exam? Wouldn't it be nice to give your readers such a note card to cut out so they don't have to take notes? Don't worry about repeating some of what you have said in the main article.

- **Quizzes, crosswords, games.** Many readers find quizzes irresistible. They love to find out what they know about a subject. And guess what? Making readers active aids their comprehension and retention.

Not every article you write will be service journalism, and those that are will not use all of these principles or techniques. Your editor may not use all, some, or any of your suggestions. But a smart editor will take advantage of such tactics to entice today's readers.

Shorts, Sidebars, and Quizzes

When it comes to writing for magazines, some writers think longer equals better. Their minds capture a stellar idea and they can't wait to pitch an editor a 2,500-word feature on the subject. That's just the nature of the freelance beast. The more words writers are asked to squeeze into an article, generally the more cash flow that follows. But many magazines don't have that kind of space, or they reserve these large features for well-established writers they've worked with previously. Where does this leave the less-experienced writer, or even a veteran word crafter, trying to break into a new publication? The short, sidebar, or quiz, that's where.

Generally, shorts, sidebars, and quizzes are straightforward, compact, don't usually require an extensive amount of research or interviews, and often pay a dollar or more per word on the national level. Shorts are common in many types of magazines. Most publications even state in their guidelines that the short is the best way to break in. Perhaps writers haven't given this idea its due. You *can* break into major magazines this way. So before you dismiss the short, know that it's a surefire way to show an editor what you can do. Depending on the publication, shorts range in length from a two-sentence snippet to six hundred words. Most are in the one hundred- to three hundred-word range. But don't be fooled. Just because they're short—some as short as seventy-five words—doesn't mean these pieces are easy to craft. Hone your skills, though, and you may just master the short article.

Once you get the go-ahead for a short, quiz, or sidebar, treat it like any other writing gig. Research, interview, and compile information just like you would for a feature article. Penning shorts is similar to writing features—just on a smaller scale. You'll need a to-the-point lead, the meat in the middle, and a closing, wrapped up tighter than ever. Mimic the magazine's style. Does the prose drip with wit or sarcasm? Are the shorts hard-nosed? Look back over your editor's notes to verify you've done the job that was requested.

Keeping to a short, limited word count can be challenging. It calls for taut, clean copy minus extraneous thoughts and excess verbiage. If you've put together a quiz, have a few friendly readers give it a dry run and ask them for feedback. You won't want to send it off to the editor if the scoring doesn't compute or the questions aren't clear. Treat your short with the respect of a feature article. Proofread, double-check, and triple-check; run a grammar and spelling program; turn it in on time, early if possible. Remember, this work shows the editor what you can do.

Peter Flax, features editor at *Backpacker* magazine, advises writers to approach shorts as if they were twice as long. A two hundred-word article, for instance, should hold as much information as a four hundred-word article. That's why the craft of writing shorts is so precise. "The writing has to be perfect," he said. "Little stories like these are their own art form, and you can achieve a level of perfection in these that you can't in longer articles."

Before you begin writing, make sure your homework's done. Do an interview with key people. Length may prohibit you from quoting them in the article, but at least you've gained knowledge about the topic. Skim through news releases and other background information. Then put everything aside and write.

Often, writers regurgitate news releases, and that's a turnoff, said Mary Jane Horton, articles editor at *Fit Pregnancy*: "Put something of yourself into the article." Consider, too, what you want readers to get out of this nugget. What's the goal of your short?

Then follow these seven tips to make your short writing sharp:

- **Get to the point ASAP.** Shorts have little room to engage readers, so state your point quickly in a way that will attract readers. It's tempting to lead with a question, but that's taking the easy way out. Challenge your imagination. Start with a snappy lead, and retain that intensity throughout the short.

- **Think simple.** The simpler you write, the better your article will be. Eliminate big words that will bog down your copy, opting instead for basic words and skipping jargon. Keep your sentences short.

- **Eliminate unnecessary words.** Write the first draft, and then hack to make your copy tight and clean. For example, rather than writing "professor of psychology," write "psychology professor." Use contractions wherever possible. If you don't need small words like *a* or *an*, get rid of them.

- **Delete people and facts not crucial to the story.** With every word being so precious, why include useless information? But do make sure that your information is accurate. Even shorts are fact-checked.

- **Choose active over passive voice.** Active voice is always better than passive, especially in shorts. For instance, "One hundred people participated in the study" sounds snappier than "One hundred people were recruited for the study." You use fewer words with active voice and get readers more involved.

- **Quote wisely.** Don't waste valuable words on long quotes or, even worse, quotes that mean nothing. If you use a quote, make sure it's relevant and important to your message.

- **Stick to the count.** If you're assigned a three hundred-word piece, don't turn in five hundred words. If you go ten or twenty words over the count, that's okay. But stick close to the assigned count.

Writing shorts may not make you a millionaire, although you can make a good living writing them. But in an editor's eye, they may make you look like a million bucks, and that's what really counts.

HOW TO WRITE A BOOK REVIEW

Book reviews are a perfect fit for writers, especially freelance writers. You can read the book on your own time, in between other jobs, while traveling, whenever. It is an article that can fit nicely into your schedule.

But how do you write a book review? What does it take to do this?

Essentially you must do three things in any book review: describe the book, analyze whether or not the book achieved its purpose, and express your own opinion about the book. If you decide to write a negative review, be prepared for the ramifications of it and decide if it is worth it. The review should be two-thirds summary of the book and one-third evaluation of the book. And don't forget to include the bibliographic information.

You must ask yourself several questions about the book before writing your review.

Continued next page

These key questions will help you get the information you need to write a useful book review for any reader. As you read these questions, realize that you may need to adjust them to fit the book you are reviewing depending on its genre.

- What is the author's purpose in writing this book? (The preface is a good place to find this information.)
- What are the key points of the book? Does the author support those points?
- Is the information accurate? How does this book fit in with other books in the same field or genre? Is this author an authority on the subject?
- What is the format of the book? What style is the book written in? What is the point of view?
- What is the theme of the book? How do the characters, plot, and setting relate to it?

These questions should get you started. Follow these suggestions and then polish your work for a useful and publishable review. See the following sample book review for inspiration.

Sample Book Review

Wordcraft: The Art of Turning Little Words Into Big Business by Alex Frankel (Crown).

There's no better example of language's power in the marketplace than the actual brand names that appear there: Verizon. Accenture. Pontiac Aztek. Viagra. It's clear that the right product names—no matter how manufactured-sounding or nonsensical—equal big money for business.

Alex Frankel's *Wordcraft: The Art of Turning Little Words Into Big Business* (Crown) offers a glimpse at the secretive world of professional namers—writers and marketers who invent the catchy product names that sometimes creep into the cultural lexicon.

How much work went into naming Lunchables? What popular tech device went through such tentative incarnations as Banjo, GamePlan, Hula, and Sling? (Answer: BlackBerry.) It's astounding to learn how much trouble large corporations will go to (and how much money they'll spend) to achieve the perfect brand name. The level of secrecy surrounding naming projects is also remarkable, as are the author's skills at worming his way into them. *Wordcraft*, with its relevant observations about what happens when language, pop culture, and capitalism intersect, is excellent journalism. It also might be the first book about brand marketing that's actually fun to read.

Art-of-Living Articles

Everyone has a story to tell. "I was agoraphobic (housebound) for several years, and miserable. I was hopeless and didn't believe I would ever get better or lead a normal life," said freelance writer Jenna Glatzer. "Then, I 'met' a woman online, Patty Miranda, who told me she had been through just what I was going through, and she had gone on to get married, travel, have kids, go to parties. Patty wrote me every day with inspirational messages and support. I promised myself that if I ever got better, I would find a way to share hope with others who were suffering." And, when she improved, Glatzer fulfilled that promise she made to herself—she wrote *Conquering Panic and Anxiety Disorders: Success Stories, Strategies, and Other Good News* (Hunter House). Glatzer has also written about overcoming her disorder for *Woman's World*, and she has contributed her story to a number of other publications.

Self-help articles and books, similar to what Glatzer has written, fall into a category commonly called "art-of-living." Stories within this broad category include three distinct categories: inspirational narratives, inspirational articles about faith and religion, and self-help articles.

Art-of-living articles generally revolve around common, personal experiences or concerns that impact the lives and emotions of the people reading them. To better understand these types of articles, a few clarifications need to be made:

- A **narrative** is a story that you tell someone to recount an event that has occurred in your life or that you have witnessed on a first-hand basis and usually involves a chronology of facts.
- An **article** is a story that acts as a personal guide through an otherwise unchartered or undiscovered area combining personal experience with factual information. However, articles are *not* a diary or a journal of information.

The key to writing art-of-living articles is to write an article that will make a difference in someone's life—to provide the reader with something to hold on to and take away into her own life.

There are three main categories that you can write in if you want to write an art-of-living story:

- **Inspirational narratives.** Everywhere you look, there is a story waiting to be discovered and told in an engaging style that piques the curiosity of the reader. Angela Adair Hoy has mastered the craft of writing inspirational narratives.

> "On Saturday night, we took our weekly jaunt down to Gifford's, the local ice cream stand. When we returned, I carried three cups of ice cream up to Zach's room for the video game fanatics (Zach, Steve, and Matt). As I was handing out the goods, I heard a CRASH outside. It brought back haunting memories of the day that Frank's friend, Mitchell, was hit by a car in front of our home on Max's first birthday."

This excerpt is from Adair Hoy's "News from the Home Office," a regular note she writes to the readers of her weekly e-newsletter, *Writers-Weekly.com*. This particular account is titled "How Small is Bangor, Maine? Well, I'll Tell Ya . . ." In each newsletter, Adair Hoy writes about something that happens in her daily life that she feels will be of interest to her readers—a group of loyal readers who have developed a curiosity for each new letter.

"We did a reader poll last year asking readers to rate the newsletter's sections," Adair Hoy said. "We were stunned to learn that 'News from the Home Office' is the most popular column."

Adair Hoy has essentially written an inspirational narrative: She uses the events (sometimes good, but also bad) that occur in her daily life and tells them in a way that entices her readers and makes them feel connected to the story. Many of her readers are not afraid to contact her about these narratives. "My aunt died last month and one reader, someone I'd never corresponded with before, mailed me a condolence card," she said. "Some readers have mailed gifts to our children in the past (one woman knitted a blanket for my son Max when he was born).

I'm humbled and always amazed that people care so much about our personal lives."

- **Inspirational articles on faith and religion.** A recent search on Writers-Market.com found more than fifty religious consumer magazines that publish inspirational articles focusing on faith and religion. One such magazine is *Catholic Parent*, whose editors say, "*Catholic Parent* is extremely receptive to first-person accounts of personal experiences dealing with parenting issues that are moving, emotionally engaging, and uplifting for the reader. Bear in mind the magazine's mission to provide practical information for parents."

Over the past twenty-five years, the publishing industry saw a decline in the number of religious magazines, but today, it seems like more people than ever are embracing some form of spirituality or religion. "There seems to be a great deal of interest in inspirational and spiritual/soul-searching types of articles," said Adair Hoy. She goes on to say that while analyzing the current magazine market for *WritersWeekly.com*, she has found that there seems to be a "a spiritual awakening across the globe, and editors are recognizing this and offering their readers alternative ways to comfort their souls."

In a March 23, 2004 article, Frank Newport, editor in chief of *The Gallup Poll*, cited that a recent Gallup Poll indicated that Americans are a predominantly Christian nation, and that "religion is very important to about six in ten Americans, and that about six in ten Americans attend church on at least a semiregular basis."

There are a number of reasons people seem drawn to inspirational articles that focus on faith and religion, but many are citing the events surrounding September 11, 2001, as well as the war in Iraq. Whatever the reason, though, many religious publications are looking for general-interest articles with an inspirational twist, which for some publications can be hard to find. The editors of *Commonweal* magazine, a biweekly journal focusing on topical issues like public affairs, religion, literature, and the arts, say, "While religious articles are always topical, we are less interested in devotional and churchy pieces than in articles which examine the links between 'worldly' concerns and religious beliefs."

- **Self-help articles.** "I get by with a little help from my friends." Who would have thought when John Lennon and Paul McCartney wrote the lyrics to the song "With a Little Help from My Friends" that they would be capturing the essence and purpose of the content contained in a self-help article? The reasons why people write self-help articles vary from person to person, but one thing is always the same: Everyone needs a little help now and again, and who better to get that help from than someone who knows exactly what you are going through and where you are coming from? "I've realized the power of sharing our stories," said Glatzer. "I've realized how much you can change people's lives—even total strangers—just by showing them that they're not alone."

Ladies' Home Journal is one magazine that looks specifically for self-help articles to round out their editorial content. The editors say, *"Ladies' Home Journal* is for active, empowered women who are evolving in new directions. It addresses informational needs with highly focused features and articles on a variety of topics including beauty and fashion, food and nutrition, health and medicine, home decorating and design, parenting and self-help, personalities, and current events."

Sometimes, self-help articles can stand alone by simply using a "this-happened-to-me" approach, while other self-help articles benefit from additional information on the topic being written about, as well as specific advice for readers on how they can cope with the topic as it relates to their own lives. In many self-help articles you will often see sidebars composed of interviews with experts, statistical data, or a table or chart listing pertinent information.

Penning a self-help article can be difficult, at times, for many writers because they are exposing a part of their life that is very personal, and it forces them to become brutally honest with themselves and those around them. But, for most writers, the end result makes the journey well worth their while. "I didn't know how honest to be because I didn't want to hurt my family," said Glatzer. "In the end, though, I decided it was important to share it all."

When writing an art-of-living article, it is important to remember that readers are not actually interested in your experience per se, but they are interested in their own experience. In order for your story to be interesting and really hook your readers, your story has to become part of your readers' experience. If you are writing for an audience that you hope will read and relate to your work, you cannot ask yourself, "What do I want to write about today?" Instead, ask, "What do my readers want to read about today?"

WRITING PERSONAL ESSAYS

The key to writing personal essays is to use your own experiences, memories, and events of daily life to exemplify a universal truth. You must be able to take your individual experience and connect it to a broader human experience that anyone can relate to. The essay should be filled with sentiment but not sentimentality. Don't go overboard on sappy, feel-good prose. Instead, make your writing strike an emotional chord with descriptive sentences and visual images. Don't wander into the realm of the cliché. While clichés are cliché because of their universality, your challenge is to tap into the universal human experience through a different avenue, not one that has already been summed up into a nice cliché.

Once you have hit upon that moment, phrase, or realization that lends itself to a common truth, then you must craft your essay. Most importantly, personal essays require that you write. Don't analyze too long or craft too much. Get the idea on paper and then look at how you can revise to make it into a strong, concise, powerful essay.

Your essay must have a theme—something that ties it all together. This needn't be overstated, but the reader must be able to recognize your theme. The theme is the universal aspect. You should also make your essay intimate. That is why so many personal essays are in first person. First person allows a reader to be closer to your thoughts and experience. Some personal essays are written in third person, but even

Continued next page

then, they must be a close third where thoughts and feelings of individuals aren't distant but rather available for the reader to tap into.

Use symbols in your essays. Take something familiar and essential to your experience and make it the center of your essay. This could be a household object, a place, or a song. Find something that can symbolize why your idea is universal. What is that one thing that transcends everyday life that made you realize that there is more to this object or phrase or memory than you originally thought? What will make others see that? Your symbol will help create unity in your essay and give a solid idea to your theme.

Have fun writing these essays. Study other personal essays and learn how to write with rhythm. Balance your ideas and emotions with well-crafted prose. Don't be afraid to revise, and don't be afraid to submit these essays to publications. Do market research to find the magazines most open to your topics and style. There are more than four hundred magazines that accept personal essay submissions, such as *Guideposts, The New York Times Magazine,* and *Modern Maturity.* Check *Writer's Market,* and also check the newsstands for even more possibilities. Flip through magazines, read the essays, and find out where your work could fit. While it can be scary submitting something that is crafted from your own personal experience, be confident and remember that those universal truths do no good inside your own desk drawer.

Crafting Pieces for Children's Magazines

Writing children's magazine pieces takes a special set of skills. Said children's magazine writer Fiona Bayrock, who specializes in nonfiction: "Writing for children is not something rookie writers do before 'graduating' to adult writing. And it's not something good writers of adult fiction can automatically do well." There are a number of special considerations writers must keep in mind when writing magazine articles for young readers. Here are some things to pay attention to as you craft magazine pieces, along with advice from a few much-published children's magazine writers.

Grab readers' attention from the first sentence. Kids are a tough audience to impress. If you don't interest them from the get-go, they'll turn the page or put the magazine down and head for their video games or the television. The opening line of a magazine piece for children needs to pique readers' interest—as well as introduce the rest of the article.

"I probably spend five times longer on the opening paragraph than any other part of an article," said Bayrock. "After the first sentence, I want readers to say something like, 'No way!' 'You're kidding!' 'Cool!' or 'Wow!' "

Bayrock uses a number of different techniques to hook her readers. "I like to dive right into the action with a surprising element, a bit of drama, or something really silly," she said. She's also not beyond deliberately deceiving her readers. "I started one article with 'Green moist-skinned aliens with big, bulging, gold eyes are invading the west coast of North America.' " Her piece was not about aliens from outer space but about bullfrogs as an alien invasive species. "Aside from being a bit of a trick (hey—it was all true!), it also served to reinforce the 'alien' and 'invasion' parts of the concept."

Freelance writer and former *Highlights for Children* editor Pam Zollman also advises writers to be creative when they're beginning a magazine piece. "The vast majority of the article submissions I received at *Highlights* started with a question, and this gets boring after a while," she said. "In fact, using a lot of questions in an article has the unintended tone of patronizing the reader. Most introductory questions are either silly or are phrased in such a way that the reader can say 'no' and move on to another article. For example, 'Have you ever wondered why clouds are fluffy?' or 'Do you like to eat ice cream?' "

Be aware of length restrictions and focus your articles. Children's magazine articles are short, ranging from several hundred words to two thousand-word pieces for the teen audience. Submitting material that's way over or way under a magazine's prescribed word count will likely mean instant rejection.

With these word-count limits in mind, writers must narrow their focus when it comes to covering a topic. "Don't try to cover everything about an entire species, or the history of the wheel, or the entire life-to-death experience of a person, in four hundred words," said Zollman. "There's just not enough room to adequately cover those types of topics. Instead, narrow the focus to a scientist studying a weaver bird building twenty-eight nests, trying to find one that will attract a mate; to the reason why Yellowstone National Park has so many geysers; to a children's festival in Japan; to one event that helped to shape a person's life or career."

According to Bayrock, it shouldn't be hard for writers to find some aspect of a topic to focus on when writing nonfiction for young readers. "I don't think I've ever come across a subject that was too dull to write about for kids. There's always some quirky, unusual, or funny kid angle to be had," she said. "It's just a matter of finding what that is—bungee jumping mussels, earthquakes are like Rice Krispies, a messy room makes for good acoustics."

Bayrock also recommends using humor when writing for young readers. "I use humor and wordplay a lot, and insert puns liberally. I have fun." And that fun comes through in her magazine articles.

Be aware of the age group a magazine targets. Children's magazines are published for audiences ranging from prereader to teens. Be sure you're writing appropriately for the age level of the magazines you're targeting.

Don't talk down to readers. This is a big no-no when it comes to writing for children. Respect your audience. "Don't be didactic, condescending, or talk down to kids," said Bayrock. "They have radar about that sort of thing and won't stand for it." And neither will editors. "Write simply and clearly using the right vocabulary for the job, but no dumbing down."

Don't try to force a moral. It's certainly okay to teach children a lesson through a magazine piece, particularly in material aimed at a religious audience. But show, don't tell. Don't hit your reader over the head with a lesson or a moral.

Let kids solve their problems. In short fiction for young readers, don't let adults interfere too much in the story. Just as in children's books, kids need stories in which kid characters solve their own problems without adult intervention or adults solving problems for them.

Nonfiction should incorporate principles of fiction. "This does not mean you should use fictional characters or talking animals in your nonfiction," said Zollman. "Instead, write an exciting or interesting story about a person or an animal or an event, making the reader feel as if he or she were there." A good nonfiction children's magazine piece should include an intro that hooks a reader, just like fiction. The conclusion should be satisfying and loose ends should be tied up.

"Dialogue in fiction quickens the pace of a story and makes it more fun to read. In nonfiction, quotes do the same trick, as long as they actually add to the article and help move it forward. Using these techniques should keep your article from sounding too 'dry' or 'encyclopedic,' " said Zollman.

Write for contemporary kids—and look to them for inspiration. Your material should be relative to the modern kids' world, not your childhood. While it's fine to draw on your own childhood for ideas and inspiration, details that are dated won't make it with today's young readers. "I've written lots of pieces that came from memories of my own childhood fears, wants, and interests—I've combined some of my own situations with those of my daughter and turned them into stories," said Kathryn Lay, a children's writer with more than one thousand published pieces to her credit.

Do solid research for nonfiction pieces. Look to experts when writing nonfiction. "One advantage of having an expert in a particular field review your articles is that you can interview him or her as one of your primary sources," said Zollman. In addition to interesting quotes, anecdotes, etc., "he or she might be able to give you information that can't be found in encyclopedias or in a casual search at the library or on the Internet."

An expert is not only a scientist or someone working in a specific field. Serious hobbyists can also serve as "experts." For a piece for *Spider* called "Cave-A-Thon," Kathryn Lay turned to the father of one of her daughter's friends who is a spelunker. "I was able to pick his brain and come up with a fun story."

Added Bayrock, "Don't settle for less reliable information or 'good enough' writing because 'it's just for kids.' Kids deserve accuracy and quality, and editors expect nonfiction for kids to be as good as or better than adult nonfiction. Some of the best nonfiction writing is for kids because it's tight, to the point, and every word has been carefully chosen and earned its place in the article. Kids are far more discerning than adults. They won't stay with a poorly written story to see if it gets better."

CHAPTER TEN:
WORKING WITH AN EDITOR

If you leave your publishing day job to hit the freelance trail, you might think you'll be going it alone. You'll leave behind editors, graphic artists, page designers, publishers, ad sales people, and the camaraderie of the publication's support staff.

But even though you may leave corporate America, you never leave the team mentality behind. You'll still have to work closely with the editors and staff at several publications. You'll send story pitches their way and field their replies. You'll brainstorm leads, ideas, future sections, and your contributions to their editorial calendars—sometimes scheduled a year in advance. With some publications, you may collaborate with the graphics editors, helping coordinate photo shoots and discussing layout and design elements.

Why will you have to do all this? Certainly today's freelancer has all the tools to be an efficient—and solo—journalist. The Internet lets you conduct effective, thorough research, and e-mail helps you stay in touch with sources, editors, contacts, and peers. The PC has become a glorified word processor, which you can then use to spirit off your finished works instantaneously to editors half a world away. With these tools, you can do your work quietly, without any further demands on your time or mental energy.

Sure, at its core, that's the business of writing. But the spirit of freelancing is to be a team player, an integral, indispensable part of your clients' organizations. By partnering with your editors and client publications, you give yourself a greater sense of self-worth, of belonging, of being a respected and needed team player.

You and Your Editor

Here are some tips for "partnering" with your editors and forming positive working relationships with any of them.

- **Be professional.** Meet your deadlines with clean, well-reported, and well-researched copy. If something is amiss with your article, let your editor know sooner than later.
- **Have team spirit.** From the beginning, foster a feeling of shared success. Read and know the publication and offer your insights, ideas, and thoughts on its content and stories. Bring interesting story ideas to the table and discuss your thoughts and how they might fit the publication's needs.
- **Know the calendar.** Get an editorial calendar and propose ideas that correspond with the topics listed and the seasons. For example, for a December issue of a business magazine, propose a story on year-end tax planning. For a family magazine's June issue, propose summer travel or vacation tips.
- **Be on the lookout.** Whether you're reading, watching the news, or driving the kids to school, always have the radar on for ideas. Many editors rely on freelancers to have their ears to the ground for trends and other news.
- **Discuss your ideas.** E-mail is an efficient way to communicate, but follow it up with a telephone call to the editor. Conversational give-and-take helps cross-pollinate and ferment good ideas, and it helps develop closer relationships.
- **Take tough assignments.** Be willing to take the assignments that no one else wants. Be able to ferret out a full story from a scrap of news. If you are well organized and keep updated lists of sources and contacts, even tough assignments shouldn't be that tough (just don't let your editor know that). Deliver a good piece and watch your editor's trust, and your assignments, grow.
- **Be flexible.** Be ready to move up a deadline—or take on a hard-to-meet deadline. Your editor will remember it.

- **Solicit feedback.** Ask your editors about your work—what they think about your raw copy, how your ideas are fitting into their coverage areas, how you're meeting their needs. Invite them to be blunt where needed and to point out mistakes or supply you with readers' comments or letters to the editor regarding your work. Not only will you become a better writer for it, they will respect your desire to learn.
- **Meet with your editors.** Visit your clients. If you have a big client or two in a major city that would require air travel and a hotel stay, think of the expense as "business development." At the very least, it's tax deductible. At best, you could land additional work.
- **Stay in touch.** Editors move. Publications fold. When an editor changes jobs, immediately hit the Web site or newsstand to learn more about their new publication. After a week or two, send a welcome note and some article queries.
- **Be understanding.** If a publication you write for folds before your article runs or you are paid, don't call and demand an immediate kill fee. E-mail the now-former editor to get the scoop. It may be that funding for the publication has dried up.

  Express your sympathy and willingness to help the editor in the future. You may be able to amicably negotiate a kill fee even if it hadn't been in the contract (though you should always make sure this is contracted).
- **Welcome rewrites.** Or at least don't begrudge your editor's request for a little time spent tweaking the piece to match the publication's expectations. Look at your contract; rewrites are probably included. Besides, look closely and you'll probably see the merit of their requested changes.

All this good karma aside, freelancing is a two-way street. Being a partner with your editors implies that they will partner with you as well. It's important to know what you should and should not expect of this partnership. As a freelance writer, in general you cannot expect:

- **Handholding.** Editors are busy, just like you, and in many cases editing copy is no longer the major part of their day. The editor wants your assignment. He doesn't want to know that your daughter just took her first steps or that you just clipped your dog's nails.
- **Direction beyond the original assignment.** That's why it's important to completely understand the assignment when it's made.
- **Editing control.** The editor, not you, will determine the headline, pullouts, and design. While many editors find it helpful when freelancers provide headlines at the top of their articles, those headlines seldom are used.

While it's important to serve your editors' needs and be flexible, you should not become a slave to their whims. If they continually call you with short deadlines or due dates that then result in articles sitting for weeks before they're reviewed for the first time, inquire if there's a way to rework future deadlines. Freelancers are entitled to and should expect:

- **A written agreement.** This should outline rights sold, payment, article focus, and delivery mode. If you don't get one, write the editor a letter detailing your understanding of the agreement.
- **Communication throughout the process.** You should see a copy of your article as it will appear in print or online, and you should have an opportunity for feedback. The editor also should be able to tell you when he anticipates your work will appear in print or online.
- **Treatment as a fellow professional.** Freelancers are important to most magazines, and you should be treated with respect and courtesy. Life is too short to work with an editor who berates you or lies to you.

The more you make yourself a part of the team, the better positioned you will be to speak up if you see your edited copy reading differently than you had intended. The relationship you've built will bolster the weight of your opinions.

Remember that even though you work alone, you still have much to learn, and your editors have much to teach. Freelancing is a team effort, one where you work in tandem with your editors to create a better product. You can maintain the camaraderie of the team while having the free spirit of a freelancer. It's like having the best of both worlds.

Be a Team Player

Here are quick tips for being a team player while freelancing:

- Propose ideas to the editors, make suggestions, and acknowledge the successes of the publication.
- An editor switching publications doesn't mean the end of a relationship. Send him a card of congratulations and some story ideas.
- Consider meeting your clients face-to-face occasionally, even if it means flying to another city. Personal interaction furthers your relationship and increases chances for new work.
- Don't shy away from tough assignments and tight deadlines. Those are the stories editors appreciate most—and remember.
- Diplomacy can help you reap benefits later. Avoid burning bridges.

Keeping Your Editor

A writer's first sale to any magazine is special. Now comes the tricky part: How do you keep those assignments and acceptances coming? Here's a little secret. Editors don't necessarily want writers whose work makes them stop and gape in amazement and envy. They want writers who are low maintenance. Editors spend a lot of time in meetings with a lot of people. They don't have as much time as they'd like to edit, much less nurture writers. Learn from the following tips and you'll find your way into an editor's e-mail address book and telephone speed-dial list.

1. Do understand the terms of the assignment or acceptance of your work before you sign the contract. This is the time to ask questions about the article's focus, due date, word count, and submission format. Be sure you understand whether you're to provide any accompanying material, such as photographs or sidebars. Further, if the editor doesn't bring it up, this also is the time to ask what rights are being purchased and how much you'll be paid. Ask whether you'll need to submit an invoice and whether the publication pays on acceptance (as soon as the editor approves the article) or publication (after the article appears in print or on the Web site).

2. **Do find out how the editor likes to communicate with writers.** Some prefer e-mail; for others, phone calls and faxes are fine. Ask your contacts if there is a time of day or week that works better for them. Some editors set aside one day per week with no meetings to handle editing and assigning.

3. **Don't contact the editor repeatedly after you've received the assignment.** He's on to other assignments and meetings. If a key interview falls through, contact the editor. If you got a killer quote from one of the subjects, don't contact the editor to share the good news. He'll see it when you turn in the article.

4. **Do turn in your assignment on time, or even a little early.** This can't be emphasized enough. Make sure it has the focus the two of you discussed and is within 10 percent of the assigned word count. If the editor asked for an e-mailed manuscript saved as text-only, don't send it in WordPerfect format, and don't send a fax.

5. **Don't quibble over the way your work is edited.** Some publications will send galleys of your article before it's published. If inaccuracies were introduced into the article or direct quotations were changed, it's worth asking why. But don't fly into a snit because the publication uses serial commas and you don't like them.

6. **Do learn from the editing.** Compare the galley with the submitted work. How was it restructured? What was cut? What was moved to a sidebar? How was your lead and conclusion changed? Knowing what the editor wants makes it easier to deliver just that in your next assignment.

7. **Do wait until your first assignment has been accepted before proposing additional articles.** Editors get nervous when the writer to whom

they've just assigned one article comes up with five more ideas before turning in the first one. It's good for the writer to be a little circumspect as well; after all, you don't know yet whether you're going to like working for this editor or this publication.

Damage Control

Now you know how to work with and keep an editor. You know all the tricks, and you plan to follow them perfectly. But you're also human, and despite your best intentions, sometimes you make mistakes. How you handle your errors shows as much about you as does your effective use of literary devices. With that in mind, here's how to save face, preserve integrity on the job, and minimize the damage when the worst does occur.

- **Deadline trouble.** For a delay of any length, editors want to hear about it sooner rather than later so, if necessary, they can rearrange the publication calendar. Though no editor will be happy with the news, most will understand if the delay is minimal or if it's outside your control like when an interview gets rescheduled at the last minute. Just apologize and advise the editor when it will be completed, and ask if that's acceptable. Many editors build in some extra time for assignments, especially for writers with whom they haven't worked before. "As long as they tell us, it's not a big deal," said Michelle Badash, director of consumer content for HealthGate.com.

No matter what the reason, the delay is at best an inconvenience for them. This is a business relationship, and they're not interested in your personal situation. "If you're going to be late, (the editor) is owed some kind of explanation," Badash said. But you needn't get into details about dear Aunt Millie's appendectomy; "family illness" will suffice.

Be aware that by being late, you're seriously jeopardizing the possibility of a long-term relationship with this editor. One final bit of advice from Badash: "Nothing better stand in your way of meeting that second deadline—especially if you're new."

- **Reporting errors.** If you make a reporting mistake, you may be tempted to let it go, hoping your editor never finds out. But even slip-ups you consider "minor," like misspelling a name or getting a title wrong—not to mention larger errors like misquotes—aren't inconsequential to the people involved and, as you have learned, can lead to legal problems.

Come clean with your editor. If the article is online, he can likely correct the mistake quickly. An upfront approach also allows you to maintain some level of professionalism. "It shows honesty; it shows good judgment," said Debra Aho Williamson, contributing editor to *Advertising Age* and the *Industry Standard*.

• **Misdirected query.** When sending out multiple query letters, occasional slip-ups—like getting the publication wrong or sending the wrong query to the right editor—can happen. "To be honest, the little mistakes don't bother me," said Nancy Price, editor of Myria.com, ePregnancy.com, GeoParent.com, and *Pregnancy* magazine. "What's more important is that the person can write well, [and] they know our publications."

If you do discover you've misdirected a query, follow up. "If they're serious about wanting to work with me, I think they should recontact me," said Williamson.

• **Incomplete query.** Whether your query is electronic or print, send the missing information. One caveat from Price: "Don't send the same message again unless there's a note at the top telling me there's some new information—I get a lot of duplicate e-mail messages as it is, and I might accidentally delete it." The same recommendation goes for snail-mail submissions.

Despite their intimidating reputation, editors can be understanding. Making an occasional honest mistake usually won't blackball you from that publication for life, especially if you've built a good record of professionalism.

Problem Editors

Though most editors can and will be understanding, realize that you may still run into some problem editors. Every writer has editors, but since freelancers work with so many publications and so many editors, they have a greater chance of running into a problem editor.

Overall, your experiences with editors will be professional, cordial, and even educational. But it goes without saying that certain relationships are less than pleasant. Here are five common kinds of "problem editors" who can make your job more difficult—and some solutions that can make your job easier.

1. Smooth talkers. Some editors can sweet-talk you into doing just about anything. And sometimes, you're so happy to receive enthusiastic feedback, you'll do just about anything for just about nothing in return.

Smooth talkers tell you they love your ideas but want you to do more research, conduct more interviews, or write more material. They can't make commitments to publish or pay, but you do more work happily, only to learn too late they "won't be needing that article after all."

Next time a smooth talker suggests that you spend more time revising an article you've submitted, give that editor a list of the additional research, interviews, and writing you'd be happy to do—as soon as you have a commitment in writing to publish the article for a set fee. Flatout refusing to do extra work won't win you brownie points, but refusing to do that work without a commitment will show that you're a hard worker but not a sucker. And make sure a kill fee is included in the deal so you won't go away empty-handed even if your editor opts to eighty-six the piece in the end.

2. Penny-pinchers. Penny-pinchers can be delightful editors until the last step: payment. There are always excuses about why your payment is late. Sometimes it's a bank error, other times a check-writing cycle that you narrowly missed. The more you hear these excuses, the less likely you are to believe them.

Contact other freelancers who have written for the outlet to see if they've had similar experiences—perhaps this is a trend. You can also write to the publisher explaining what you submitted and what fee was agreed upon, and ask nicely when payment can be expected. If the publisher offers similar excuses, the publication is probably having trouble paying its bills. If a publication is in hot water or regularly stiffs contributors, don't submit more work. Freelancing is a job, not a volunteer position.

If the money eventually comes, perhaps the editor's story was true, or maybe your letter to the publisher helped grease the bookkeeping department's wheels. In this case, you can give this editor a second chance, but make sure you receive a written contract before doing any work. And never turn in an article until your previous jobs have been paid.

3. Backseat writers. Every good editor rewrites copy at some point to punch up a lead, clarify a point, or tweak syntax. But backseat writers overhaul your article from beginning to end—changing not just a word or a sentence but entire swaths of prose—until it's unrecognizable as your own. When you see the finished article, all that remains of what you submitted is your byline, which now hardly seems accurate.

If you've been radically revised by a backseat writer, first check what's been changed. Has your editor added or removed humor, "dumbed down" your wording, or made it more "inside" for a readership knowledgeable in a certain area? Make a list of the changes that seem arbitrary or gratuitous. Then make another list—this one is difficult—of the editor's changes that improved what you wrote.

Next, discuss what you've found with your editor—not to attack the decisions but to learn what is expected of you so your next assignment can be more in line with what the editor wants. Explain the trends you noticed in revisions—this will show you're paying attention. Note the changes that improved your work—this will show you appreciate rewriting as a rule. Then ask gently about the changes you don't understand—and listen, don't argue.

Next time you turn in an assignment, ask to see a copy before it goes to press, if possible. Using the same process you used before, walk through the article with your editor. If you disagree with any changes, make it known now, before it's too late. An editor who knows that you care about style, accept reasonable rewriting, and appreciate the occasional editorial improvement will be more likely to concede to your objections and retain your individual voice.

4. Mysterious characters. These editors give vague assignments and leave you to figure out the specifics. You might relish this freedom and flexibility when you get the assignment, but you won't be so pleased when you turn in your piece and hear, "This isn't exactly what I had in mind."

When you accept an assignment from a mysterious character, send your editor a note outlining what you understand the assignment to be, using as many specifics as possible: deadline, length, fee, tone, sources, and content. Wait to hear back before you start work.

Then, as you work on your article, submit periodic updates explaining what sources you've already used, what material you're planning to include, and any changes you think are necessary to the original plan. You might also include a basic overview of your article's structure, including your lead and main points. Again, wait to hear back before proceeding. This way, you can change direction midstream if need be, and your editor won't be surprised when you turn in the finished product.

5. Silent types. More frustrating than editors who shoot down every idea or blow you off with a perfunctory form letter are silent types who won't communicate at all. They're never available when you call, and they don't return messages, even with a simple yes or no.

Dropping by the publication's office might be your first instinct, but it's often seen as pushy, and your editors will likely be in different cities anyway. A better idea is to make sure all your communications include a response deadline or gentle ultimatum: "If I haven't heard back by June 1, I'll assume you're not interested in this query," or "Since my article hasn't been published in the six months since I submitted it, I'll assume you don't plan to publish it, so I'm wondering when I should expect my kill fee."

This gives your editor a reason to call you promptly. But it also gives you a deadline for moving on if your editor doesn't call—so you can submit your query elsewhere or start pestering that silent type about receiving your kill fee.

Failing everything else, you can simply stop working with an editor; as a freelancer, you've got thousands of other editors to court. But before you throw in the towel, give your editor one more chance and see if you can't work it out. If you can find the solution, your "problem editor" might be no problem at all.

Writers Editors Hate

Just as you don't want to work with a problem editor, editors don't want to work with problem writers. What prospective writers need to know isn't simply how to be a freelancer but how *not* to be a freelancer: how to avoid alienating editors, respond to criticism, and overcome professional weaknesses.

Identified here are five types of freelancers editors hate. These categories are not mutually exclusive; more importantly, they are not immutable. Once you identify the problem, you can try to solve it.

1. Cheerleaders. Cheerleaders have never met a subject they didn't like. Every review is a rave, every situation positive, every person interviewed beyond reproach. A cheerleader might write: "Newcomer Jane Doe is the greatest jazz singer since Ella Fitzgerald, and her brilliant album is sure to sweep the Grammys."

WHAT MAGAZINE EDITORS HATE

To perk up your chances of getting plum assignments, avoid these groan-inducing practices:

- **An "every word is precious" mentality.** If you think your work is perfect when you hand it in, you may be in for a rude awakening. Editors edit, and even if your story reads beautifully as is, they often make changes to fit the style of the magazine, meet space constraints, take out material covered in other articles, etc. If you get upset over restructured sections or semicolons vs. dashes, you're going to get a reputation. However, do speak up if changes have been made to the content or voice/tone that you feel strongly just "aren't you." It's your byline on the thing, so don't be afraid to speak up—nicely.

- **Being a slave to word counts.** Editors often go back to writers with a request to elaborate on certain points here, scale back on others there. When these requests fall within the scope of the original assignment, professional writers understand this and get to work. They don't demand more money because they're "being asked to do extra work" or if they turn in something that's now three hundred words over the limit. The revise should still fit within the word count, and if the editor felt there wasn't room to cut back, she wouldn't have mentioned it.

  Sometimes, though, the demands can get unreasonable. If you have your original assignment letter (always get a letter in writing), refer to it and respectfully explain how you've delivered on it. Show exactly how the requested revisions go beyond that, and you should get the extra payment you deserve.

- **Missing deadlines without prior warning.** If you're going to miss a deadline, give the editor fair warning with a reasonable excuse—and a firm deadline by which you'll get your copy in. For writers who've proven themselves reliable with deadlines in the past, editors will be understanding about the occasional missed one. But if you're a new writer, do everything in your power to meet—or beat—that deadline. If you absolutely can't, be professional about it and give as much notice as possible.

- **Pitching obvious or generic story ideas.** If you want to write for a parenting magazine and pitch the editor with an idea for a feature called "How to Discipline Children," you'll need a strong hook, as well as the background or journalistic experience to deliver on it. Without these, a rejection letter is almost guaranteed because that editor gets fifty such pitches per year (if not per month). Try narrowing your focus or offering a unique point of view, then offer as much detail as you can about how you'd organize the piece and whom you'd interview. List actual names you know you can get instead of vaguely referencing "experts in the field." Then tell the editor why you're just the writer to do it.

In short, cheerleaders write like publicists, overstating every comparison and overusing superlatives. Perhaps cheerleaders are afraid of alienating a source, a publicist, or the reader. Whatever the reason, their writing makes cheerleaders unreliable and unlikely to get assignments from responsible editors.

If you're a cheerleader, try to avoid writing reviews or other criticism and stick to articles based more on reporting than on evaluation. If you find that high praise is warranted, find a source to back you up. If you think a local PTA president has a bright future in politics, for example, find a state senator to quote about the president's potential instead of making your own unfounded assertions.

Request an assignment in a field about which you have few strong personal feelings. If you're passionate about jazz, try your hand at a piece about folk musicians; if you're an ardent activist, look for an article that avoids partisan politics. You don't need to avoid your interests forever, but stepping outside your passions briefly will help you sharpen objectivity and regain credibility in your editor's eyes.

2. **Prima Donnas.** Prima donnas hate to be edited. "When I turn in an article, it's finished!" they say. Prima donnas often are excellent writers who turn in near-perfect copy but throw tantrums when a single comma is removed. Other prima donnas turn in abysmal work requiring major surgery but resent the editor's efforts to save the article. In the end, it doesn't matter. Any writer who won't let an editor edit won't get a second assignment.

If you've had serious run-ins with just one or two editors, it's likely their fault. If you're consistently arguing with every editor over every article, take a look in the mirror. You could be a prima donna.

First, note the changes your editor is making. Are they technical (avoiding abbreviations, separating quoted paragraphs), stylistic (using soft leads, omitting second person), or structural (rearranging paragraphs, revising sentences)?

Next, talk to your editor about general rules of style and tone for that publication. Perhaps this editor prefers service journalism or never runs Q&A-style interviews. Listen to the answers without arguing; the editor is telling you how to write for this publication, not opening a debate on the subject.

Lastly, ask to see your edited piece before it goes to press. Again, this is not always possible. Keep your last-minute changes to an absolute minimum, and choose your battles carefully—knowing that you may not win. Editors who see that you care about your work but respect their position will be more willing to heed your concerns in the future.

3. Pests. "I'm sorry to bother you again, but . . ." Pests drop in unannounced, phone repeatedly without waiting for messages to be returned, and call on deadline days. Even a good writer can be a nuisance.

First, ask editors for their preferred mode of communication: e-mail, fax, phone, or letter. Then ask what days are best and worst for submitting queries and getting questions answered. Take both these considerations seriously; even an e-mail can be a bother on a deadline day, while on a slow day, an editor might enjoy having lunch with you. Second, put all your questions—and your editor's answers—in writing. This way, you won't need to keep calling to double-check details. Finally, wait to hear back from your editor before following up. It's great to appear eager, but it's not so great to look impatient.

4. Free Spirits. Free spirits don't stick to editors' guidelines. They turn in a story twice as long as assigned, a week past deadline. An article that was supposed to be a hard-hitting, multiple-source news story ends up a first-person humor column.

If you're a free spirit, confirm your assignment in writing before getting started: length, tone, deadline, approach, sources. Ask your editor for similar, already published stories as models.

If the guidelines don't seem logical, ask the editor for an explanation before writing. An assignment's parameters may seem arbitrary to a free-lancer, but there are usually solid reasons an editor frames a piece a specific way.

If you still believe your idea for the story is superior, write two versions. One version of the story must conform to the exact guidelines your editor has spelled out, but the other can be different or longer. Include a note explaining why you believe your version is superior. It's a lot of extra work, and you won't always win. But sometimes you will persuade your editor without shirking the assignment you agreed to write.

5. Invisibles. Now you see them, now you don't. Invisibles disappear whenever there's a problem: a missed deadline, a needed revision, a question. Invisibles always make excuses about malfunctioning answering machines, disconnected phone lines, unreliable e-mail providers, and destructive computer viruses. Whatever problem you're having, you must make yourself visible to your editor; she'd rather know there's a crisis than be left in the dark.

Confirm receipt of every article you submit, and submit articles in multiple formats—e-mail and fax, for instance—so you're not blamed when you really do have technical problems.

Most of all, keep your editor apprised of all difficulties as early as possible. If you're going to miss a deadline, let your editor know immediately. Be sure you have a good explanation, as well as a backup plan, including a new deadline. As mentioned several times already, missing deadlines is always a bad idea, but being out of touch is much worse and a sure way to end your relationship with an editor.

As a freelancer, you don't have to stay with a particular editor if it's not working out. But before you walk away from a potentially promising professional relationship, take a long look at yourself and see how you might appear from the other side of the desk. You'll never have perfect connections with every editor, but if you can see yourself through your editor's eyes for a moment, then with a little bit of effort you may find your writing career going more smoothly.

Chapter Eleven:
Business and Rights-Related Issues

Writers who have been successful in getting their work published know that publishing requires two different mind-sets. The first is the actual act of writing the manuscript. The second is the business of writing—the marketing and selling of the manuscript. This shift in perspective is necessary if you want to become a successful career writer. That said, you need to keep the business side of writing in mind as you continually develop your writing.

This chapter discusses the writing business topics and rights-related issues that affect anyone selling a manuscript or trying to make a living as a freelance writer. This information is not exhaustive, so be sure to check the mentioned resources or with lawyers to answer all questions you still have.

Make Money Writing

You finally get that assignment you want from the magazine you've been querying for the past year. Now it's time to write it—where do you start? How about with an old, but oh-so-true, cliché—time is money.

Magazines usually base pay on word count. The editor couldn't care less if it takes you four hours or four days to get it done, as long as you give him the quality and content desired. That means it's up to you to make the most efficient use of time possible. The faster you get the work done, the more you make per hour and the more time you have to do other freelancing and make even more money.

If you are a professional writer, you want to make lots of money in a profession not usually known for that. You have to be organized to accomplish your goal. You need to get organized to maximize your output and minimize your effort. Start by developing a timeline.

Put together your action plan. How much are you getting paid for this article? How much do you want to make per hour? Divide the second figure into the first to decide how long you'll devote to this project. Say you're getting $750 for a one thousand-word story. You want to earn $125 an hour, so that means you should devote six hours to this project.

Next, think about how much time you'll need to write the story. If you've always been a fast writer, assume you can turn out one thousand words in about an hour, then spend maybe another hour or two rereading and editing, double-checking facts, and putting the first draft into final form. So in this example, that would leave you about four hours for interviews. Unless you're writing about something extremely technical, figure no one interview will go more than a half an hour.

So, you can do eight half-hour interviews for this story. That sounds about right. After doing years worth of articles, you'll come to the realization that any expert has about two hundred words of usable copy she can convey in a half-hour interview. If you get your eight good interviews, you'll have at least 1,600 words, more than enough to winnow your piece down to an information-packed story quoting a variety of solid sources.

By taking this formulaic approach, you'll find that you can increase the money you earn writing. For example, Robert Bly started freelancing full time in 1982, and except for that first year and the next, he has earned more than $100,000 a year as a freelance writer for over twenty consecutive years. In 2001, he grossed $500,000, as he did the year before that. He continues to prosper because he has figured out how to think like a businessman as well as a writer.

This illustrates that making a six-figure income is a realistic goal for even an average freelance writer. Bly's never written a best-seller, nor has he sold a script to the movies or television, but he knows how to make the most possible money out of his work. Follow these suggestions to help you achieve your moneymaking goals for the year.

1. Get serious about money. If money is not a concern, you can write whatever you want, whenever you want, as much or as little as you want, without regard to the fee you will be paid, how long it will take to write the piece, or the likelihood that you will sell the piece.

But if you want to consistently make $100,000 a year as a freelance writer, you need to avoid the poverty mentality that holds so many writers back from earning a high income. A doorman in New York City earns around $30,000 annually. If an unskilled laborer can make $30,000 just for opening a door, surely you can earn $50,000 to $100,000 for your skills.

2. Set daily revenue goals. To make $100,000 a year, you need to earn $2,000 a week for fifty weeks. For a five-day workweek, that comes to $400 a day. Will people pay you $400 a day for writing-related work? Do you have to make $400 each and every day? No. Some days you'll be writing queries or doing self-promotion and earn nothing. Other days you'll get into a writing groove, finish a $1,000 article in six hours, and still have time to write more queries. You're safe as long as your average revenue is $400 a day, or $2,000 a week, or about $9,000 a month.

3. Value your time. If you earn $100,000 a year and work forty hours a week, your time is worth at least $50 an hour. You should base decisions about how you spend your time on that figure. If you spend an extra half-hour to go out of your way to save $10 in office supplies, it costs you $25 in lost productivity, and you are $15 in the red.

The only thing you get paid to do is write, research, and think for your clients and publishers. All other activities are nonpaying and therefore should be farmed out to other people who can do them better and more cheaply than you can. If your time is worth at least $100 an hour, then virtually any service you can buy for under $100 an hour—including lawn services, handymen, and tax preparation—you should outsource. You don't need to hire a full-time secretary to outsource routine office work and administrative tasks. Plenty of bright high school and college students are eager to work with writers for the glory, glamour—and a relatively modest fee.

Of the two resources, time and money, time is the more valuable. You can always make more money. But time is a nonrenewable resource. Once it's gone, you can't get it back.

4. **Be more productive.** Develop habits that help you get more done in less time. The easiest is simply to get up and start work an hour earlier than you do now. That first hour will be your most productive, because you can work without interruptions before the business day starts.

Nancy Flynn, author of *The $100,000 Writer* (Adams Media), maximizes her productivity by avoiding in-person meetings unless absolutely necessary. "You can accomplish a tremendous amount—including establishing and maintaining successful business relationships—via telephone, e-mail, and fax," she said.

5. **Nix writer's block.** Profitable writers write consistently, every day, whether the mood strikes them or not. The best way to maintain a steady output and avoid writer's block is to have many projects on various subjects and in different formats.

Try this fail-proof method. If you're writing a magazine ad and get stuck on the headline, put it aside and switch to a different writing assignment you are working on for another publication. If you need more info to proceed with the second assignment, put that aside and work on yet another.

6. **Get paid more.** You may read articles and letters in writer's magazines that go something like this: "I was writing for a long time for a magazine that paid ten cents a word. Finally, I told the editor that I could not work for less than fifteen cents a word. At first he said no, but I stuck by my guns and, by gosh, he paid it. See, you can get paid more for your writing!"

The practice of going to low-paying markets and trying to convert them into high-paying markets is unproductive. Even if you get an extra five cents a word—which in this example represents a 50 percent pay hike— you're talking about only $50 more for a one thousand-word article.

If you really want to start making big money from your writing, don't haggle over nickels and dimes. Don't try to get a penny-a-word market to pay two cents a word, then feel pleased that you doubled your fee. Instead, target high-paying markets and assignments, such as large-circulation consumer magazines.

Moving to higher-paying assignments accelerates your climb to the $100,000 a year mark. It's much easier to meet your goal of $400 a day when you get $2,000 per project instead of $200.

When considering the profitability of assignments, calculate your earnings per hour rather than per project or per word. If it takes you ten eight-hour days to do a $2,000 feature article for a glossy magazine, you make $25 an hour. If another magazine hires you to write simple articles for their publication at $500 each, and you can do two per day, you make $125 an hour.

7. Create a demand. To earn six figures as a freelance writer, you have to be pretty busy most, if not all, of the time. Writers who suffer prolonged periods without work will have a difficult time meeting their revenue goals. To ensure a full writing schedule, you have to create a demand for what you are selling. And one way to make sure you are always in demand is to specialize.

You can specialize in a subject: gardening, content management, wastewater management, investments, interpersonal skills, health and fitness. Or you can specialize in a format or medium: how-to articles, children's articles, or writing for online venues.

Must you specialize? No. But as a rule, specialists earn more than generalists, are more in demand, and have an easier time finding work than generalists.

A few more words about specializing:

- Being a specialist and a generalist are not mutually exclusive. You can develop a specialty—even several specialties—and still take on general assignments.
- The narrower your specialty, the greater your value to clients and editors who need someone to write on those subjects. An example of a narrow focus is mutual funds, a subtopic within the broader area of investing and personal finance.

- The less popular your specialty is with other writers, the greater your competitive edge. If you are only one of a handful of known experts on your topic, the demand for your writing services will exceed the supply, and you can pick and choose your assignments.

8. **Get repeat business.** The most profitable assignments in freelance writing are repeat assignments from current clients. Why? Because you are familiar with the client and his organization, what you need to learn about him diminishes with each new assignment. You can charge the same price per job, or maybe even more if he likes you. And you can do the jobs much faster because of the knowledge you have accumulated.

How do you get lucrative repeat assignments?

Give every writing job your best effort. The more satisfied the client, the more likely he is to give you another job.

Provide excellent customer service. Don't be a prima donna. Clients avoid working with writers perceived as difficult or demanding.

Ask the editor for another project. Often you won't get the work unless you ask.

Making significant amounts of money as a writer is very possible, but it won't just happen. You must work hard to create opportunities and improve your efficiency as a writer. Believing you can do it is essential. Don't let the stereotypical notion of the struggling writer limit you. You can break that conception and make a healthy living as a dedicated freelance writer.

Getting Paid on Time

Waiting for checks is one of the most nerve-racking parts of being a writer. As a writer you probably rely heavily on the creative side of your brain. Business and finances are not something you probably enjoy dealing with. You like to think that your creative efforts will always be rewarded fairly. Yet even when your rights are carefully spelled out in a contract, there's no guarantee that payment will arrive when it's due.

One skill that writers acquire is patience. But you needn't be too patient.

No matter how poor the publisher's cash flow, it's usually better than yours. So when the wait gets too long, here are some steps you can take:

1. **If payment is thirty days past due.** Call and/or write immediately. You need not be confrontational. Simply send a late notice or call to check on the status of payment or to make sure your invoice wasn't lost. If you call, be sure to get a commitment from the editor or accounting office on when the payment will be sent.

2. **If payment isn't in your mailbox by the time promised.** Call and talk to the person in charge of payment. Be polite but firm. If you're told the check is on its way, get specifics about when it was mailed or when it will be mailed. This is a good time to let them know you won't be able to send any more work until payment is received. Your leverage increases greatly if you're working on another assignment that's needed soon.

3. **If payment isn't forthcoming after the second time you call or write.** If the money you are owed warrants it, send a final notice informing the publisher that you will have to turn the account over for collection or legal action if payment isn't received by a specified date. Take that "further action" promptly if the deadline passes. It could be a letter from a lawyer, or you may want to hire a collection agency.

If the amount in question does not warrant hiring an attorney or collection agency, you may be able to get help from certain writer's organizations if you are a member. Some writer's organizations will send letters on behalf of members who have not been paid for published work. A letter from a third party is an attention-getter that will sometimes disgorge a check from many slow payers.

4. **If all else fails and there's little hope of seeing the money owed you.** You can get some sense of satisfaction (and save others from a similar problem) by alerting your fellow writers about the problem publisher. Several organizations will note nonpayments in their newsletters. You can spread the word rapidly through online forums and bulletin boards frequented by writers. The threat of such disclosure can even work in your favor.

If you learned about the publication in a directory, inform the directory's staff of your problem. They may also write on your behalf, or at least consider deleting the publication from the next edition of their directory.

Finances and Taxes

You will find that as your writing business expands, so will your need to keep track of writing-related expenses and incomes. Keeping a close eye on these details will prove very helpful when it comes time to report your income to the IRS. It will also help you pay as little tax as possible and keep you aware of the state of your freelance writing as a business. It's essential that you maintain your writing business as you would any other business. This means that you need to set up a detailed tracking and organizing system to log all expenses and income. Without such a system, your writing as a business will eventually fold. If you dislike handling finance-related tasks, you can always hire a professional to oversee these duties for you. However, even if you do hire a professional, you still need to keep all original records.

The following tips will help you keep track of the finance-related tasks associated with your freelance business.

- Keep accurate records.
- Separate your writing income and expenses from your personal income and expenses.
- Maintain a separate bank account and credit card for business-related expenses.
- Record every transaction (expenses and earnings) related to your writing.
- Begin keeping records when you make your first writing-related purchase.
- Establish a working, detailed system of tracking expenses and income. Include the date, the source of income (or the vendor of your purchase), a description of what was sold or bought, how the pay-

ment was rendered (cash, check, credit card), and the amount of the transaction.

- Keep all check stubs and receipts (cash purchases and credit cards).
- Set up a record-keeping system, such as a file folder system, to store all receipts.

You can't be too meticulous in your record keeping. The more thorough you are, the easier it will be when it comes time to do your taxes. You will be very grateful that you put in the effort up front because becoming a freelancer means saying goodbye to the days you spent thirty minutes filling out your annual taxes. As soon as you make any money freelancing, you'll have to fill out the long form 1040 and Schedule C for business profit or loss. If you plan to deduct car or equipment expenses, you'll have another even more complex form to fill out.

Below is some general information regarding what is tax deductible in your writing business, but to find out more, visit the IRS Web site at www.irs.gov.

Tax-Deductible Expenses

Auto expenses. If you work from your home you can deduct mileage from home and back to any interview, trips to the library for research, or travel for any business function. This is true even if you don't qualify for the home office deduction. If you work from an office outside the home, however, you can't deduct mileage for commuting to the office.

You can calculate auto expenses using the standard mileage rate or the actual-cost method. To use the standard mileage rate, multiply the mileage driven by the current mileage rate (37.5 cents in 2004). The rate frequently changes but is stated each year in the instructions that come with Schedule C, the IRS form for reporting business income and expenses. Using the standard mileage rate is the easiest method in terms of record keeping.

As the name implies, the actual-cost method measures what it really costs you to operate your car. For this method you'll have to keep receipts for all automobile expenses, including gas, maintenance and repairs, insurance, taxes, loan interest, and depreciation of the car's cost.

If you use the car for both business and personal reasons, you calculate the percentage of business miles each year and deduct that percentage of your costs. There are limits to how much of your car's value you may write off each year. For details you'll need a current copy of IRS publication 917.

Home office expenses. Qualifying for the home office deduction means jumping through regulatory hoops and increasing your risk of an audit. But the tax savings can be worth it. You may be able to deduct a percentage of your mortgage interest or rent, utilities, and upkeep for your home each year.

To qualify for the deduction you must use an area of your home regularly and exclusively for business. Occasional or incidental use of your home office won't cut it, even if you don't use the space for anything else.

"Exclusive use" means just that—no games on your personal computer, no personal calls from the phone in your office. No relatives rolling out sleeping bags there on the weekend. Some furnishings are banned in a home office, like televisions and sofas. The IRS sees them as signs of personal use. Although it is best to have an entire room set aside for a home office, a portion of a room set aside exclusively for business also satisfies the Internal Revenue Code.

The most accurate way to calculate the business portion of your home is to divide the square feet of the work area by the total square feet of your home. Expenses you can deduct include the business percentage of:

- mortgage interest
- utilities and services, such as electricity, heat, trash removal, and cleaning services
- depreciation of the value of your house
- home security systems
- repairs, maintenance, and permanent improvement costs for your house

- all costs of repairs, painting, or modifications of your home office (Repairs you can write off the first year. Permanent improvements are considered capital expenditures and subject to depreciation over several years.)

One other word of caution—you can't use home office expenses to put you in the red. They can't be used to help create a tax loss.

Before you take any home office deductions, figure out what the tax savings will be. If the savings are minor, you may not want to bother. What you lose in taxes you may gain in peace of mind. You can get more information from IRS Publication 587.

Other expenses. The IRS applies the "ordinary" and "necessary" rules in judging the validity of a business expense. This means the expenses should be ordinary for your profession and necessary for carrying out your business.

Office equipment is a necessary—and often major—expense for free-lance writers. Computers, desks, chairs, shelves, filing cabinets, and other office furnishings are deductible expenses if you use them in your business. These can be deducted even if you don't opt for the home office deduction. IRS publication 534 provides more details on how to depreciate business property.

Among the largest costs for freelancers are phone expenses. The IRS prohibits deductions for your personal phone line, even if you use it for business. But you can still deduct the cost of long-distance business calls, even if they're from a personal line. You can also deduct the cost of a second line or other services used exclusively for business, such as a distinctive ring or voice mail.

If you entertain sources or clients you can deduct 50 percent of that expense. You must keep a log of the date, location, person entertained, and business purpose of the entertainment for every item you deduct. If you travel in connection with your writing, you can deduct the cost of transportation, lodging, and meals.

Other deductible expenses include the cost of:

- dues to professional organizations
- costs of newspapers, magazines, and journals used for your business
- research, copying services, and online databases
- office supplies
- postage for business use
- cleaning supplies for your office
- legal, accounting, and other professional services
- business licenses

If publishers or clients reimburse you for some of your expenses, remember to keep records of those payments and either report them as income or subtract them from the expenses you report.

Getting Professional Help

As mentioned before, business tax forms are a lot more complicated than ordinary tax forms, so you may want professional help. If so, your options include tax-preparation services and accountants. You may also get tax preparer training offered by H&R Block or other services, which can save you money and even allow you to start a sideline preparing taxes.

If you're incorporated or face particularly complex business issues, you may need help from a certified public accountant. Small- or medium-size CPA firms are most likely to be familiar with issues that concern you. Franchise tax services provide a consistent, mass-produced product. They're the cheapest option, but they may be less familiar with some of the unusual situations of freelancers.

Rights and the Writer

Beyond concerns of income and business issues, a freelance writer must also have a good working knowledge of the rights that go along with writing. A creative work can be used in many different ways. As the author of the work, you hold all rights to the work in question. When you agree to have your work published, you are granting a publisher the right to use your work in any number of ways. Whether that right is to publish the manuscript for the first time in a publication or to publish it as many times and in many different ways as a publisher wishes is up to you—it all depends on the agreed-upon terms. As a general rule, the more rights you license away, the less control you have over your work and the money you're paid. You should strive to keep as many rights to your work as you can.

The primary right in publishing is the right to publish the work itself. All other rights (movie rights, audio rights, book club rights, etc.) are considered secondary, or subsidiary, to the right to print publication. In contract negotiations, authors and their agents traditionally try to avoid granting the publisher subsidiary rights that they feel comfortable marketing themselves. Publishers, on the other hand, want to obtain as many of the subsidiary rights as they can.

The marketing of electronic rights can be tricky. With the proliferation of electronic and multimedia formats, publishers, agents, and authors are going to great lengths to make sure contracts specify exactly which electronic rights are being conveyed (or retained). Compensation for these rights is a major source of conflict because many magazines routinely include electronic rights in the purchase of all rights, often with no additional payment.

Writers and editors sometimes define rights in a number of different ways. The following are a classification of terms as they relate to rights.

First Serial Rights—Rights that the writer offers a newspaper or magazine to publish the manuscript for the first time in any periodical. All other rights remain with the writer. Sometimes the qualifier "North American" is added to these rights to specify a geographical limitation to the license.

When content is excerpted from a book scheduled to be published, and it appears in a magazine or newspaper prior to book publication, this is also called first serial rights.

One-Time Rights—Nonexclusive rights (rights that can be licensed to more than one market) purchased by a periodical to publish the work once (also known as simultaneous rights). That is, there is nothing to stop the author from selling the work to other publications at the same time.

Second Serial (Reprint) Rights—Nonexclusive rights given to a newspaper or magazine to publish a manuscript after it has already appeared in another newspaper or magazine.

All Rights—This is exactly what it sounds like. All rights mean that an author is selling every right they have to a work. If you license all rights to your work, you forfeit the right to ever use the work again. If you think you may want to use the article again, you should avoid submitting to such markets or refuse payment and withdraw your material.

Electronic Rights—Rights that cover a broad range of electronic media, from online magazines and databases to CD-ROM magazine anthologies and interactive games. The contract should specify if—and which—electronic rights are included. The presumption is that unspecified rights remain with the writer.

Subsidiary Rights—Rights, other than book publication rights, that should be covered in a book contract. These may include various serial rights; movie, television, audiotape, and other electronic rights; translation rights, etc. The book contract should specify who controls the rights (author or publisher) and what percentage of sales from the licensing of these rights goes to the author.

Dramatic, Television, and Motion Picture Rights—Rights for use of material on the stage, in television, or in the movies. Often a one-year option to buy such rights is offered (generally for 10 percent of the total price). The party interested in the rights then tries to sell the idea to other people—actors, directors, studios, or television networks. Some properties are optioned numerous times, but most fail to become full productions. In those cases, the writer can sell the rights again and again.

Sometimes editors don't take the time to specify the rights they are buying. If you sense that an editor is interested in getting stories but doesn't seem to know what his and the writer's responsibilities are, be wary. In such a case, you'll want to explain what rights you're offering (preferably one-time or first serial rights only) and that you expect additional payment for subsequent use of your work.

Contract Negotiations

If you've been freelancing, you know that contracts and agreements vary from publisher to publisher. Very rarely will you find two contracts that are exactly the same. Some magazine editors work only by verbal agreement; others have elaborate documents you must sign in duplicate and return to the editor before you even begin the assignment. It is essential that you consider all of the elements involved in a contract, whether verbal or written, and know what you stand to gain and lose by agreeing to the contract. Maybe you want to repurpose the article and resell it to a market that is different from the first publication to which you sold the article. If that's the case, then you need to know what rights you want to sell.

In contract negotiations, the writer is usually interested in licensing the work for a particular use but limiting the publisher's ability to make other uses of the work in the future. It's in the publisher's best interest, however, to secure as many rights as possible, both now and later on. Those are the basic positions of both parties. The negotiation is a process of compromise on questions relating to those basic points—and the amount of compensation to be given to the writer for his work. If at any time you are unsure about any portion of the contract, it is best to consult a lawyer who specializes in media law and contract negotiation.

A contract is rarely a take-it-or-leave-it proposition. If an editor tells you that her company will allow no changes to the contract, you will then have to decide how important the assignment is to you. However, most editors are open to negotiations, so you need to learn how to compromise on points that don't matter to you and stand your ground on those that do matter. Veteran freelancers know that often rights are more important in contract negotiations than pay is. Make sure you protect the bread and butter.

Carefully consider all contract proposals. Take this example from an online publication. Under the section pertaining to ownership of any work it gives this clause: The publisher owns "all rights, including copyright, therein throughout the universe." Forever. In all media. Even if it hasn't been created yet—even in the Andromeda Galaxy. In return, the publication pays the writer a fee and grants him a limited, nonexclusive license to use the work for the sole purpose of promoting himself and his work.

If you get a contract like this, call to discuss these passages. If the editors are unmoved, just say no.

Once, signing away rights meant that after initial publication, an article would collect dust. Now print and Internet publishers are looking to reap financial gain from the work they contract.

Where does that leave the writer? With a fleeting byline and a check stub. Every freelance writer who produces content for a publishing company increasingly is faced with the issue of ownership and licensing rights. The problem is that "Contracts 101" isn't taught in college journalism or English classes. Pulling off these deals calls for the savvy that comes only with time and experience.

The "universal rights" contract is just one example of what you should turn down. Many are quite the same, as are the editors' responses. After writer Jeffery Zbar declined to sign a similar contract without first changing the terms to something slightly more favorable, an editor said, "I don't understand why you would expect to have any right to the article. After all, we're paying you for it."

Sure, the money is nice. And most publishers will provide a brief bio and mention or link back to your Web site. But your words are worth more than money alone. These are your creations. Especially in the area of columns and opinion, they are your thoughts. Unlike staff writers, whose work typically becomes the property of the publisher, freelancers decide for themselves whom they work for and literally on what terms.

Writers have to figure out the back-end potential for each article they pen. Will you resell your writings? Will you self-publish an anthology or adapt the work to audiocassette or CD-ROM? Will writing for that particular publication benefit your career more than holding out for better terms? Is it better to get the money and relinquish the rights—or stand your ground?

Before entering contract and rights negotiations, here are a few points to consider:

- **Learn the negotiating game.** Contract negotiation isn't personal; it's all about business. To become a savvy negotiator, don't wait until you're in serious discussions to perfect your prowess. Practice with each new contract.

- **Don't be shy.** Don't ask, don't get. Writers are often quick to think that if a publisher demands something, or leaves something out of a contract, that's just the way it is. If you want something in a deal, demand it. If you don't like something, strike it. If both sides want the deal enough, they'll find common ground.

- **Find common ground.** If a publication wants all rights, see where the wiggle room lies. Will the editor settle for exclusive rights for a certain time period, after which she can retain a nonexclusive license to the content? It remains your property, but the publication can use it. Or maybe the editor will settle for rights in a specific subject area, like competing publications. This way, if you find a publication with no competing interests, you can resell the work.

- **Consider each publication and contract individually.** No two situations are the same—even with the same publication. Zbar writes a weekly marketing news column as well as a monthly home office feature for a metro daily newspaper. The legal department wanted all rights to both. He agreed to give the paper all rights to the marketing column and thirty-day exclusivity to the feature. His thinking: He can't use the news articles a day after they've run, and the newspaper likely won't use the home office features at all. They agreed, and he's been able to resell the home office features, give them away for marketing purposes, and even repackage them as a book.

- **Consider what it's worth.** Is it worth more than just the money? On your pro/con list, weigh ownership and usage rights, exposure for your work, the cachet of your name being associated with a given publication, and the potential to work with the publisher in the future.

- **Consider the stage of your career.** If you're new, you might not have the negotiating strength that a more established writer has earned. Be humble where appropriate.

- **Know the industry standard.** What's reasonable to demand? On certain projects (especially contract writing assignments for corporate clients), don't expect any rights; it's straight work-for-hire. With publications, it's not unreasonable to expect to retain some rights.

- **Call your attorney.** Until you become a savvy negotiator who's seen a few contracts, run each by a lawyer. It may cost you, but it's better to make sure no one is slipping in some language unfavorable to your needs—or outside the terms negotiated. And the experience will help you learn the ropes.

- **Don't rush to sign.** Even if an editor says she needs an answer right away, take time to consider your options.

- **Know where your line in the sand is.** If rights mean that much to you, no amount of money may make the difference. If it boils down to principle, make sure you can live with your decision. Don't sweat lost contracts. The funny thing about work lost because you stood your ground is that you'll rest easy knowing you did what was right.

- **Hit these sites for more information and guidance:** The National Writers Union (www.nwu.org), a trade union for freelance journalists, book authors, poets, novelists, business-technical writers, and fiction writers; the American Society of Journalists and Authors (www.asja.org), a leading association of nonfiction writers and publisher of Contracts Watch, a free electronic newsletter on contracts and rights; and Writer's Digest (www.writersdigest.com).

Negotiating on Your Own

Everything within a contract is fair grounds for negotiation. Remember these five phrases the next time you are negotiating a contract, and they will help you get the results you're hoping for.

1. "That sounds a little low." A timeless classic. This follows a golden rule of writing: Keep it simple. No matter what figure is proposed, just state those five words and then shut your mouth. Since no one can stand uncomfortable silences, your tight lips will force the editor to say something in response. Either he will make a new offer, ask you what you need, or tell you that's the best he can do. If it's the latter, employ one of the next phrases.

2. "To make it worth my time, I would need . . ." This one lets you take control of the situation. If you've already figured out approximately how much time and effort this piece will require, you should be able to determine how much you expect to be paid for it. Make sure that you've done some research and that your figure is in the realm of what that particular market typically pays. (Asking for a figure that's 20 percent more than the average payment for an article of your word count and scope is reasonable; asking for 200 percent more is not.) Don't bother mincing your words; state your figure and let the editor decide.

3. "Considering the amount of research required, can we agree to . . ." Heavily researched pieces often have potential reprint markets. If an editor has asked for all rights, or exclusivity in any way, use this as a bartering chip. Mention that you can only give exclusivity if the editor raises the fee; otherwise, you'll accept the fee for one-time rights (or whatever rights you find suitable) only. You may also barter for free advertising space, links to your Web site, etc.

4. "I'm expecting more for this piece." Another simple statement that puts the ball back in the editor's court. Again, follow this one with silence, and allow the editor to come up with a new figure. This statement introduces the possibility that you could decide to sell the piece elsewhere if the editor doesn't meet your requirements.

Continued next page

5. "Can we work on that?" For pop psychology fans, this one brings the editor onto your "team." By using the word "we," you've asked the editor to partner with you in coming up with more acceptable terms. This question opens the door to a variety of improvements; you may choose to talk about fees, rights, word count, sidebars, etc.

Whichever phrases you use, keep in mind that your tone and professionalism will matter. You must convey the impression that you are self-confident and aware of the value of your work. And, with a few successful negotiations to your credit, you may be able to stop acting and start believing.

Copyright

Besides the rights in a contract, writers must also understand copyright. Copyright law exists to protect creators of original works. Copyright law is designed to encourage the production of creative works by ensuring that artists and writers hold the rights by which they can profit from their hard work.

The moment you finish a piece of writing—or in fact, the second you begin to pen the manuscript—the law recognizes that only you can decide how the work is used. Copyright protects your writing, recognizes you (its sole creator) as its owner, and grants you all the rights and benefits that accompany ownership. With very few exceptions, anything you write today will enjoy copyright protection for your lifetime, plus seventy years. Copyright protects "original works of authorship" that are fixed in a tangible form of expression. Copyright law cannot protect titles, ideas, and facts.

Some writers are under the mistaken impression that a registered copyright with the Library of Congress Copyright Office is necessary to protect their work and that their work is not protected until they "receive" their copyright paperwork from the government. This is not true. You don't have to register your work with the Copyright Office for it to be protected. Registration for your work does, however, offer some additional protection (specifically, the possibility of recovering punitive damages in an infringement suit) as well as legal proof of the date of copyright. Adding a copyright notice allows you to defeat claims of "innocent infringement." You must register your work with the Copyright Office before you can file suit against someone who steals your work. If you wait to register your work until after the theft takes place, you may not be able to recover attorney fees and some damages from the defendant.

To register a copyright, first you must request the proper form from the Register of Copyrights at the Library of Congress. Follow these steps to register your work.

1. Request and complete the proper form, either Form TX for books, manuscripts, online work, and poetry, or Form PA for scripts and dramatic works.
2. Put into one envelope: your completed application form, $30 payment to "Register of Copyrights," and a nonreturnable copy or copies of the material to be registered.
3. Send the package to the Library of Congress Copyright Office at the address on page 230.

Most magazines are registered with the Copyright Office as single collective entities themselves; that is, the individual works that make up the magazine are not copyrighted individually in the names of the authors. You'll need to register your article yourself if you wish to have the additional protection of copyright (your name, the year of first publication, and the copyright symbol) appended to any published version of your work. You may use the copyright notice regardless of whether your work has been registered with the Copyright Office. But remember, editors know your work is copyrighted as soon as you write it, so don't insult their intelligence or integrity by including the symbol on your submissions.

One thing you need to pay particular attention to is work-for-hire arrangements. If you sign a work-for-hire agreement, you are agreeing that your writing will be done as a work for hire, you will not control the copyright of the completed work—the person or organization who hired you will be the copyright owner. These agreements and transfers of exclusive rights must appear in writing to be legal. However, it's a good idea to get every publishing agreement you negotiate in writing before the sale.

MORE COPYRIGHT INFORMATION

For more information about copyrights contact: Library of Congress, Copyright Office, 101 Independence Avenue Southeast, Washington, DC 20559-6000. Tel: (202) 707-3000. Web site: www.copyright.gov.

The Copyright Office Web site makes available all copyright registration forms and informational circulars, plus other announcements and general copyright information. The Web site also provides a means of searching copyright registrations and recorded documents from 1978 forward.

You can also use the Forms and Publications Hotline [(202) 707-9100] to request application forms or informational circulars. The Fax-on-Demand service [(202) 707-2600] allows you to use any Touch-Tone phone to order up to three circulars and/or announcements via fax. (Applications forms are not available via fax.)

Fair Use

Aside from protecting their work, the copyright issue of most concern to writers is the doctrine of fair use. This principle allows you to quote briefly from someone else's work. It's important to note, however, that the rules of fair use have never been clearly defined by the courts, nor have they been spelled out in law. Fair use can only be judged in the context in which it occurs. Standard industry guidelines say that you can quote one hundred words from a short work (short story, essay, or article) and three hundred words from a book-length work. These are cumulative counts, so if you quote from the same work in two different sections of your article, you must add the total word count of the two excerpts. Songs and poetry have even stricter rules about using any words or lines. If you are unsure of the limits for any work, obtain permission before quoting from any copyrighted material.

To get permission to quote from copyrighted material, you must submit a request to the copyright owner, which usually means contacting the publisher. In a brief letter, explain exactly what you want to quote, and note when and where it was first published. Be sure to include information about how you will use the material and the name of the publication in which it will appear. In most cases, you will be granted permission on the condition that you credit the original source. In some cases you may have to pay a fee, which can range from a few dollars to a few hundred dollars. You must decide whether the material is worth the cost involved.

The Public Domain

Sometimes you will be able to use a work that is no longer copyrighted. These are works considered to be in the public domain. Maps, photo-

ADDITIONAL RESOURCES

Online Resources

- U.S. Copyright Office: www.copyright.gov
- Cottrill & Associates' copyright table: www.progenealogists.com/copyright_table.htm
- Public domain usage rules: www.copylaw.com/new_articles/PublicDomain.html
- The Midwest Chapter of the American Society of Media Photographers take on copyright, photography, and the Web: www.chimwasmp.org/photoweb/copyrite.htm
- Alexander Media's site of public domain images, both free and for fee: www.pdimages.com
- University of North Carolina chart on when material goes into the public domain: www.unc.edu/~unclng/public-d.htm

Further Reading

- *The Copyright Permission and Libel Handbook: A Step-by-Step Guide for Writers, Editors, and Publishers* by Lloyd J. Jassin and Steven C. Schechter (John Wiley and Sons)
- *Getting Permission: How to License & Clear Copyrighted Materials Online & Off* by Richard Stim (Nolo Press)
- *Patent, Copyright & Trademark, 3d Edition* by Stephen Elias (Nolo Press)
- *The Public Domain: How to Find & Use Copyright-Free Writings, Music, Art & More* by Stephen Fishman (Nolo Press)

graphs, drawings, engravings, woodcuts, documents, newspaper articles, magazines, novels—the possibilities for enhancing your writing are boundless. But so are the potential legal minefields you face in using works you didn't create yourself.

As mentioned, any creative work is protected by copyright law for a given number of years, regardless of whether the author or creator is living. When the copyright expires, the work becomes part of the public domain. When that happens, these works may be used without anyone's permission and often without a fee. Some works are never eligible for copyright and are always in the public domain, such as works produced by the U.S. government.

Determining when material has passed into the public domain isn't always easy. Different rules apply depending on when—and if—the work was published. Any work published before 1923 is now in the public domain and cannot be retroactively protected. That said, be certain the version you use is the original and not an adaptation. The derivative work might be protected under a separate copyright, but the underlying original public domain work would be free to use.

The rules are different for unpublished works. For those created before January 1978, copyright protection lasts for the life of the author/creator plus seventy years, but in no case did that copyright expire before December 31, 2002.

Lloyd J. Jassin, coauthor of *The Copyright Permission and Libel Handbook* (see page 231), writes that you should know the answers to the following questions before assuming a work is in the public domain:

- When was the work created?
- Who created the work (an individual, two or more individuals, or an employee)?
- Is the author still alive? If not, when did he die?
- When was the work registered or published?

Jassin cautions that seeing an illustration or text on the Internet does not mean the work is in the public domain. There is much infringement on the Internet, and a work could have been posted without the owner's knowledge or consent.

Public domain is not to be confused with fair use—the privilege to use copyrighted materials under certain circumstances. If a work is part of the public domain, no permission is required and no fees can be assessed. For a full discussion of the subject, see "A Writer's Guide to Fair Use in Copyright Law," by Howard Zaharoff (*Writer's Digest*, January 2001) at www.writersdigest.com.

The basic rules for using public domain texts, illustrations, and photographs are the same. Establish whether or not the item is free from copyright by verifying the creation date, publication status, and ownership. While it would be wonderful if there were a massive, online public domain database, there isn't. But you can check the records of the U.S. Copyright Office online to see if a copyright was registered and renewed. Go to www.copyright.gov, then click on the link "Search Records." From there, follow the prompts. Currently, there are three databases available at this site:

- **COHM:** Works registered for copyright since January 1978. Included are books, films, music, maps, sound recordings, software, multimedia kits, drawings, posters, sculptures, and so forth. Also included are renewals of previous registrations, originally published from 1950 on. Updated weekly.
- **COHS:** Serials (such as periodicals, magazines, journals, newspapers) registered for copyright since 1978. Updated twice yearly.
- **COHD:** Documents relating to copyright ownership, such as name changes and transfers. Updated weekly.

The information in the databases is searchable by author and title. However, copyright renewals on works published from 1923 to 1949 are not all online. Renewal records for books only are at the Online Books Page (www.digital.library.upenn.edu/books/cce/). Otherwise, you need to find a copy of the hardcover volumes called *The Catalog of Copyright Entries*, available in some large public and university libraries.

There are thousands of works and images in the public domain for you to enhance your work. Finding them may be the most challenging part of your assignment, but it can be well worth your time and your budget.

Using Art

Some public domain images may be used to enhance your writing for free, but in some cases they are in private collections and the owner will charge you a royalty fee for usage. When a photograph becomes public domain depends on several factors, including whether the photograph is unique, if it has been published, and when it was created. Keep in mind that a photograph does not require a copyright symbol to be protected under the law. Under copyright law, a photographer is considered the "author" or creator of photographic works, and as such, the legal copyright holder. If you want to make copies of a photograph, alter it, or publish it, you need the photographer's permission.

You need to proceed carefully when using old images, family photographs, and other illustrations; don't assume they are in the public domain. If you want to use a photograph taken or published after 1978, obtaining permission can be a simple procedure if you can contact the current copyright holder. Send the photographer a letter requesting permission and outlining how the image will be used. In most cases, you will have to pay a royalty (usage fee) for the right to publish the image.

Suppose you find a line drawing, engraving, woodcut, or photograph published in another book, newspaper, city directory, or elsewhere. If the illustration is in a recently published work, check the author's credits to see the source of the original. If it was originally published before 1923, then the illustration is in the public domain.

Several professional organizations including the Professional Photographers of America have agreed to adhere to a set of copyright guidelines outlined by the Photo Marketing Association International. A complete set of the responsibilities of consumer and professional photographers is on the Kodak Web site at www.kodak.com/global/en/consumer/doingMore/copyright.shtml or the ASMP Web site at www.asmp.org.

A Final Word

As you have seen, writing for magazines includes more than just having an idea and putting words on paper. There is so much to consider if you want to do it successfully. But if you take everything into consideration, then your chances at success are so much greater. Once you get your idea accepted and your article written to fit perfectly with your publication's needs, you still have more to do. You can work on selling reprints and rewrites, and of course querying for your next article. But constant querying and successful submissions alone will not make you successful. Don't forget to put time into developing your freelance business as well. Market yourself, keep accurate records, and make sure you are getting paid on time. Make sure you are retaining the rights to your work that you need to continue to profit from it. As with anything else, you will gain knowledge through experience. So jump right in, armed with the information you now have, and continue to learn as you go. And never forget that you are capable of freelance success.

CONTRIBUTORS

Coleen Armstrong is a freelance writer and home editor at *Cincinnati Magazine.*

Karen Asp is a health and fitness writer who most recently has written for *Shape, Fitness, Cooking Light*, and *Fit Pregnancy*. She is also the author of *Exercise or Obsession? Women Talk About When Too Much Goes Too Far* (MightyWords).

Wendy Hart Beckman is a full-time freelance writer based in Cincinnati. She has published over two hundred articles in such publications as *Qualified Remodeler, Cincinnati Magazine, M.D. News*, and *Builder/ Architect.*

Robert W. Bly is the author of more than fifty books including *Secrets of a Freelance Writer: How to Make $85,000 a Year* (Henry Holt). He is an independent copywriter and consultant with more than twenty years experience in business-to-business, high-tech, industrial, and direct marketing.

Kathryn S. Brogan is the editor of *Writer's Market, Writer's Market Deluxe Edition*, and *Guide to Literary Agents.*

Michael Bugeja is director of the Greenlee School of Journalism and Communications at Iowa State University. He is former associate director of Ohio University's E.W. Scripps School of Journalism and a Writer's Digest advisory board member. He is the author of *Guide to Writing Magazine Nonfiction* (Allyn & Bacon), *The Art & Craft of Poetry* (Writer's Digest Books), and *Living Without Fear: Understanding Cancer and the New Therapies* (Whitston Press).

Gordon Burgett is the author of *Sell & Resell Your Magazine Articles* (Writer's Digest Books), *The Travel Writer's Guide* (Communications Unlimited), *Publishing the Niche Market* (Communications Unlimited), and *How to Sell More Than 75% of Your Writing* (Prima). He lives in Santa

Maria, California. His Web site is www.gordonburgett.com.

Sharon DeBartolo Carmack is a certified genealogist, editor of Family Tree Books, and contributing editor to *Family Tree Magazine*. She is the author of eight books and numerous articles.

Rebecca Chrysler is a graduate student at the University of Michigan's School of Education. She was awarded a fellowship by Northern Michigan University for its master's in creative writing program. She has worked as assistant editor to *Children's Writer's & Illustrator's Market* and *Artist's & Graphic Designer's Market* and as a staff reporter to a local newspaper in northern Michigan. Her work is also featured in *TD Monthly* magazine and *Novel & Short Story Writer's Market.*

Jack Clemens is an associate editor of *Writer's Digest* magazine. He writes "The Last Word," a monthly column that examines the writing styles of well-known authors, and edits the magazine's upfront section, "Ink-Well." A graduate of James Madison University, Jack has also worked as an advertising copywriter, newsletter editor, and itinerant bookseller.

Andrea King Collier has written for numerous publications, including *The New York Times Book Review* and *Epicurean*, as well as *Wonder Years*. Her memoir, *Still With Me*, was published by Simon & Schuster.

Mary Carmen Cupito is coauthor of *Writer's Market Companion, 2d Edition*. She has worked as a reporter for *The Cincinnati Post, The Columbus Dispatch*, and *The St. Petersburg Times*. Since leaving full-time reporting, she has written many freelance articles for magazines, newspapers, and other publications. Mary teaches journalism at Northern Kentucky University.

Sandra Dark is the author of seven novels and two hundred articles that have appeared in such magazines as *Kiwanis, Working Woman, Nation's Business, Organic Gardening*, and *Prevention.*

Greg Daugherty is a magazine editor and newspaper columnist. His books include *You Can Write for Magazines* (Writer's Digest Books).

Julie Duffy is the author of *21st Century Publishing* (Booklocker). She is the former director of author services at Xlibris and has had articles appear in *Inscriptions Magazine* and on WritingWorld.com. She is the publisher of a writer's and publisher's resource site at www.jdwrite .com and its e-mail newsletter, *The 21st Century Publishing Update!* She has a master's in history from the University of Edinburgh, Scotland.

Lain Chroust Ehmann has published over three hundred articles for publications such as the *Christian Science Monitor, Woman's World, Family Life, The Boston Globe, Runner's World,* and *The Industry Standard.* She can be reached at Lainie9@mediaone.net.

Kelly James-Enger's freelance work has appeared in more than fifty national magazines including *Redbook, Continental, Health, Woman's Day,* and *Self.* She is also the author of books including *Ready, Aim, Specialize! Create Your own Writing Specialty and Make More Money* (The Writer Inc.) and *The Six-Figure Freelancer* (Random House) and the novels *Did You Get the Vibe?* and *White Bikini Panties* (Strapless). She lives in Downers Grove, Illinois; visit www.kellyjamesenger.com to contact her.

Jason Fargo is a New York-based writer and editor who specializes in business and financial topics.

Joe Feiertag is coauthor of *Writer's Market Companion, 2d Edition.* He is a public relations professional and former journalist who has built a highly successful career as a freelance writer and editor. He also has taught writing at the college level.

Linda Formichelli is coauthor of *The Renegade Writer: A Totally Unconventional Guide to Freelance Writing Success* (Marion Street Press) and runs the *Renegade Writers* e-newsletter, which shares her rule-breaking freelance success secrets. Sign up at www.twowriters.net. She has written for over ninety magazines, such as *Woman's Day, Wired,* and *Family Circle.*

John N. Frank has spent nearly thirty years as a professional journalist, covering a wide variety of beats ranging from real estate to Wall Street to technology. He is currently the Midwest bureau chief for *PRWeek* magazine, a trade publication for the public relations business, and he freelances for food publications and accounting Web sites.

Eric Freedman is a Pulitzer Prize winner and has published articles in more than 125 U.S. and foreign publications. He is author of *What to Study: 101 Fields in a Flash* (Kaplan) and *How to Transfer to the College of Your Choice* (Ten Speed Press). He teaches journalism at Michigan State University.

Jane Friedman is executive editor for Writer's Digest Books and former managing editor of *Writer's Digest* magazine. Her work has appeared in *Writer's Digest* magazine, *Salon*, *Novel & Short Story Writer's Market*, *Poet's Market*, *The Evansville Review*, and *The Formalist*.

David A. Fryxell is the author of *How to Write Fast (While Writing Well)*, *Elements of Article Writing: Structure and Flow*, and *Write Faster, Write Better* (all Writer's Digest Books). He is the editor and publisher of *Desert Exposure* magazine.

Jenna Glatzer is editor in chief of AbsoluteWrite.com and WriterOnline.net. Her books include *Outwitting Writer's Block and Other Problems of the Pen* (The Lyons Press) and *Make a Real Living as a Freelance Writer* (Nomad Press). She is also the author of *The More Than Any Human Being Needs to Know About Freelance Writing Workbook* (Booklocker).

Kristin D. Godsey is the editor of *Writer's Digest* magazine. She holds a master's degree in journalism from Northwestern University and has written and/or edited for national magazines including *Good Housekeeping* and *Glamour*.

Kelly Milner Halls is a freelance writer based in Spokane, Washington. Her work has appeared in dozens of children's magazines, including *Highlights for Children*, *Boys' Life*, *U.S. Kids*, *ASK*, *Dig*, *Teen People*, *Guidepost for Teens*, and others. She has also written for *The Washington Post*, *The Chicago Tribune*, *The Atlanta Journal Constitution*, *The Denver Post*, *Writer's Digest*, *Family Fun*, *New Jersey Monthly*, *Wyoming Magazine*, and other adult publications. She has ten children's books published including her latest, *Albino Animals* (Darby Creek Publishing), and she also works as a PR consultant at Darby Creek. Halls also works as YA novelist Chris Crutcher's personal assistant. E-mail her at KellyMilnerH@aol.com.

Brad Herzog is the author of hundreds of national magazine articles, numerous children's books, and the award-winning travel narrative *States of Mind* (John F. Blair). He is author of the travelogue *Small World* (Pocket Books).

Wayne Hoffman has been a freelancer for more than fifteen years and has published articles in more than fifty publications, including *The Washington Post*, *The Advocate*, and *The Nation*. He is former associate editor at *Billboard*.

Steven James is an award-winning author and popular conference speaker. He has written seventeen books and hundreds of articles and stories that have appeared in over seventy-five different magazines and publications. He lives with his family in Tennessee.

Mark H. Massé is an associate professor of literary journalism and a writing coach at Ball State University. A widely published freelance author since 1978, Massé has written for *The New York Times*, *Ladies' Home Journal*, *Hemispheres*, *Men's Health*, *Golf Journal*, *Catholic Digest*, and *Modern Short Stories*.

Lauren Mosko is editor of *Novel & Short Story Writer's Market*. Her work has also appeared in *Children's Writer's & Illustrator's Market*, *Artist's & Graphic Designer's Market*, *Songwriter's Market*, and *I.D. Magazine*. When she's not hunched over her desk writing and editing, she teaches news media and composition classes at the University of Cincinnati.

Deborah J. Myers is a full-time freelancer living in New York. Her articles have appeared in magazines including *Classic Auto Restorer*, *Quality Digest*, *Colorado Homes & Lifestyles*, and *College Monthly*.

Jennifer Nelson is a full-time freelancer in Florida. Her work has appeared in *Writer's Digest*, *Parenting*, *Woman's Day*, *Fitness*, *Shape*, *Health*, *Self*, *The Christian Science Monitor*, and many other publications.

Tom Neven has worked in newspapers, magazines, and books for twenty years. He has written and edited for, among others, *The Washington Post*, Time-Life Books, Reader's Digest Books, *Focus on the Family* magazine, and *The Denver Post*. Tom has an MA in journalism from the Columbia University Graduate School of Journalism. His latest book is *Do Fish Know They're Wet?* (Baker Book House).

Erin Nevius is the associate editor of Family Tree Books. Her work has appeared online on WritersMarket.com as well as in such publications as *The Artist's Magazine, Writer's Digest, Family Tree Magazine, Photographer's Market*, and *The Family Tree Guide Book to Europe.*

Hank Nuwer is author of *Wrongs of Passage* (Indiana University Press), *High School Hazing: When Rites Become Wrongs* (Grolier/Franklin Watts), and *The Hazing Reader* (Indiana University Press). He has written and rewritten pieces for *American Legion, Outside, Modern Maturity, Harper's*, and *GQ.*

Sinara Stull O'Donnell has been writing full time since 1999 and has been published in *The Wall Street Journal Online, Succeed, 'Teen, Sam's Club Source*, and other publications.

Eileen Ogintz is a nationally syndicated columnist and creator of "Taking the Kids." She has written for numerous magazines, authored six books, and spent nearly twenty years as a reporter at major newspapers including *The Chicago Tribune.*

Steve Outing is an online writer and Internet content entrepreneur. He is a senior online editor at the Poynter Institute for Media Studies and an interactive media columnist for *Editor & Publisher Online.*

Janine Palley is freelance writer from the San Francisco Bay area. Her work has appeared in *The San Francisco Chronicle, The San Francisco Examiner, NewAge Journal, Intuition, The San Francisco Guardian*, and many others.

Timothy Perrin, a British Columbia-based freelancer, is executive director of WritingSchool.com. He is also author of *Better Writing for Lawyers* (Law Society of Upper Canada) and contributor to *Agents, Editors, and You* (Writer's Digest Books). He has published over 150 articles in publications such as *Continental, Omni, Reader's Digest, Your Money*, and *Homemaker's.* He is one of the founding instructors of the Professional Writing Program at Okanagan University College in British Columbia, Canada.

Michael Polak has published articles in many antique publications.

He is the Western region news editor for *Bottles & Extras* magazine. He is the author of the fourth edition of *Bottles: Identification and Price Guide* (Krause) and *American Patriotic Memorabilia* (Random House).

Alice Pope has been editor of *Children's Writers & Illustrator's Market* for more than a decade. She also serves as managing editor of Writer's Digest Books' Market Books department, is a former regional advisor for the Society of Children's Book Writers and Illustrators, and is a regular speaker at children's writing conferences.

Don Ranly, Ph.D., is professor of journalism and head of the magazine program at the University of Missouri School of Journalism where he has taught for the past thirty-one years. He is coauthor of *News Reporting and Writing* (8th ed.), *Telling the Story: The Convergence of Print, Broadcast and Online Media* (2d ed.) and *Beyond the Inverted Pyramid* (all with Bedford/St. Martin's) and author of *Publication Editing* (Kendall/Hunt). He has compiled a book of readings *The Principles of American Journalism* (Kendall/Hunt).

Peter Reilly is senior editor of *The National Enquirer*. He also has worked for *Star*, *The National Examiner*, and *Globe* and is the coauthor of *Really Bad Swing Thoughts* (Andrews McMeel).

Melanie Rigney is the former editor of *Writer's Digest* magazine.

Will Romano is a freelance writer living in New York. He has been published in *The New York Post*, *The New York Daily News*, *Guitar Player*, *Toy Shop*, *Small Business Opportunities*, and *Modern Drummer.*

Michelle Ruberg is an editor for Writer's Digest Books. She has written and done public relations work for *Applause! Magazine* and has also worked as a writing consultant. She has a Master of Arts in English from Xavier University.

Joe Stollenwerk is the manager of educational programming for Writers Online Workshops and has developed a number of writing workshops, including the Advanced Nonfiction Book Writers' Workshop. Joe holds a Master of Arts in English and a Master of Education, both from Xavier University. He is a contributing editor of *Writer's Digest* and formerly served as the executive editor of the special interest publication *Start Writing Now*.

Tony Seidman is a veteran freelance writer who has written thousands of stories for publications ranging from *The New York Times* and *Variety* to *American Karaoke, Gourmet Retailer, Reputation Management*, and *Tape/Disc Business*.

Maureen Taylor is a member of the American Society of Picture Professionals and the author of numerous books and articles on photo history and genealogy, including *Preserving Your Family Photographs* (Betterway). Her columns appear in *Ancestry, The Computer Genealogist*, Geanealogy.com, and *New England Ancestors*.

Britta Waller is senior editor of *Sky*, the inflight magazine of Delta Air Lines, and the managing editor of Delta Shuttle's *The Shuttle Sheet*. Her writing has won awards from The Press Club of Cleveland and Women in Communications.

Judy Williams is a Vancouver, B.C.-based freelance writer with over five hundred magazine and newspaper clips in trade and consumer publications.

Ben Yagoda directs the journalism program at the University of Delaware. He is the author of *The Sound on the Page: Style and Voice in Writing* (HarperResource), *About Town: The New Yorker and the World It Made* (Da Capo Press), and *Will Rogers: A Biography* (University of Oklahoma Press) and is the coeditor, with Kevin Kerrane, of *The Art of Fact: A Historical Anthology of Literary Journalism* (Scribner). He has written for magazines that begin with every letter of the alphabet except J, K, Q, X, and Z.

Jeffery D. Zbar is a freelance writer specializing in small office/home office and teleworking issues and is the author of *Your Profitable Home Business Made E-Z* (Made E-Z Products) and *Home Office Know-How* (Upstart Publishing). He also had a business column appear in *Writer's Digest* magazine.

INDEX